Unit 3   Positive Personality

Singin', Sweatin', and Storytime

Literature-based Movement and Music for the Young Child

Rebecca E. Hamik
and Catherine Wilson

Published in partnership with
MENC: The National Association for Music Education

ROWMAN & LITTLEFIELD EDUCATION
A division of
ROWMAN & LITTLEFIELD PUBLISHERS, INC.
Lanham • New York • Toronto • Plymouth, UK

Published in partnership with MENC: The National Association for Music Education

Published by Rowman & Littlefield Education
A division of Rowman & Littlefield Publishers, Inc.
A wholly owned subsidiary of The Rowman & Littlefield Publishing Group, Inc.
4501 Forbes Boulevard, Suite 200, Lanham, Maryland 20706
http://www.rowmaneducation.com

Estover Road, Plymouth PL6 7PY, United Kingdom

British Library Cataloguing in Publication Information Available

Library of Congress Cataloging-in-Publication Data
Hamik, Rebecca E., 1962–
  Singin', sweatin', and storytime : literature-based movement and music for the young child / Rebecca E. Hamik and Catherine M. Wilson.
    p. cm.
  "Published in partnership with MENC: The National Association for Music Education."
  ISBN 978-1-60709-265-0 (cloth : alk. paper) — ISBN 978-1-60709-266-7 (pbk. : alk. paper) — ISBN 978-1-60709-267-4 (electronic)
  1. School music—Instruction and study—Outlines, syllabi, etc. 2. Games with music. I. Wilson, Catherine, 1968– II. Title.
  MT10.H24 2009
  372.87'044—dc22   2009014526

∞ ™ The paper used in this publication meets the minimum requirements of American National Standard for Information Sciences—Permanence of Paper for Printed Library Materials, ANSI/NISO Z39.48-1992.
Printed in the United States of America

Contents

Unit 4   Skills and Thrills

Unit 5 Games, Songs, and Seasons of Other Lands

Unit 6 Holidays and Special Times

Introduction

Music and physical activity are a part of all of us from the time we are born and all throughout our human life. From feeling our hearts beat, feeling our rhythmic breathing when we are relaxing, walking and running with a rhythm, reading with a rhythm to our first songs of nah-nah-nah-nah-nah-nah, all of us are musical, rhythmic, physical beings. It is woven into our very nature through the beating of our hearts. As a music teacher, PE teacher, or a regular classroom teacher of young children, if you believe this with every fiber of your being, then this book is for you. If you enjoy children's books, lots of movement, and singing, you can bring all of these wonderful elements together to create a classroom that is welcoming, child centered, and highly enriching for your young students.

This curriculum is designed to include literature with an appropriate PE and music activity for the young child. All of the activities are standards based, so you can be assured that you are teaching the essential skills needed in music and PE class. The National Standards for Music Education are from *National Standards for Arts Education* by the Consortium of National Arts Associations (MENC, 1994). The National Standards for Physical Education are from *Moving into the Future: National Standards for Physical Education*, 2nd edition, by the National Association for Sport and Physical Education (McGraw-Hill, 2004).

The book is designed in units so that you can review the focus of each unit with your students every day. Review is particularly important so that skills taught are remembered. Because each lesson includes books, movement, and music, you are teaching to visual, kinesthetic, and aural learners. There is also a section for special days and holidays. The book is flexible to meet the needs of your students.

Although some of the skills of music and PE are related in this book, not all of the music and PE plans are related to each other. In many situations with this age group, it is much more productive to team teach so that two adults can demonstrate for the students a particular skill in music or in PE. If the music skill for the day is singing in a round or if the skill is throwing and catching in PE class, it is helpful to have another capable adult teaching in the classroom or in the gym with you. Most activities can be done with large or small groups. If you are a general classroom teacher and you must teach alone, there are suggestions for managing your group. Some lessons work well with the assistance of student teachers, parent volunteers, and teaching assistants. This will be noted in these particular lessons.

Many of the lessons in the book introduce concepts that would not ordinarily be introduced until later grades. The important thing to remember is that education is a layering process. If you teach the students some terms and concepts they will need later, it will be easier for them to remember next year when you bring the terms and concepts back. Give the students musical and physical experiences, even if they cannot do them perfectly yet. Give them the chance to try things, and encourage them. You are giving them the background to be healthy people enjoy physical activity. You are also helping them to become excellent musicians.

The most important thing you will teach students is that music, physical activity, and reading are a lot of fun. Music and exercise will keep you and your students healthy and happy. Have fun with our book and with your precious students.

General Information

If you are team teaching, it is essential that you and your teaching partner spend ten or fifteen minutes each day looking at the lesson plan for the next day. Decide who will give an overview of the previous lesson with the students, who will read the story, and how new skills will be demonstrated. Decide which activities will be done as a large group and which activities you would like to do in smaller groups. Take turns visiting the school library to pick up the books you will need one week in advance. This will give you time to find another story if the book you would like to use is checked out. Most of the books that are listed in the literature list are easy to find, but they might be popular. Sometimes an alternate suggestion is listed. Make sure you have the equipment and resources necessary for each lesson in advance so that you have time to think of alternate items or resources if you cannot get the exact materials that are listed.

The lesson plans in the book are flexible. If you have other units that need to be taught throughout the year, feel free to use the lessons in this book to reinforce other concepts and skills you must teach. Although the book is chronological, most lessons can be taught out of sequence. However, Unit 1, My Body and Melodic Voice, and Unit 4, Skills and Thrills, are basic movement concepts that must be taught sequentially for young children. Unit 1 must be taught before Unit 4. If you skip any of the lessons in Unit 1, make sure you have taught all of the basic movement concepts in Unit 1 before moving on to the skills in Unit 4. If you do not have enough class sessions to go through all of the lessons during the school year, choose the lessons with the standards that are most important during early childhood.

These young children you will be teaching are emotionally me-centered. They are concerned with their needs and wants, and they are not concerned with other things or people around them. They are not developmentally at a social stage yet. This will change as the school year progresses. They are still trying to figure out how their body works physically and how to control it. Some students will be able to hop, leap, and skip. Others will not. Because young children are trying to learn how to control her body, most PE lessons do not include equipment until all movement concepts have been taught. Musically most of the students will chant in rhythm, but most of them will not be able to sing yet as we understand singing. The first songs they will be able to sing are like the "chase me" songs (nah-nah-nah-nah-nah-nah). Many of them will not be able to pat to the steady beat of a song yet. Again, all of these things will change as the year progresses. (Because the young child needs practice singing and keeping a steady rhythm, singing and gross motor movements while keeping a steady beat on instruments are emphasized.) Emotionally they cannot always separate reality from fantasy. They might think that nonliving objects really do have feelings. When you are pretending with them, it is important to tell them at the end of rhymes or songs that might end in a way they would perceive to be scary that everything is OK. For example, in "Three Little Monkeys," make sure they know that Mr. Crocodile did not really eat the monkeys. You could also change the ending. After Mr. Crocodile eats the monkeys, he sneezes and out they come, laughing and covered in crocodile slobber. Use your imagination with these young students!

Most of the lessons in the book will take about forty-five to sixty minutes to complete if you read the story, do the PE portion of the lesson, and then the music portion. Some lessons might be a little bit shorter or a little bit longer depending on the length of the story and how the children understand and respond to the activities. Feel free to repeat lessons that need extra time or that were favorites of your class. If you ever have any extra time, review past lessons, songs, and stories.

Literacy and the Young Child

Reading to your young students and discussing literature with them every day is not only informative and enjoyable, but it also has many desirable outcomes. By the end of kindergarten, most children who have had daily exposure to age-appropriate literature will be able to:

- Understand and respond to stories that are read aloud to them.
- Relate the story to their lives.
- Discuss what could happen next if the story were to continue.
- Identify characters and events from the story.
- Retell a story using their own words.
- Understand that stories have a beginning, middle, and an end.
- Have a greater understanding of people from other countries and cultures.
- Understand that people in other countries have different celebrations and values.
- Relate to people from other countries and cultures.
- Start to gain a historical perspective of major world events.
- Learn the difference between reality and fantasy.
- Understand what types of events can really happen and what kinds of events cannot happen.
- Understand that some stories are true, and others are fiction.
- Understand that some books are for information, and other books are for entertainment.
- Understand that being able to read is an important life skill.

MY BODY AND MELODIC VOICE

Lesson 1

Slow, Fast, Largo, and Presto

National Standards for Physical Education: Demonstrates understanding of movement concepts, principles, strategies, and tactics as they apply to the learning and performance of physical activities.

National Standards for Musical Education: 6, Listening to, analyzing, and describing music.

Equipment: None.

Lesson Focus:

- Freeze, listening, slow, and fast in PE.
- Largo and presto in music.

Related Literature: *The Hare and the Tortoise* by Carol Jones.

READ THE STORY

Read the story aloud to the class.

PE ACTIVITY

Tell the students they are going to move like the Hare and the Tortoise. When you say *hare*, they will need to move quickly, and when you say *tortoise*, they will need to move slowly. Start off trying it with the children staying in place.

When they start moving around the gym, tell them to freeze like an ice cube when you say the word *freeze*! Try that again. (Practice until you see that they understand the concept.)

The students can walk and run in different ways. Have them try walking on their tiptoes, on their heels, and so on. Have them freeze before you call out a new way to move.

PE MUSIC

The Learning Station; *Physical Ed*, song #14 "The Run Walk Song."

MUSIC ACTIVITY

Introduce the word *tempo* to the class. Tell them that the tempo of a piece of music tells you how slow or fast the piece is. Discuss the words largo (slow) and presto (very fast) and how these words relate to the Tortoise and the Hare. The Tortoise moves slowly, and the Hare moves quickly.

Play a recording of "In the Hall of the Mountain King" from *Peer Gynt Suite* by Edvard Grieg for the class. Ask them if the piece begins slowly or quickly. Ask them to tell you if the piece starts largo or presto. Ask them what happens as the music continues. Ask them if the music ends largo or presto. (The piece begins at a slower tempo and ends at a fast tempo.)

Tell the students the story of Peer Gynt as they move in place to the music. Have the students walk in place as the music begins. As the music progresses, have them jog, and then run in place to the tempo of the music.

If you are a classroom teacher with limited space, the music portion of this lesson can be done as described. The PE portion of the lesson can be done outside, or the students can do the movement in place.

If you have paraprofessionals or other adults assisting in your classroom, have them assist students who have a difficult time grasping the concepts of fast, slow, and freeze.

Lesson 2

Space Awareness and a Steady Beat

National Standards for Physical Education: Demonstrates understanding of movement concepts, principles, strategies, and tactics as they apply to the learning and performance of physical activities.

National Standards for Music Education: 2, Performing on instruments, alone and with others, a varied repertoire of music.

Equipment: Rhythm band instruments for music.

Lesson Focus:

- General space and self-space in PE.
- Maintaining a steady beat in music.

Related Literature: *Peter's Chair* by Ezra Jack Keats or *My Secret Place* by Erica Magnus.

READ THE STORY

Read one of the selected stories aloud to the class.

PE ACTIVITY

Introduce your general space rules.

1. Share the space.
2. Move safely.
3. Stay "inside the fence" or boundary. (General space is the area within the gym that the children are encouraged to travel through. Boundaries are established for safety reasons.)

Practice moving through general space and "freezing" on command. You can use music for your start and stop cues. If the students are having trouble understanding the boundary concept, have them walk the fence or the boundary lines.

Next, use the story to explain the meaning of self-space. Self-space is like a personal island, an area where the student can move his or her body staying in one spot without touching anyone. Maybe students have a special place where they can go to be alone and not have to share. Peter had grown out of his chair, and your students are growing, too. They need more space to do things without touching others.

Have the students explore their self-space. Stretch and see how much room they need. Stand tall in their self-space. Hop up and down or jog around, and so on.

The students should now understand that when they are moving around the gym and staying inside the fence, they are moving in general space. When they are by themselves and staying in their own space to do activities, they are in self-space.

PE MUSIC

Jim Gill's *The Sneezing Song and Other Contagious Tunes*, song #8 "The Silly Dance Contest."

MUSIC ACTIVITY

Tell the students that music has a steady beat. Discuss the steady beat of familiar songs they know. Play the song "La Boomba," and have the students pat their legs to the steady beat. Play the song again, and have the students move forward in four counts and back in four counts. Have them clap on beat four. Tell them to stay in their self space. This will take practice. Have the students enjoy the movement and the music.

When the students are moving well to the steady beat of the music, teach them to play a steady beat for "La Boomba" using rhythm band instruments.

It will take the students several times through this lesson before they maintain the steady beat to the song.

If you are a classroom teacher with limited space, tell the students to take "baby steps" when moving forward and backward on the song "La Boomba." The PE portion of the lesson may proceed as described. Tell the children to be aware of classroom furniture.

If you have paraprofessionals or other adults assisting in your classroom, have them help students who need physical assistance keeping a steady beat, playing a rhythm, or understanding general space and self-space.

Lesson 3

Levels, Directions, and Moving to a Beat

⟶ ·ᴗᴗᴗᴗᴗᴗᴗᴗ· ⟵

National Standards for Physical Education: Demonstrates understanding of movement concepts, principles, strategies, and tactics as they apply to the learning and performance of physical activities.

National Standards for Music Education: 2, Performing on instruments, alone and with others, a varied repertoire of music.

Equipment: Drum and rhythm sticks for music.

Lesson Focus:

- Freeze on command; levels and directions in PE.
- Keeping a steady beat in music.

Related Literature: *Beach Ball-Left, Right* by Bruce McMillan.

READ THE STORY

Read the story aloud to the class.

PE ACTIVITY

Begin class today with a review of the command *freeze*. Use a drum instead of your voice to signal the freeze. Practice moving safely and using the three general space rules.

Teach the students that their body moves at three different levels. Compare it to a house. High level is the upstairs, medium level is the first floor, and low level is the basement. Let the students explore moving in each of these levels, on your command, staying in general space "inside the fence."

Teach them the six directions they can move: forward, backward, right, left, up, and down. Again, allow the students to explore moving in these different directions. It is fun to tell them you are having a little quiz, or that you need help understanding ways to move, and shout out a direction or level to see if they can follow it.

PE MUSIC

A fun way to practice walking in different directions or on different levels it to use the Sesame Street CD *Hot! Hot! Hot! Dance Songs*, #8 "A New Way to Walk."

MUSIC ACTIVITY

Review Lesson 2 by having the students clap their hands or pat their legs to the steady beat of "La Boomba." Again, tell the students that music has a steady beat. Also tell them that music has rhythm, just like words have rhythm. With rhythm sticks, have the students echo play a rhythm after you, using a four-beat pattern.

Next, have the students clap, pat, or dance to the song "Spicy Hot." Tell them to stay in their self-space while dancing and moving at medium or low levels. Summarize the lesson by having a discussion about steady beat and rhythm. Ask them to clap the steady beat of "Spicy Hot." Then have them clap the rhythm of the words of the phrase "spicy, spicy hot."

If you are a classroom teacher with limited space, these lessons can be done as described if you remind the students to be careful when moving around classroom furniture. If you can go outside or find a larger space for the activities, that is best.

If you have paraprofessionals or other adults assisting in your classroom, have them assist students who are having difficulty understanding how to move at high, medium, or low levels or how to keep a steady beat.

NOTE

The movement in this PE lesson prepares the students for high and low musical sounds in Unit 1 Lesson 5.

Lesson 4

Body Control and Dynamics

National Standards for Physical Education: 2, Demonstrates understanding of movement concepts, principles, strategies, and tactics as they apply to the learning and performance of physical activities; 4, Achieves and maintains a health-enhancing level of physical fitness; 6, activity provides enjoyment.

National Standards for Music Education: 6, Listening to, analyzing, and describing music.

Equipment: Paper plates and pictures of ice skaters and skiers from magazines for PE.

Lesson Focus:

• Levels and body control in PE.
• Forte and piano in music.

Related Literature: *Cross-Country Cat* by Mary Calhoun.

READ THE STORY

Read the story aloud to the class.

PE ACTIVITY

Tell the students that they are going to be like the Cross Country Cat today. See if they can tell you the different levels in which the cat and other animals move in the story. Take time to let them practice moving like the other animals.

Show the students pictures from old sports magazine of skaters and skiers. This is a great way to show levels in real-life situations. Give them the opportunity to skate. Use paper plates for skates. They can move around the gym pretending to be skaters.

Use the command *dogs* for crawling low and *cats* for leaping high. Have the students stand in a personal space while you give the two commands and assess if they can move on two different levels. Students should be able to do this activity for a minute at a time to keep a health-enhancing level of fitness. They should also be willing to try new movements without hesitation.

MUSIC ACTIVITY

Talk about the words *loud* and *soft*. Tell the students that music has many different dynamic levels. Dynamics are how loud or soft the music is. Introduce the words *forte* (loud) and *piano* (soft). Tell the students that these are Italian words for loud and soft and that the Italian language is used frequently to describe music. Speak loudly, and ask them if it is forte or piano. Speak softly to them, and have them tell you if you are forte or piano. Ask them if you are using a speaking or singing voice. Ask them to show you the difference between their singing and speaking voices.

Play the song "Forte/Piano" for the students. Have them put their hands over their ears on the word forte. Have them put their finger to their lips as if to say *shh* on the word piano. Play the song again. Assess whether the students understand the difference between forte and piano.

After this activity, review keeping a steady beat with the pieces that the students are familiar with.

If you are a classroom teacher with limited space, and cannot find a larger space, the music portion of the lesson can proceed as described. To do the PE portion of the lesson, remind the students how to move safely in the classroom.

If you have paraprofessionals or other adults assisting in your classroom, have them help you demonstrate moving on different levels. They can also assist at demonstrating dynamic levels. They can help monitor students who need special assistance.

Body Awareness and Singing High and Low

National Standards for Physical Education: Demonstrates understanding of movement concepts, principles, strategies, and tactics as they apply to the learning and performance of physical activities; 5, Exhibits responsible personal and social behavior that respects self and others in physical activity settings.
National Standards for Music Education: 1, Singing, alone and with others, a varied repertoire of music.
Equipment: Orff Instruments for music.
Lesson Focus:

* Recognizing of body parts in PE.
* Identifying high and low sounds in music. (The PE lessons in Unit 1 Lessons 3 and 4 have helped to prepare the students for the musical concept of high and low sounds.)

Related Literature: *Even More Parts* by Tedd Arnold.

READ THE STORY

Read the story aloud to the class.

PE ACTIVITY

The students are going to focus on identifying body parts. Start with some that you assume will be relatively simple (have them touch their nose, mouth, eyes, and so on). Next introduce some that the students may not know by name (e.g., shin, calf, or thigh).

If they are successful at identifying a single body part, have them touch two different body parts together. For instance have the students touch their thumb to their knee. Give students a chance to make up some of their own combinations and share them with the class.

PE MUSIC

The Learning Station; *Tony Chestnut and Fun Time Action Songs*, song #1 "Tony Chestnut."
Jim Gill sings *Do Re Mi*, song #5 "Toe Leg Knee."

MUSIC ACTIVITY

Ask the students to show you the difference between their speaking voice and their singing voice. Tell the children that their voices can sing both high and low notes. Play high and low pitches on the piano. Have them tell you which pitches are high and which are low. Next, have the children show you a high level and a low level with their bodies. Show the students how to sing a scale using Curwen hand signs.* Move your hand up as the notes go higher and down as the notes go lower. Have them sing the scale with you. Sing the notes *do*, *re*, and *mi*. Then sing the notes *la*, *ti*, and *do*. Ask them which part of the scale is higher. Have them sing the scale with you on numbers. Have the students move their hands up when the notes are high. When the notes are low, have them move their hands down.

When you are confident that the students can identify high and low pitches, show them how to play a bass xylophone, an alto xylophone, and a soprano xylophone. Ask them which instrument produces a higher sound and which instrument produces a lower sound. Let the students try each instrument in small groups. Close this part of the lesson singing high and low by singing the scale on numbers and with Curwen hand signs one last time.

If you are a classroom teacher with limited space, both of these lessons may proceed as described. If you do not have xylophones or other pitched instruments, fill tall glasses with various amounts of water. Have the students tell you which pitches are higher and which are lower.

If you have paraprofessionals or other adults assisting in your classroom, have them assist students who are having trouble identifying body parts. They can also assist students who are having trouble striking one note at a time on the xylophones.

NOTE

*Curwen hand signs can be found at www.classicsforkids.com.

Lesson 6

Moving My Body and Singing High and Low

National Standards for Physical Education: 2, Demonstrates understanding of movement concepts, principles, strategies, and tactics as they apply to the learning and performance of physical activities; 4, Achieves and maintains a health-enhancing level of physical fitness.

National Standards for Music Education: 1, Singing, alone and with others, a varied repertoire of music; 2, Performing on instruments, alone and with others, a varied repertoire of music; 4, Composing and arranging music within specified guidelines.

Equipment: Orff instruments for music.

Lesson Focus:

- Moving in different directions and levels and understanding what a skeleton is in PE.
- Understanding high and low pitch and matching pitch in music.

Related Literature: *I Can Move* by Mandy Suhr.

READ THE STORY

Read the story aloud to the class.

PE ACTIVITY

This lesson involves some review. As the students are getting ready to move through general space, review the three rules for moving safely. Have them move through general space. As they are moving, incorporate the use of the six different directions (i.e., forward, backward, right, left, up, and down). Have them move in these directions on different levels. For example, have them move forward at high level.

Refer to the book *I Can Move* and the picture of the skeleton. Help the students to understand that they must have bones to keep their body upright and to move. Have them describe what it would be like if they did not have a skeleton.

PE MUSIC

Jim Gill sings *The Sneezing Song and Other Contagious Tunes*, song #12 "Spaghetti Legs."

MUSIC ACTIVITY

Before you begin this activity, set your Orff instruments up in a horseshoe so that you can easily see each student. Take all of the bars off of the instruments except those bars that make up the I chord in the key of F major (i.e., F, A, and C).

Talk about the many ways that music moves. Review high-sounding and low-sounding notes with the children. Next, show the children how to strike the instruments correctly with the mallets. Put an equal number of children at each instrument. Give each child a number according to how many children you have at each instrument. If you have three children at each instrument, give each child a label of 1, 2, or 3. Have the group of children experiment with the notes by playing high and low sounds. Have them start when you say *one, two, ready, play*. Encourage them to play using a steady beat and to make up patterns. Encourage them also to match some of the pitches that they play with their singing voice. Have group 1 stop when you say *one, two, three, stop*. Have individual students play for you some high or low notes. If they can match pitches on the notes that they play, have them demonstrate this for the class.

When group 1 is finished, have the group 2 students play in the same way. When all groups have played, have each group move clockwise to the next instrument and repeat the process, listening for and identifying high and low sounds, inventing patterns, and matching pitches. Insist that no one play out of turn. If a child plays out of turn, he or she must miss the next instrument rotation and sit down. Summarize the lesson by reviewing and singing high and low notes. Sing a major scale using Curwen hand signs, and also have the students sing a scale using numbers.

If you are a classroom teacher with limited space, and you do not have access to a larger space, remind the students how to move safely in your classroom. If you do not have Orff instruments, fill glass jars with varying amounts of water. Have a bucket for dumping out water, and a pitcher for filling jars with more water. Let the students try striking the jars of water with a pencil or a pen. Let them see what happens to the pitch when they add water to the jar or when they dump water out of the jar.

If you have paraprofessionals or other adults assisting you, they can help with the management of the water and jars.

NOTE

We chose having the instruments in the key of F major because there are many songs that the children play on the instruments in this key. You may use any key you like, as long as there are many notes on the instruments that the children can match with their voices. If you do not have all of the children playing on the same chord, you will become irritated by the sounds.

Pathways, Staccato, and Legato

National Standards for Physical Education: 2, Demonstrates understanding of movement concepts, principles, strategies, and tactics as they apply to the learning and performance of physical activities; 5, Exhibits responsible personal and social behavior that respects self and others in physical activities.
National Standards for Music Education: 3, Reading and notating music.
Equipment: Scarves for music.
Lesson Focus:

- Straight, curved, and zigzag pathways in PE.
- Staccato (detached) and legato (smooth) in music.

Related Literature: *Red Riding Hood* by James Marshall.

READ THE STORY

Read the story aloud to the class.

PE ACTIVITY

Tell the students that they are going to move on different pathways just as Red Riding Hood did in the story. Discuss how they got to the gym or how they got to school. Draw the pathways on a whiteboard as you are explaining them.

Start with a straight pathway. Tell them that Red Riding Hood's mom told her to go straight to Granny's. Draw it on the board and have them draw it in the air with a "magic crayon finger." Next introduce the curved pathway. See if they can tell you some of the things that Red Riding Hood had to go around while moving through the woods. Draw the curved pathway on the board. Have the students draw with their magic crayon finger. The last pathway to teach is the zigzag. Pretend that Red Riding Hood would zigzag if she had to go up the hill and back down the hill. Draw the zigzag on the board. Again, have the students draw with their magic crayon finger.

Have the students form a line to play Follow the Leader. You are the leader. Tell them a story about Red Riding Hood as they are following. Practice going straight to Granny's and curving around trees and rocks. Show them sharp-pointed turns going up the hill and down.

PE MUSIC

Tom Chapin, *Zig Zag*, song #3 "Zig Zag."

MUSIC ACTIVITY

Tell the students that music has many ways that it can "travel," or "move," just like the different pathways. Little Red Riding Hood sometimes walked, skipped, hopped, and ran on her way to her grandmother's house. Introduce the terms *staccato* (detached, or like a hot potato) and *legato* (attached or smooth, like leaves falling). Bounce the ball like you are trying to handle a hot potato. Then toss it to each student, saying the word *staccato*. Have them repeat the word as they toss the ball back to you. Sing the "Staccato Bounce!" song for the children, and then have them sing it with you. Have the students hop to the steady beat of the song.

Next, using a scarf sing the "Legato Leaves" song while you wave the scarf in the air. Have the students wave their scarves in a smooth, legato way as they sing or listen to the song.

Summarize the lesson by asking the students the meaning of staccato and legato.

If you are a classroom teacher with limited space, the music lesson may proceed as described. Consider "touring" your school as you play Follow the Leader.

If you have paraprofessionals or other adults assisting in your classroom, have them be a "line ender" when you play Follow the Leader to ensure that everyone stays with the class. During the music portion of the lesson have them also toss a ball to students using the word *staccato*. The assistants can also help students wave their scarves.

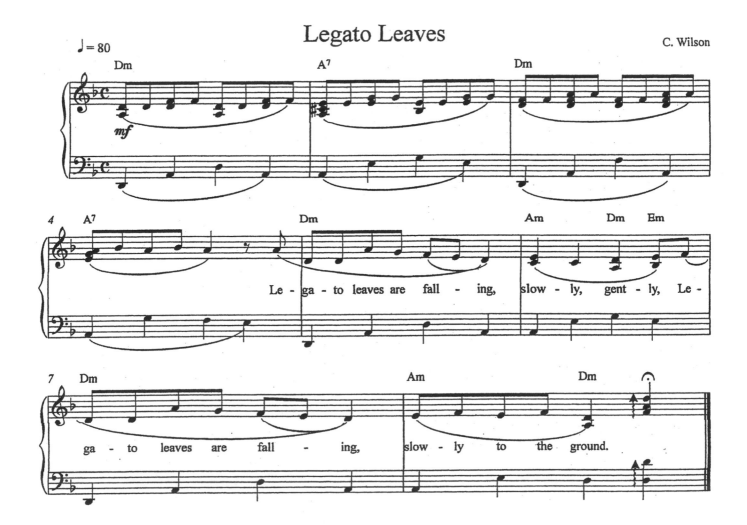

Staccato Bounce!

C. Wilson

Relationships, Crescendo, and Decrescendo

—✦—

National Standards for Physical Education: 2, Demonstrates understanding of movement concepts, principles, strategies, and tactics as they apply to the learning and performance of physical activities.
National Standards for Music Education: 6, Listening to, analyzing, and describing music.
Equipment: None.
Lesson Focus:

• Relationships with self (body awareness) and objects (proximity) in PE.
• Crescendo (gradually get louder) and decrescendo (gradually get softer) in Music.

Related Literature: *Elephants Aloft* by Kathi Appelt.

READ THE STORY

Read the story aloud to the class.

PE ACTIVITY

This book helps children understand relationship word meanings. The students like to find the bird and see what its relationship is to the elephants. After reading the story, help the students understand their relationship to the objects around them. For instance, point out to them that they are sitting on the floor or beside a friend.

Set up a small obstacle course for the students to practice their relationship words. Examples of relationship words are *above*, *around*, *behind*, and *under*. Have them go under a table, over a hurdle, between the mats, and so on. Lead them through the course before they attempt it on their own. Discuss the relationship word and then let them go through the course on their own.

MUSIC ACTIVITY

Introduce the words *crescendo* (gradually get louder) and *decrescendo* (gradually get softer) to the students. Play a major scale for them on the piano or on another instrument. You can also sing a scale for them using Curwen hand signs or numbers. Intentionally get louder or softer. Have them raise their arms gradually as they hear you get louder, and have them lower their arms as you get softer. Be sure that as you are playing or singing the scales you are sometimes louder when you are lower and softer when you are higher so that they do not confuse high pitches with high volume and low pitches with low volume.

Play "Carmen's Theme" on the piano (from the opera *Carmen* by Bizet). If you do not have a piano, sing it or play it on another instrument. Have the children raise their arms in the air when you crescendo, and lower their arms when you decrescendo. Show the students that a crescendo looks like this: <. A decrescendo looks like this: >. Have some students draw a crescendo and a decrescendo on your whiteboard or blackboard.

Summarize the lesson by discussing crescendo and decrescendo. Have the students identify a crescendo and a decrescendo in other familiar songs.

If you are a classroom teacher with limited space, proceed with the PE portion in a smaller area using what is available to make an obstacle course. The students will need to move at a slower pace for safety purposes. The music lesson can proceed as described.

If you have paraprofessionals or other adults assisting in your classroom, divide your students into smaller groups and have the other adults be leaders also.

Carmen's Theme

Lesson 9

Body Shapes and Melody Shapes

National Standards for Physical Education: 2, Demonstrates understanding of movement concepts, principles, strategies, and tactics as they apply to the learning and performance of physical activities.

National Standards for Music Education: 6, Listening to, analyzing, and describing music.

Equipment: Pencils and paper for music.

Lesson Focus:

• Wide, narrow, round, and twisted in PE.
• Melodies have shape in music.

Related Literature: *Brown Rabbit's Shape Book* by Alan Baker.

READ THE STORY

Read the story aloud to the class.

PE ACTIVITY

Discuss the different shapes that were presented in the book. Explain to the students that their body can make shapes also. Introduce the following shapes:

1. *Wide*: describe it using an alligator's mouth, or when a doctor says to open wide. Have the students make the shape standing, sitting, and lying.
2. *Narrow*: describe it like an uncooked spaghetti noodle. Have the students make the shape standing, sitting, and lying down.
3. *Round*: describe this shape like a basketball. Have the students make the shape standing, sitting, and lying down.
4. *Twisted*: describe this shape like a pretzel, or use the example of a twisted old tree. Have them make the shape standing, sitting, and lying down.

   Next, have the students play a game with you. Call out one of the shapes and have them make a statue as quickly as possible. Use all four shapes in different order.

PE MUSIC

Hap Palmer, *Sally the Swinging Snake*, song #3 "Everything has a Shape."

MUSIC ACTIVITY

Explain to the students that melodies have a shape. Melodies go up and down, fast and slow, staccato and legato. There are many musical elements that give a melody "shape."

Teach the students the song "Hot Cross Buns." Explain that this melody has a high note, a middle note, and a low note. When the note is high on the word *hot*, have the children put their hands way up in the air. When the note is in the middle on the word *cross*, have the children put their hands on their hips. When the note is low on the word *buns*, have the children touch their toes. "One a penny" is low, so the children would touch their toes. "Two a penny" is in the middle, so the children would have their hands on their hips. Have the children repeat the song several times using the motions so they have a physical and an aural sense of high, medium, and low pitches.

Next, give the children a piece of paper and a pencil or crayons. Have the children draw a line of the melody they heard. If there is time, they can make their melody pretty by decorating it. Ideally, notes that are high would be higher on their melody line.

Summarize the lesson by talking about how melodies have shape. Discuss once again the different elements that give melodies shape.

If you are a classroom teacher with limited space, the lessons can proceed as described.

If you have paraprofessionals or other adults helping in your classroom, have them assist students who need help moving like a particular shape or doing the high, medium, and low movements to the song "Hot Cross Buns."

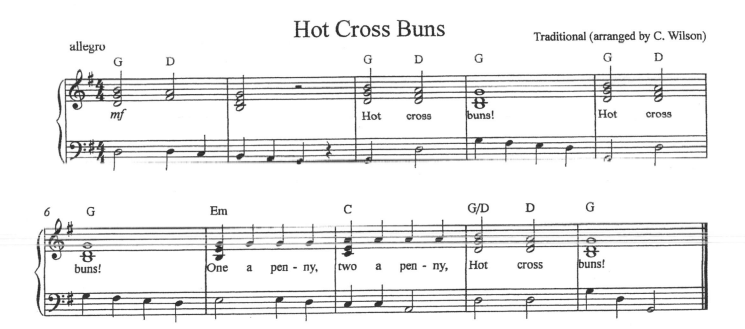

Hot Cross Buns

Traditional (arranged by C. Wilson)

Lesson 10

Flow and Musical Melody

National Standards for Physical Education: 2, Demonstrates understanding of movement concepts, principles, strategies, and tactics as they apply to the learning and performance of physical activities.

National Standards for Music Education: 1, Singing, alone and with others, a varied repertoire of music; 2, Performing on instruments, alone and with others, a varied repertoire of music.

Equipment: Orff instruments for music. If Orff instruments are not available, use boom whackers or make drinking glass xylophones.

Lesson Focus:

- Bound and free flow in PE.
- Playing and singing melodies in music.

Related Literature: *Applebaums Have a Robot!* by Jane Thayer or *Hello, Robots* by Bob Staake.

READ THE STORY

Read one of the selected stories aloud to the class.

PE ACTIVITY

Tell the students that today they will learn about flow. Use an example of a water hose. When you turn on the spigot, the water will flow continuously until turned off; this is *free flow*. If you take the water hose and put a kink in it, the water stops. If released, the water will begin to flow again. This is called *bound flow*. Have the children do the hand movements with you like they are kinking the hose.

Tell the students that movement can be bound and free. If they are batting a ball to get it over the fence, that is one fluid movement or free flow. If they are bunting, or stopping the swing so the ball does not go far, that is bound flow.

Now have them take their arms and raise them a little higher over their head each time you count a number. When you get to ten have them drop their arms in one movement. Going up choppy would be bound flow, and coming down in one movement would be free flow.

Have them experiment with the movement by doing a creative dance, the dance of the "robots and the butterflies," using the robots as bound flow and the butterflies as free flow. Play a song that has a strong beat, and tell the students when you want them to change from a robot to a butterfly.

Extending the Lesson

If time allows and the children understand the concept, give them each a heavy-duty paper plate. Practice bound flow by putting the plate against their hand and stopping the motion. The plate will fall off. Next have them put the plate against their hand and move it constantly; the plate will stay put. This would be free flow.

MUSIC ACTIVITY

The music activity during this lesson is an extension of Unit 1 Lesson 9. Talk about melodies and the musical elements that describe how a melody travels (i.e., high, low, staccato, legato, in steps, leaps, skip, and so on). Have the students review the song "Hot Cross Buns" by singing and using their hands to indicate if the note is higher (hands above head), in the middle (hands on hips), or lower (hands touch toes).

Next, show the children the Orff instruments. Make sure that the only bars on the instruments are B, A, and G, so that the children do not become confused. Review rules for holding mallets correctly. Have the children point to the notes B, A, and G, so that they can identify them when they will play. After you are sure they know where the notes are, sing a phrase of "Hot Cross Buns." Have the children repeat the phrase after you by singing and playing on the instruments. Go through this process several times. When it sounds like the children know the song with the notes, have them play the entire piece. When they sing, tell them the importance of singing the note that they play. See how many children can match the pitch that they play. If the children are doing very well, play the melody of "Hot Cross Buns" with them on the piano, making an accompaniment with chords. You may have to repeat this lesson several times to get to this point.

Summarize the lesson by discussing melodies and things that are heard when listening to different melodies. Explain that music is written on a staff to show how the melody travels. Tell the students that they will see how melodies are written on paper in a lesson coming soon!

If you are a classroom teacher with limited space, the lessons may proceed as described. If you do not have any classroom instruments, use a combination of buckets and cans in sets of three: a high-pitched, a medium-pitched, and a low-pitched bucket or can. Have the students play the high, medium, and low sounds with the corresponding pitches using a wooden spoon.

If you have paraprofessionals or other adults assisting in your classroom, have them assist students who need help understanding free and bound flow. They can also assist students with proper playing technique (e.g., mallet grip, strike the bow, bucket, or can in the center).

Lesson 11

Force and Expression

~~~⟋⟍~~~

National Standards for Physical Education: 2, Demonstrates understanding of movement concepts, principles, strategies, and tactics as they apply to the learning and performance of physical activities.

National Standards for Music Education: 4, Composing and arranging music within specified guidelines; 6, Listening to, analyzing, and describing music.

Equipment: None.

Lesson Focus:

• Strong and light force in PE.
• Improvisation and loud and soft in music.

Related Literature: *Thundercake* by Patricia Polacco.

READ THE STORY

Read the story aloud to the class.

PE ACTIVITY

Talk to the students about using force in movement. Strong force takes a lot of muscle, and light force is more relaxed. Have the students make strong muscles. Have them squeeze their muscles tight and then relax them to see how they go from firm to soft.

Give the example of sumo wrestlers. They are big and strong. When they wrestle they are using strong force. If a sumo wrestler is doing a ballet dance, that is light force. Search the Internet and magazines for suitable pictures of strong and light force to show for your students.

Have your students do different movements using both types of force. For instance, pretend to throw a ball from center field to home plate (strong). Then pretend to throw a ball a few feet to a small child (light). You can come up with several examples including things they may do at home. Dusting the furniture takes light force. Carrying out the trash takes strong force.

Have your students come up with examples in relation to sporting activities. When would you use strong and light force in soccer or in football? Have the students get up and pretend they are doing these different scenarios.

Tie the book into the lesson by linking it to the difference in force between a rain shower and a thunderstorm.

Extending the Lesson

If you are working cooperatively with the classroom teacher, give every child a copy of the *Thundercake* recipe so they can make a cake in class or at home.

MUSIC ACTIVITY

Discuss the words *forte* (loud) and *piano* (soft) with the students again from Unit 1 Lesson 4. Review the song "Forte/ Piano." Tell the students that they are going to use their bodies as percussion instruments to create a rainstorm. Divide the children into five equal groups. Explain to the children that each group is responsible for a sound and that they should become louder or softer as you direct them with your hand. The sound for the storm will be created in layers. Direct group 1 to rub their hands together. While they continue, direct group 2 to snap their fingers. Both of those groups continue, while group 3 lightly claps their hands together. While those three groups continue, have group 4 pat their hands on their laps. Finally, have group 5 stomp their feet. Have them get louder and then softer while they listen to the storm. To hear the "storm," they should not talk. Slowly, have the storm finish by taking out group 5, then 4, then 3, then 2, and lastly, group 1. Try different combinations of groups together, and also try layering them in different ways to come up with other "stormy" forte and piano sounds.

Summarize the lesson by discussing the words forte and piano. Discuss how many different things, even parts of your body, could be used as percussion instruments to make forte and piano sounds.

If you are a classroom teacher with limited space, both lessons may proceed as described.

If you have paraprofessionals or other adults assisting in your classroom, have them place themselves among the students to help with examples of strong and light force and forte and piano sounds.

Lesson 12

Relationships and Harmony

—⟨⟨⟨⟨∿⟩⟩⟩⟩—

National Standards for Physical Education: 2, Demonstrates understanding of movement concepts, principles, strategies, and tactics as they apply to the learning and performance of physical activities; 5, Exhibits responsible personal and social behavior that respects self and others in physical activity settings.

National Standards for Music Education: 1, Singing, alone and with others, a varied repertoire of music.

Equipment: None.

Lesson Focus:

• Relationships (proximity) with others and leading and following in PE.
• Harmony in music.

Related Literature: *Harry and the Terrible Whatzit* by Dick Gackenbach, *Stand Tall, Molly Lou Melon* by Patty Lovell, or *Enemy Pie* by Derek Munson.

——————

READ THE STORY

Read one of the selected stories aloud to the class.

PE ACTIVITY

This lesson focuses on doing relationship activities with a partner. The first relationship to teach is face to face. Demonstrate standing face-to-face with a partner. Talk with the students about standing in front of the mirror in the morning when they get ready for school. Ask them what they do to get ready when they look into the mirror. Put the children in pairs. Have them pretend that their partner is a mirror. Every time they move, their partner is going to mirror them. Play this game for several minutes. Have the students take turns being the mirror. Lead them through this activity with suggestions such as brushing their teeth or combing their hair.

The next relationship is lead and follow. One person in each pair of students is the leader. Their partner stands behind them. Have them play Follow the Leader. The follower should match what the leader is doing. Make sure that the children understand not to go too fast because their partner needs to be able to stay with them. Switch after several minutes.

Discuss how the book relates to the lesson by reviewing relationship words. Read a page or two and have the students raise their hands when they hear a relationship word.

PE MUSIC

The Learning Station; *Tony Chestnut* CD, song #6 "Mr. Mirror."

MUSIC ACTIVITY

Tell the students that music requires cooperation from all participants. Tell the students that the difference between a song that is sung in unison and a song that is sung in harmony is that a song is sung in unison when everyone sings the same note at the same time, and that a song is sung in harmony when two or more people sing two different notes at the same time. Teach the children the song "Down by the Station." First teach the children the words and the rhythm. Next teach the children the tune. Explain to the children that singing a song in a round can create harmony. When singing in a round everyone sings the same song, but groups start at different times. Divide the students into two groups. Have the children speak the song "Down by the Station" in a two-part round. When they are comfortable with speaking in a two-part round, have them sing the song in a two-part round.

Discuss leading and following. Explain the role of the conductor in music. The conductor is the musical leader. When the students watch you, the conductor, for their cue to start singing, they are following while you are leading. Teach the students how to conduct a four-beat pattern with their right hand. Do not expect perfection at this age. Let the children enjoy the experience.

Let individual students conduct the group while singing "Down by the Station."

If you are a classroom teacher with limited space, both lessons can proceed as described.

If you have paraprofessionals or other adults assisting in your classroom, have them help students who have trouble following their partner during the mirror game. If your adult helpers are comfortable with singing, have them lead part one during the round chanting or singing while you lead part two.

Lesson 13

Traveling and Phrasing

National Standards for Physical Education: 2, Demonstrates understanding of movement concepts, principles, strategies, and tactics as they apply to the learning and performance of physical activities; 1, Demonstrates competency in many movement forms and proficiency in a few.

National Standards for Music Education: 6, Listening to, analyzing, and describing music.

Equipment: Scarves for music.

Lesson Focus:

- Traveling in different ways in PE.
- Phrasing; just like people, music "travels" and is expressive.

Related Literature: *Gingerbread Man* retold by Jim Aylesworth or *Ready, Set, Skip!* by Jane O'Connor.

READ THE STORY

Read the story aloud to the class.

PE ACTIVITY

Review from Unit 1 Lesson 2 the general space rules so that the students remember how to move safely through the gym. Explain that locomotor movements are ways to get from one place to another without using something mechanical. Have the students name what they think moving with something mechanical would be. For instance, planes, boats, and scooters are mechanical. Next have them think of ways that the gingerbread man moved in the story. Have them name different ways they like to get from one place to another.

   Play some upbeat music and have the students do the locomotor movements of your choice while the music is playing. Have them freeze when the music stops. Continue to call out movements until you have covered the basics (e.g., run, jog, walk, march, gallop, and skip).

PE MUSIC

The Learning Station, *Physical Ed*, song #14 "Run Walk."

If the students are proficient at performing the locomotor movements, try to do a locomotor dance. Give them two or three locomotors and have the children put them together in a pattern to music. Next, let them come up with their own locomotor dance pattern.

MUSIC ACTIVITY

Tell the students that music is made up of phrases. Phrases are like musical sentences. Just as the students speak to each other in sentences, music "speaks" in phrases. The notes travel higher and lower, just as their voices move higher and lower as they speak and sing. Teach the students the traditional song "My Bonnie Lies Over the Ocean." Have the students sing the song several times, being expressive with their voices. Have them tell you when their voices go higher and louder during the phrase and when their voices go lower. Next, hand the students each a scarf, and assign them a self-space in the room. As you play or sing "My Bonnie Lies Over the Ocean," have them move the scarf up and down with the phrasing of the song. Conclude the lesson by having the students sing and move with their scarves to the song.

Play other music that the students are already familiar with. Have them move to the music and the phrasing in different ways, such as running, walking, galloping, marching, skipping, and jogging.

If you are a classroom teacher with limited space, you may want to use a larger space (i.e., hallway, cafeteria, or outside) for the PE portion of the lesson. The music lesson may proceed as described.

If you have paraprofessionals or other adults assisting in your classroom, have them help students with locomotor movements. The assistants can also demonstrate ways to move the scarves on the song "My Bonnie Lies Over the Ocean."

Lesson 14

Animal Walks and Animal Sounds

———

National Standards for Physical Education: 1, Demonstrates competency in motor skills and movement patterns needed to perform a variety of physical activities; 2, Demonstrates understanding of movement concepts, principles, strategies, and tactics as they apply to the learning and performance of physical activities.

National Standards for Music Education: 1, Singing, alone and with others, a varied repertoire of music; 6, listening to, analyzing, and describing music.

Equipment: None.

Lesson Focus:

- Levels, speed, and directions in PE.
- Animal sounds in music.

Related Literature: *Wiggle Waggle* by Jonathan London.

———

READ THE STORY

Read the story aloud to the class.

PE ACTIVITY

Have the students find a self-space in general space. Tell them they are going to practice some new locomotor movements. The new movements will be exploring the different ways that animals move.

The students saw examples of animal movements in the story. Using the story as a guide, have the students do the movements and the sounds the different animals made. For example, have them clomp like the elephant. Walk around the gym and show them the pictures of the story again as they are imitating the animals.

Have the students mimic other animals. Now have the students try to guess which animal other students are mimicking.

Next, have them try moving like the animals in different directions, at different levels, and at different speeds. Ask them what animals might be fast or what animals travel only at low level. This is a great review for the movement concepts.

MUSIC ACTIVITY

Tell the students that just as animals have styles of walks, they also make different sounds. Ask them to show you some of the sounds they know animals make. Teach the students the song "Old MacDonald." Have the students sing the song with the different animal sounds. Have the students move like the animals as they sing.

Teach the children the Spanish folk song "Mi Chacra." This song will be taught in Unit 5 Lesson 1. They will enjoy making the animal sounds in this song also. Talk with them about children in different countries all over the world, and tell them that children all over the world love songs and games about animals.

If you are a classroom teacher with limited space, remind the students how to move safely in your classroom.

If you have paraprofessionals or other adults assisting in your classroom, have them help supervise the students to ensure they are following the general space rules.

HAPPY, HEALTHY, MUSICAL ME

Lesson 1

My Heart and a Steady Beat

National Standards for Physical Education: 3, Participates regularly in physical activity; 4, Achieves and maintains a health-enhancing level of physical fitness; 6, Values physical activity for health, enjoyment, challenge, self-expression, and social interaction.

National Standards for Music Education: 2, Performing on instruments, alone and with others, a varied repertoire of music.

Equipment: Rhythm band instruments for music.

Lesson Focus:

• Keeping a steady beat in music.
• Fast and slow and heart rate and pulse in PE.

Related Literature: *Wiggle* by Doreen Cronin or *The Heart* by Anne Fitzpatrick.

READ THE STORY

Read one of the selected stories aloud to the class.

PE ACTIVITY

Tell the students that the heart is a muscle. It is the strongest muscle in the body because it works all of the time. Because it is a muscle it must be exercised. Ask them if they can pull their heart out and make it do push-ups.

Have them try to find their pulse. Explain that this is the speed that their heart is beating. The thumb side of the wrist and the side of the neck are the easiest and the most commonly used places to find a pulse. (Most of them will have a hard time finding a resting pulse.)

Next, have them start moving. They can jog in place or play Stop and Go to music. The important thing is to have them move. Tell them to stop and feel their neck or chest. If they have worked hard enough, they should be able to feel the "thump" in their chest.

Have them sit down and explain that the only way to exercise the heart muscle is to make it beat faster. Give them some examples of what they could do to get their heart rate up. See if they can think of other ways to exercise their heart muscle.

PE MUSIC

Hap Palmer, *Sally the Swinging Snake*, song #3 "Wiggy Wiggy Wiggles."

MUSIC ACTIVITY

Have the students speak the rap "Heart Rap." It will be easiest first if you have them repeat each phrase after you. Explain to them that just as their hearts keep a steady beat, most music keeps a steady beat, too. Tell them that just as their heart rate speeds up and slows down, music also speeds up and slows down.

Pass each child a rhythm band instrument. If you do not have enough instruments, divide the children into groups, and give each group a turn to play the instruments. Demonstrate keeping the steady beat as you say the "Heart Rap." Have the children keep a steady beat as you say the rap. Then have the children say the rap and keep the steady beat with the instruments. It will be difficult for many of them to keep the beat and speak the rap at the same time. Keep practicing until they get more comfortable. It will be easier for a while if you speak it for them and just have them play the instruments. If you cannot be heard over the instruments, give the children turns at playing in small groups while you and another group speak the rap.

Next, teach the children the song "Head and Shoulders." Practice singing the song slowly at first and then practice singing the song fast. See if they can do "Head and Shoulders" fast enough to exercise their heart. Teach the children musical words for describing the tempo of a song (i.e., largo, andante, allegro, presto). It is easier for the children to understand tempo words when you tell them that a largo is like a slow walk; andante is like taking a walk; allegro is like jogging; and presto is like running as fast as you can.

Have the children sing and listen to different songs they have already learned. Have them clap or play rhythm band instruments to the steady beat, and ask them what the appropriate musical word to describe the tempo of the song might be. Have the children move around the room to the songs as well.

HEART RAP

My heart is a muscle
It goes thump, thump, thump
The beat goes faster
When I run and jump

When I lay down
And rest my feet
My breathing slows
Like my heart beat

Thumpity thump thump
On it repeats
It keeps on a pumpin'
To a steady beat

Thu Thump
Thu Thump
Thu Thump
Thu Thump

If you are a classroom teacher with limited space, remind the children how to move safely around your classroom or find a larger space for the PE portion of the lesson. If you have no rhythm band instruments, have the children bring a shoebox to use for a drum. Wooden spoons make excellent beaters.

If you have paraprofessionals or other adults assisting in your classroom, have them help students find their pulse. When doing "My Heart is a Muscle," have the assistants repeat the phrases after you to show the students how the steady beat drives the rap.

The Skeleton and Singing a Spiritual

National Standards for Physical Education: 3, Participates regularly in physical activity; 4, Achieves and maintains a health-enhancing level of physical fitness; 6, Values physical activity for health, enjoyment, challenge, self-expression, and social interaction.
National Standards for Music Education: 1, Singing, alone and with others, a varied repertoire of music.
Equipment: Printout of skeleton for PE (included).
Lesson Focus:

- Bone health and the skeleton in PE.
- Singing a spiritual in music.

Related Literature: *The Skeleton Inside You* by Philip Balestrino.

READ THE STORY

Read the story aloud to the class.

PE ACTIVITY

This lesson focuses on the bones and their relationship in the skeleton. If you have a poly skeleton puzzle, let the students put it together with your guidance. You can also use a printout of a skeleton. Have the students identify the bones by their common names. Ask them to identify the leg bones, the arm bones, and other bones. If you are using the printout, have them color the different bones different colors. Have them work as a group and put the puzzle together with your guidance.

It is interesting to watch them try to figure how the bones form a skeleton. Soon they will begin to understand where the bigger bones are located.

Use the song "Bones" by Jim Valley from Rainbow Planet. Have the students do some creative dance to the song. There are some directions in the lyrics.

MUSIC ACTIVITY

Teach the students the spiritual "Dry Bones." The song has origins in the biblical verses from Ezekiel in the Bible. Have the students point to the bones as they sing. Repeat the song several times until they are familiar with it.

Next, review the song "Head and Shoulders." Point to each body part while singing the song. Repeat the song over and over, progressively leaving out a body part each time you sing. Substitute the syllable *Hmmmm* for the body parts that are left out. Conclude by having the children tell you how their body parts are connected.

Have the students tell you which notes were higher or lower in the songs. Have them also tell you which parts were louder or softer. Tell the students to sing the songs and move their arms to show the shape of each phrase. Ask the students if they know other songs that are about body parts or skeletons.

If you are a classroom teacher with limited space, these lessons may proceed as described.

If you have paraprofessionals or other adults assisting in your classroom, have them help students put the skeletons together. When singing "Dry Bones," have adults assist students in pointing to the right body part.

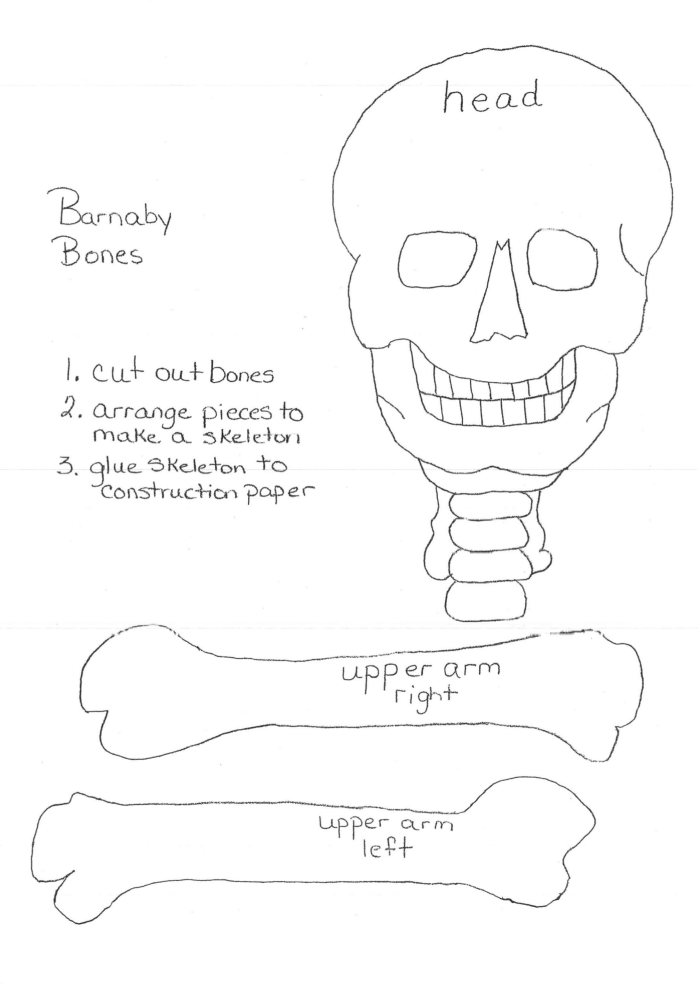

Barnaby
Bones

head

1. cut out bones
2. arrange pieces to make a skeleton
3. glue skeleton to construction paper

upper arm
right

upper arm
left

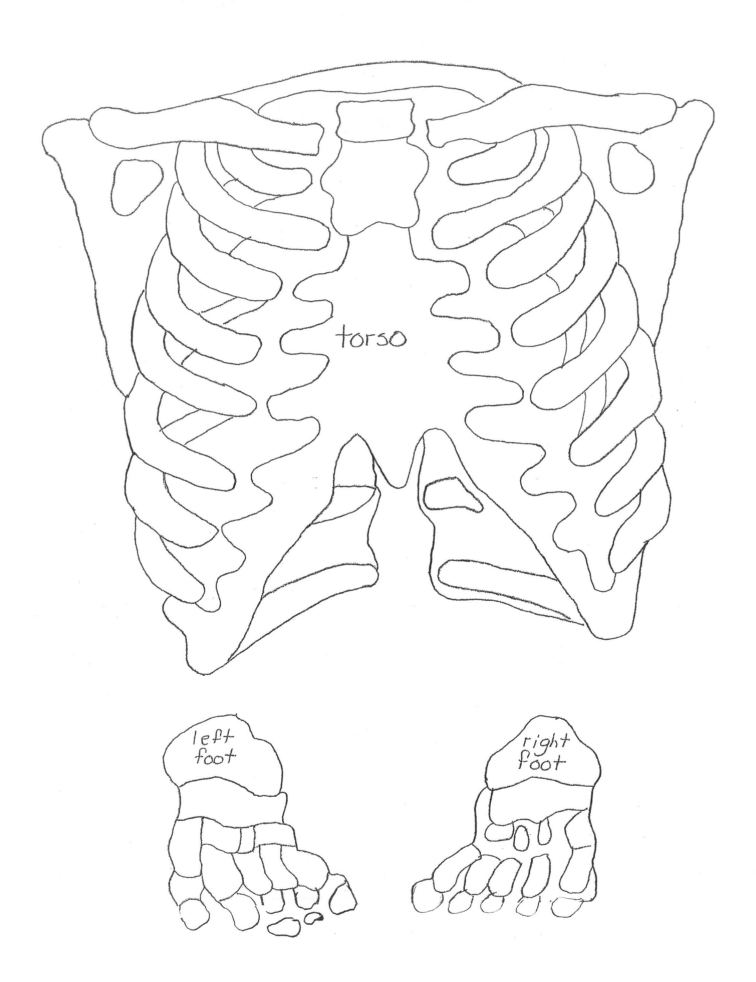

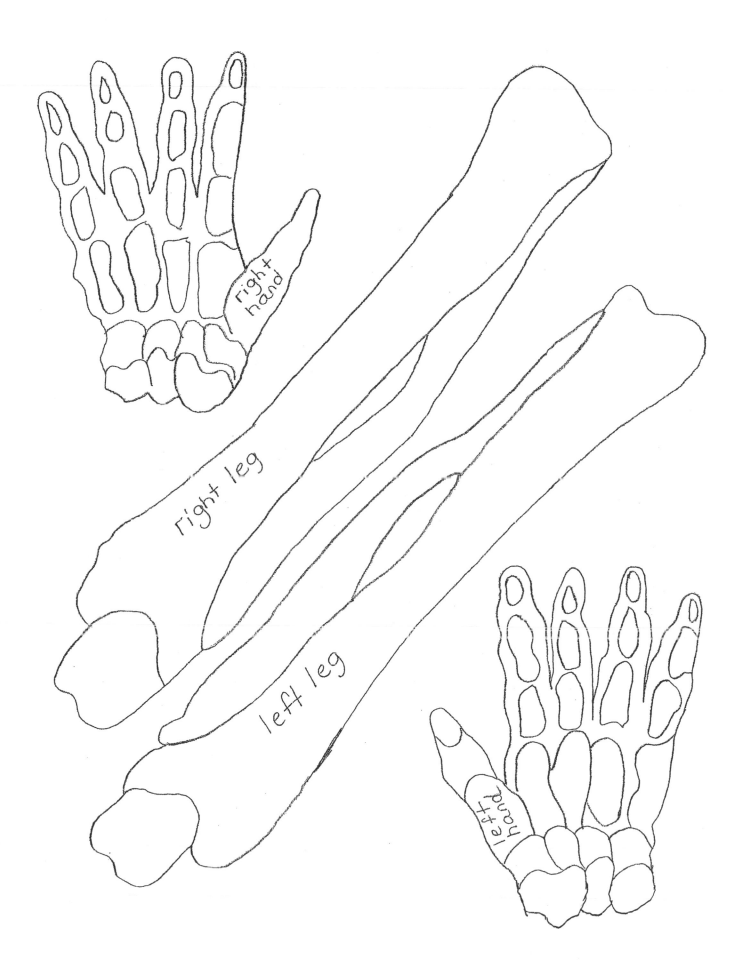

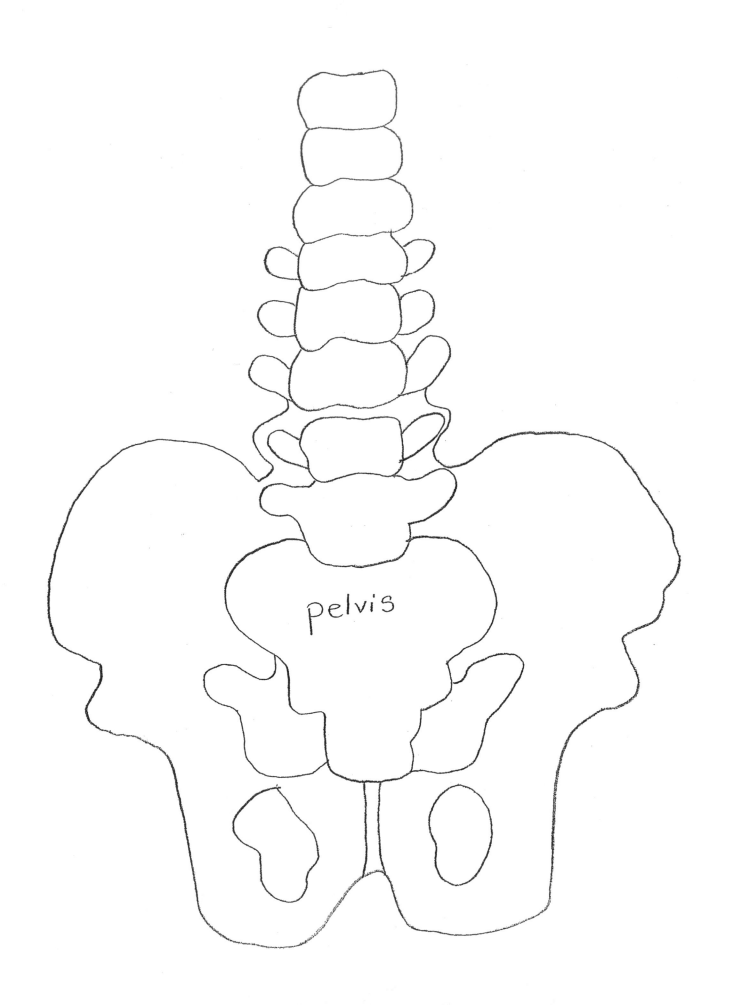

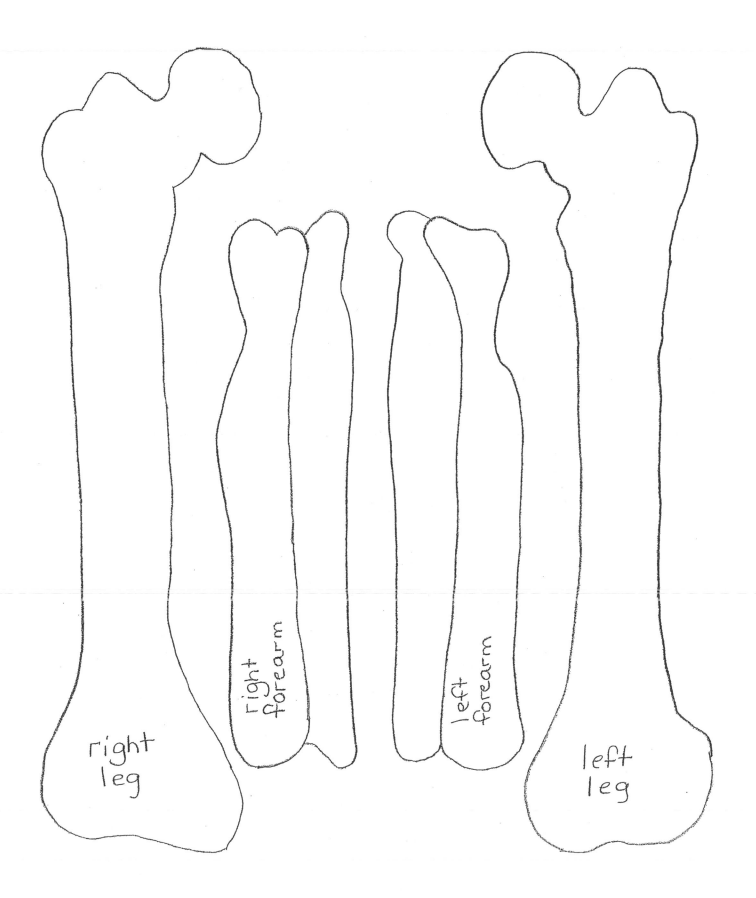

right leg

right forearm

left forearm

left leg

Lesson 3

Self-Identification and a Steady Beat

National Standards for Physical Education: 6, Values physical activity for health, enjoyment, challenge, self-expression, and social interaction.

National Standards for Music Education: 1, Singing, alone and with others, a varied repertoire of music; 2, Performing on instruments, alone and with others, a varied repertoire of music.

Equipment: Rhythm band instruments for music.

Lesson Focus:

- Understanding yourself as an individual in PE.
- Steady beat in music.

Related Literature: *No One Like You* by Jillian Harker.

READ THE STORY

Read the story aloud to the class.

PE ACTIVITY

Children at this stage in their development do not understand the characteristics about them that make them completely unique. Play the game called That's Me. Have the students stand on a line in the gym or outside. Tell them which line they will be moving to if the phrase matches their personality or a physical trait. All of the students begin on the same line. Now begin asking questions. For instance, you could say, "Anyone who has brown hair may go." The children with brown hair should respond, "That's me!" and move to the line that you designated. Continue asking questions that identify the students as individuals. They will be moving in and out of each other as they cross from one line to the next.

Review your locomotor skills and state the type of movement that you want the students to use.

MUSIC ACTIVITY

Teach the students the song "Kids Are Different." Discuss with the students how each person is special and unique and that there is no one else in the world who is just like them. Have each child tell you something that is special and unique about himself or herself. Review steady beat with the students. Pass out the rhythm band instruments. Have the students sing the song "Kids Are Different" again, and have them play the rhythm band instruments to the steady beat of the song. Sing and play the song several more times, giving students the chance to play a different instrument each time.

Ask the students the difference between the steady beat of the song "Kids are Different" and the rhythm of the words. Have them play the refrain using the rhythm of the words instead of keeping the steady beat.

"Kids Are Different"
Kids are different
On the outside
But inside, we all have feelings
So look around you
And give someone a smile
To show that you care

If you are a classroom teacher with limited space, move to an area with more space to play the game That's Me (e.g., hallway, gym, outside). If you have no rhythm instruments, use the shoebox drums from Unit 2 Lesson 1 or have the students pat the steady beat of the song on their legs.

If you have paraprofessionals or other adults assisting in your classroom, have them help students recognize their individual characteristics when you call them out during the game That's Me. They can also help students keep the steady beat of the song "Kids Are Different."

Kids Are Different

C. Wilson

Lesson 4

Muscles and Following a Conductor

—◦⦙◦—

National Standards for Physical Education: 6, Values physical activity for health, enjoyment, challenge, self-expression, and social interaction.
National Standards for Music Education: 4, Composing and arranging music within specified guidelines.
Equipment: Orff instruments, resonator bells, or boom whackers for music.
Lesson Focus:

• Muscles and how they work in PE.
• High, medium, and low sounds in music.

Related Literature: *Just Big Enough* by Mercer Mayer or *Bend and Stretch* by Pamela Hill Nettleton.

READ THE STORY

Read one of the selected stories aloud to the class.

PE ACTIVITY

This lesson focuses on muscles. If you have an age-appropriate picture of the human muscular system to show the children, it would be a good visual to help them learn about their muscles. Help them to understand how the muscles work with the bones. Muscles are attached to the bones. Bones are hard and can break. Muscle is tissue and can tear.

Have the students flex some of their muscles. The easiest muscles to flex will be the biceps. Show them that when they flex a muscle it becomes tight. This will relate back to the use of strong and light force (see Unit 1 Lesson 11). How many different muscles can the students find to flex? Have them try flexing their legs, tummy, and even their face.

Music to use with this lesson is "Pump Pump Shuffle" on the Learning Station *Tony Chestnut* CD. Either go with the suggestions on the recording or allow the children time for free movement of flexing their muscles.

MUSIC ACTIVITY

Tell the students the difference between fine motor skills and gross motor skills. Ask them if musicians use fine motor skills or gross motor skills when they are playing a xylophone. (Gross). A trombone. (Both). A piano. (Fine). Marching in a band. (Both). Ask them about other instruments as well.

Teach the student the song "My Muscles." When they are comfortable singing the song, assign each child to an Orff instrument that is in a group. Group 1 will play the notes G, B, and D. Group 4 will play the notes C, E, and G. Group 5 will play the notes D, F#, and A. Make sure that each child is responsible for only playing one note of the chord. If you have instruments with removable notes, take off the notes that the students will not be using to avoid confusion. Tell the students that you are their conductor, or musical leader. When you hold up one finger, the group 1 students will play. When you hold up four fingers, the group 4 students will play. When you hold up five fingers, the group 5 students will play. Have them play whole notes when it is their turn to play. You can prepare them to play this by having them clap on beat one while saying the words "hold that whole note." Sing the song slowly while you direct the groups of students to play at the appropriate time. You may also have half of the students play the song while the other half sing. If you have time, give the students a moment to gently play their assigned instruments and listen to the sounds they make.

"My Muscles"

My muscles help me move,
My muscles are so strong.
My muscles help me run and jump
And play this happy song.

If you are a classroom teacher with limited space, these lessons may proceed as described. If you do not have any classroom instruments, have the students play "My Muscles" using homemade drums for group 1, homemade shakers for group 4, and homemade bells (glasses partly filled with water) for group 5.

My Muscles

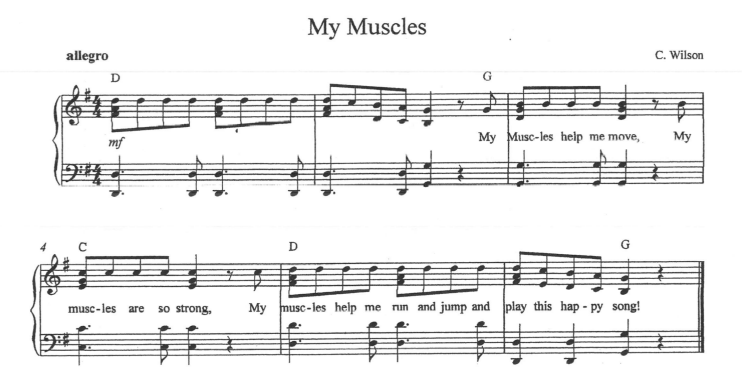

allegro

C. Wilson

My Musc-les help me move, My musc-les are so strong, My musc-les help me run and jump and play this hap-py song!

Lesson 5

Germs and Handling Instruments

National Standards for Physical Education: 4, Achieves and maintains a health-enhancing level of physical fitness.

National Standards for Music Education: 1, Singing, alone and with others, a varied repertoire of music; 2, Performing on instruments, alone and with others, a varied repertoire of music.

Equipment: A soft ball for tagging for PE, Rhythm band instruments for music.

Lesson Focus:

- Germs and how to stay healthy in PE.
- How to handle instruments without passing germs in music.

Related Literature: *You Dirty Dog* by Stephen Caitlin.

READ THE STORY

Read the story aloud to the class.

PE ACTIVITY

Children do not understand that they can prevent germs from making them sick. Explain the ways that germs can enter their body and ways they can prevent this from happening. Some examples of ways to prevent the spreading of germs are sneezing into your armpit rather than your hands and washing your hands after using the toilet.

As the flu and cold season approaches, this is an important topic. Make a point of explaining that their germs can live on desks and toys. See if the students can think of ways to not pass germs to one another and still share things.

Have the students play Germ Tag. Have one person be "it." The child who is it should carry a soft ball for tagging. Go through safety rules for tagging. If the child who is it tags a child, the tagged child must hold the spot that was touched and run to the "doctor" (teacher). The teacher asks him for a way to get rid of germs. If the child gives an appropriate answer, he may return to the game. If he does not have a good answer, cue him until you get an appropriate response.

PE MUSIC

Learning Station, *Tony Chestnut* CD, song #10 "The Shiny Clean Dance."

MUSIC ACTIVITY

Tell the students about the importance of keeping their hands out of their mouth, away from their eyes, and out of their noses. Discuss the importance of frequent hand washing. Teach the students the song "Don't Put Your Fingers in Your Mouth." Tell the students the importance of keeping their hands out of their mouths, especially while playing instruments. Tell them how many classes could possibly play on the instruments per day and how many students might play on each instrument per day. If the students do not keep their hands clean, germs can be passed quite easily.

Give each child a rhythm band instrument. Have the students gently play as many rhythm band instruments as they can in one minute by quickly but gently trading with each other. Have them count the number of instruments they played. Reemphasize the importance of good hand washing and keeping their hands out of their mouths, eyes, and noses.

"Don't Put You Fingers in Your Mouth"

Don't put your fingers in your mouth,
Don't put your fingers in your mouth,
If you do, the germs will spread,
You'll be sick and home in bed,
So please don't put your fingers in your mouth.

Don't stick your fingers up your nose,
Don't stick your fingers up your nose,
If you do, the germs will grow,
You'll feel bad from head to toe,
So please don't stick your fingers up your nose.

Don't poke your fingers in your eyes,
Don't poke your fingers in your eyes,
'Cause the germs will multiply,
You'll be sick; you'll want to cry,
So please don't poke your fingers in your eyes.

If you are a classroom teacher with limited space, find a larger space for the game Germ Tag (e.g., gym or outside). If you have no classroom instruments, use homemade drums and shakers for the demonstration of how to handle instruments without passing germs.

If you have paraprofessionals or other adults assisting in your classroom, have them be doctors while playing Germ Tag. During the instrument demonstration have them help students play each instrument and quickly pass it to the next person.

Don't Put Your Fingers in Your Mouth

C. Wilson

130 bpm

Don't put your fin - gers in your mouth,   No,
Don't stick your fin - gers up your nose,   No,
Don't poke your fin - gers in your eyes,   No,

don't put your fin - gers in your mouth.   If you do the germs will spread, you'll be
don't stick your fin - gers up your nose!   If you do the germs will grow, you'll feel
don't poke your fin - gers in your eyes!   'cause the germs will mul - ti - ply, you'll feel

sick and home in bed! So please don't put your fin - gers in your mouth!
bad from head to toe! So please don't stick your fin - gers up your nose!
sick, you'll start to cry! So please don't poke your fin - gers in your eyes!

Germs and Getting Well

—━━◍〰◍━━—

National Standards for Physical Education: 4, Achieves and maintains a health-enhancing level of physical fitness.
National Standards for Music Education: 1, Singing, alone and with others, a varied repertoire of music; 2, Performing on instruments, alone and with others, a varied repertoire of music.
Equipment: Soft ball for tagging for PE, Lummi sticks for music.
Lesson Focus:

• Taking care of yourself when you are sick in PE.
• Singing and keeping a steady beat in music.

Related Literature: *Dinosaurs Get Well Soon* by Jane Yolen and Mark Teague.

———————

READ THE STORY

Read the story aloud to the class.

PE ACTIVITY

This lesson is a review from Unit 2 Lesson 5. Once again explain the way germs are passed and ask the students what they can do to decrease the spread of germs.

Often young children put their fingers in their eyes, nose, and mouth, and then they touch shared items and each other. This contributes to the spreading of germs. Tell the students that it is important to keep their hands out of their mouths, ears, and nose. Insist that students immediately wash their hands if they put their hands in an area that produces body fluids.

Have the students "dance the germs away." (Jim Gill CD, *The Sneezing Song and other Contagious Tunes,* #1 "The Sneezing Song.") Instruct students to use their arm to muffle a sneeze, not their hands. The second song will be #4 "I Took a Bath in a Washing Machine." The students can do some creative movement or you can direct the movement.

If time allows, this would be a great opportunity to play a short round of Germ Tag that they learned in Unit 2 Lesson 5.

MUSIC ACTIVITY

Teach the song "Wash Your Hands." Discuss the importance of good hand washing. Sing "Wash Your Hands" again. Have the students clap to the steady beat while they sing along. Next, give each student a set of Lummi sticks. Have the students play the Lummi sticks, on the steady beat of the refrain as they sing. You will notice that once they start to play the Lummi sticks they might not be able to sing while they play. It takes practice to be able to sing and play at the same time, so have them try several times and be patient. These skills get better with practice.

Finish the lesson by discussing once again the importance of keeping your hands out of your mouth, nose, and eyes. Emphasize the importance of good hand washing. Have the children demonstrate clapping to the steady beat of "Wash Your Hands."

"Wash Your Hands"

(refrain)
Wash your hands,
Wash your hands,
Wash your hands to stay healthy.
Wash your hands,
Wash your hands,
Scrub-a-dub-a dub-a-dub-a-dub!
(verse one)
Wash them before you eat,
Wash them before you sleep!
Wash them right after a restroom break,
Wash them after you sneeze!
(sing refrain)
(verse two)
When ever they feel dirty,
Give them a scrub-a dub.
It takes about twenty seconds
To kill the germs and the bugs!
(sing refrain)

If you are a classroom teacher with limited space, the lessons may proceed as described.

If you have paraprofessionals or other adults assisting in your classroom, have them help students "dance the germs away." They can also help students play the Lummi sticks to the steady beat of "Wash Your Hands."

Wash Your Hands

C. Wilson

Lesson 7

Dental Health

National Standards for Physical Education: 5, Exhibits responsible personal and social behavior that respects self and others; 6, Values physical activity for health, enjoyment, challenge, self-expression, and social interaction.
National Standards for Music Education: 1, Singing, alone and with others, a varied repertoire of music.
Equipment: Signs for teeth for PE and music.
Lesson Focus:

• Healthy dental habits in PE and music.

Related Literature: *Jane vs. the Tooth Fairy* by Betsy Jay.

READ THE STORY

Read the story aloud to the class.

PE ACTIVITY

This lesson teaches the students about their teeth. Tell the children that teeth are bones. Review briefly the lesson that you taught regarding the skeleton (see Unit 2 Lesson 2). Just as bones need calcium to stay strong, calcium is also important for the teeth.

Ask the students how many of them have already lost a tooth. Give them time to discuss the different ways that the teeth fell out. Ask if the tooth fairy visited their house!

Go through the important factors of tooth health. Begin by asking the students how often they brush their teeth. If you have students who are not brushing, local dentists are usually willing to give out free toothbrushes. That may be enough to get non-brushers to start. Make sure that when you begin talking about tooth health factors you include eating a healthy diet. (Nutrition is the focus in Unit 2 Lessons 16 to 20.)

The other factors that you need to discuss besides a healthy diet and regular toothbrushing are regular visits to the dentist and wearing a mouth guard during activities that may cause injury to the teeth.

Next, do the activity called Make a Mouth. Make signs ahead of time that have letters or pictures representing the teeth for each child to hold. Have each child be a "tooth" in a mouth. Place them in the order that they would be located inside the mouth. Use two half circles to represent an open mouth so that they can see each other. If you have more students then "teeth," have some students walk around the circle and be a "toothbrush." This is the order of the teeth in pairs starting from the center of the mouth to the back of the mouth. The upper and lower teeth have the same names even though they are shaped differently.

C—Cuspid (two teeth in the center of the mouth)
B—Bicuspid (on the right and left of the cuspids)
I—Incisors (on the right and left of the bicuspids)
Dog—Canines (on the right and left of the incisors)
1—Molar (on the right and left of the canines)
2—Molar (on the right and left of the first molars)
3—Molar (on the right and left of the second molars)

Arrange the children in groups to form the entire mouth with the teeth in order. Play the following song and have the children jump up and down as their tooth sign is mentioned in the song.

"The Tooth Hop"

If you're a cuspid, jump up and down.
If you're a bicuspid, jump up and down.
If you're an incisor, jump up and down,
If you're a canine, jump up and down.
Molar 1 jump up,
Molar 2 jump up,
Molar 3 jump up and down!
If you're a happy, healthy tooth,
Jump up and down
And make some munchy, crunchy sounds.

MUSIC ACTIVITY

Discuss the importance of good toothbrushing habits. Tell the children about their teeth. Explain that the first teeth to come in are the cuspids, followed by the bicuspids, incisors, canines, then the first molars, second molars, and third molars, and finally, the wisdom teeth. Teach the children the song "I Lost My Tooth Today." Emphasize good singing and supporting the tone. Review "The Tooth Hop." Conclude the lesson with a discussion on proper toothbrushing and singing "I Lost My Tooth Today" again.

"I Lost My Tooth Today"

(to the tune of "Battle Hymn of the Republic")
I am so very happy that I lost my tooth today,
If fell out of my mouth when I was going out to play.
I picked it up and brushed it off and then I had to smile,
The tooth fairy will visit me in just a little while.

I'm so happy that I lost my tooth today,
I am growing up, that's what my mom will say.
I'm so happy that I lost my tooth today,
I have to shout, I want to yell a big hip-hip HOORAY!

If you are a classroom teacher with limited space, find a slightly larger area for the activity of making a mouth. The music lesson may proceed as described.

If you have paraprofessionals or other adults assisting in your classroom, have them help you arrange the students in the shape of the mouth for the activity. Have them point at the students when it is their turn to jump up and down.

NOTE

A helpful website to view regarding dental health is www.colgate.com.

The Tooth Hop

Lesson 8

Dental Health

—◈—

National Standards for Physical Education: 4, Achieves and maintains a health-enhancing level of physical fitness; 5, Exhibits responsible personal and social behavior that respects self and others in physical activity settings.
National Standards for Music Education: 1, Singing, alone and with others, a varied repertoire of music.
Equipment: None.
Lesson Focus:

• Dental health in PE and music.

Related Literature: *The Tooth Fairy's First Night* by Anne Bowen.

———————

READ THE STORY

Read the story aloud to the class.

PE ACTIVITY

Do a quick review of the healthy dental habits that were discussed in Unit 2 Lesson 7.

Have the students play the Tooth Fairy Tag. Depending on the number of students that you have, decide how many groups of students will be playing at the same time. Limit each game to no more than ten to fifteen students. If you have thirty students, have two or three groups playing at the same time, each in a designated area. Have one of the students be the tooth fairy and stand in the designated area. The tooth fairy will carry a nerf noodle to use as a magic wand. Scatter beanbags around the tooth fairy's designated area. These will be the teeth. Have the remaining students stand on a "starting line."

On the command *I need some teeth*, the remaining students try to get into the tooth fairy's area and "steal" a "tooth." They may only take one at a time. If they get a tooth, they need to put the beanbag tooth back at the starting line and try to get another tooth. The tooth fairy in the meantime will try to tag the students with the magic wand. If a student gets tagged, she must go to an adult and give her a healthy dental habit.

Change the student who is "it" (the tooth fairy) every few minutes and replace the teeth in the designated area.

MUSIC ACTIVITY

Review the song "I Lost My Tooth Today." Talk to the children about visiting the dentist. Tell the children that if they have trouble with their teeth, a dentist can help them feel better. Teach the children the song "Ouch, I Have a Sore Tooth." Emphasize good singing. Teach the children how to support the tone by breathing like they are sniffing a delicious roast beef. Tell them that their shoulders should remain relaxed and that their abdominal area should expand, like it does when they call for a friend across the playground. Have them practice calling to a friend by having them call "Hello!" in unison after you count to three. Have them feel the expansion in their abdominal area as they do the calling exercise. Conclude the lesson by singing "Ouch, I Have a Sore Tooth" and "I Lost My Tooth Today." Review "The Tooth Hop."

It is hard for children this age to understand the concept of supporting the tone when they sing at this early age. Education is a layering process, and by introducing the concept now, it will not seem as strange or new in future years. It will eventually have meaning for the students.

If you are a classroom teacher with limited space, find a larger space (e.g., gym or outside) to play Tooth Fairy Tag.

If you have paraprofessionals or other adults assisting in your classroom, have them supervise one of the groups playing Tooth Fairy Tag. During the music lesson have the assistants demonstrate calling *hello* back to you. If you play an instrument to accompany the singing, use your assistants as song leaders.

I Lost My Tooth Today

Ouch, I Have A Sore Tooth!

C. Wilson

I don't know. So off to the den - tist here I go._____ ter.

Lesson 9

School Safety, Quarter Notes, and Eighth Notes

—⬭⬭⬭—

National Standards for Physical Education: 3, Participates regularly in physical activity.
National Standards for Music Education: 6, Reading and notating music.
Equipment: Rhythm chart with quarter notes and eighth notes for music.
Lesson Focus:

- Safe ways to get to school in PE.
- Rhythms in music.

Related Literature: *This Is the Way We Go to School* by Edith Baer.

READ THE STORY

Read the story aloud to the class.

PE ACTIVITY

Discuss the different ways that your students get to school. Find out if they travel by car, if a bus picks them up, or if they walk or ride a bike. If they are walking, find out with whom they walk.

Talk about safety issues for each situation. For students riding in a car, talk about getting out of the car on the curbside, not in the street. If students are riding in a bus, talk about the importance of staying seated and not disturbing the bus driver. Seat-belt safety should also be discussed.

Go over safety in numbers. It sometimes is not a good idea to walk alone. It is also not a good idea to walk in a remote area. Talk about safe routes that are more populated in case of an emergency. This is also a good time to go over safety tips while crossing the street and why using the crosswalk is important.

If you find that this is too much information to teach in one class period, you may want to extend the lesson into another day.

Review the locomotors taught previously. Let the students know that they can walk to school and get health benefits. They can also skip, jog, hop, and so on.

MUSIC ACTIVITY

Discuss how walking and music both have a rhythm. Usually when people are walking to get somewhere, their feet keep a steady rhythm as they walk along. Show the children rhythm card one with the quarter notes in measure 1. Explain that a quarter note gets one beat just like the syllable *ta* gets one beat when you speak it. Have the children speak the syllable *ta* on each quarter note as you point to it. Tell them to speak the syllable only when you point to it. Next, show them measure 2 of rhythm card one with the quarter notes and the eighth notes. Tell them to speak the syllables *ti-ti* when they see a pair of eighth notes. Have the students speak the rhythm on the cards using the syllable *ta* for the quarter note and *ti-ti* for the eighth note pairs.

When the students are speaking the rhythms on the cards well, have them find a self-space on the floor. Have the students speak the rhythm on a card and then have them "walk" and "run" to the rhythm on the card. The students walk the quarter notes and run the eighth notes. Conclude by reviewing quarter notes and eighth notes.

If you are a classroom teacher with limited space, these lessons may proceed as described.

If you have paraprofessionals or other adults assisting in your classroom, have them help small groups of students figure out creative ways of getting to school. Next, have the students act out how they could get to school while staying in a self-space. Paraprofessionals can also work with small groups of students during the rhythm card activity.

NOTE

This is a great opportunity for your school to get involved in the Walk to School program. If you are not familiar with this program go to the website, www.walktoschool.com.

Rhythm Cards

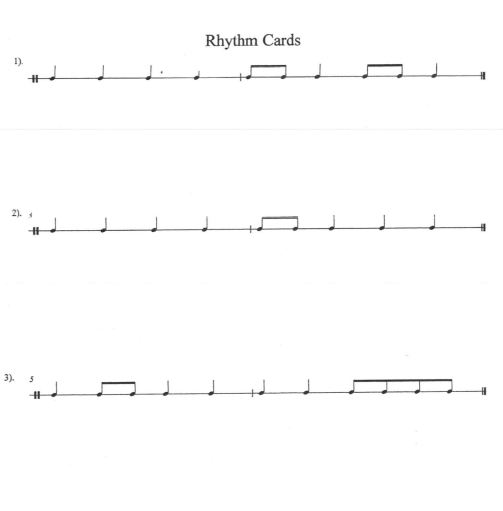

Five Senses: Touch and Quarter Notes and Eighth Notes

National Standards for Physical Education: 5, Exhibits responsible personal and social behavior that respects self and others.

National Standards for Music Education: 6, Reading, notating, and interpreting music.

Equipment: Small bags and objects to feel for PE, Rhythm cards with quarter notes and eighth notes and hand drums or rhythm sticks for music.

Lesson Focus:

• The sense of touch in PE.
• Learning about half notes and half rests in music.

Related Literature: *Moses Goes to a Concert* by Isaac Millman.

READ THE STORY

Read the story aloud to the class.

PE ACTIVITY

Split up your students into groups of four. Have one small bag containing an object for each group. Spread out the groups so that they cannot hear each other's conversation.

Explain to the students that they are going to try to name the object in the bag without looking at it. They must rely on their sense of touch. Make sure they understand not to make any comments until every one in their group has had a chance to put their hand in the bag. When all four students have felt the object in the bag have them describe it to each other. This can be difficult at this age. Usually they just want to start guessing instead of giving descriptive words. After they think they have solved the mystery, have the groups switch the bags and begin again.

Pick objects for the bags that have either a unique shape or texture. Make sure that it is a common object but not something so easily figured out. Koosh balls or other small PE and musical equipment works well.

MUSIC ACTIVITY

Review the rhythm cards from Unit 2 Lesson 9 by having the children speak the rhythms on the cards using the syllables *ta* and *ti-ti* on the quarter notes and eighth notes. Teach the children the "Five Senses Jive." Briefly discuss the five senses, and discuss the sense of touch. Show them what a quarter rest looks like, and tell them that a quarter rest gets one beat of silence.

Next, have the students find a self-space on the floor. Have the children speak the rhythm on the rhythm card and then move to the rhythm using a running step for the eighth notes, a walk for the quarter notes, and a stop sign (arms crossed in front of face) for the quarter rests.

Pass out hand drums or rhythm sticks. Have the students play the rhythms from the cards on the instruments. If you do not have enough instruments, or if there are too many students to monitor well, have the students divide into groups and line up behind each instrument. Have the students play the rhythms on two cards. Then have the students who played move to the end of the line and the students next in line will play.

Take up the instruments after the students have had a chance to play. Review the "Five Senses Jive." Conclude the lesson by talking about the note values of quarter notes, eighth notes, and quarter rests. Tell the children that rhythm is "the skeleton" of music. If there were no rhythm to music, it would not have the same appeal.

"Five Senses Jive"

1 . . . 2 . . . 3 . . . 4 . . . 5,
This is the senses jive!
Listen loud and clear,
So that everyone will hear.
Your skin and fingers feel and touch,
Hot and cold it's just too much!
Sweet and spicy is the thing
That your sense of smell will bring.
Whistles, laughter, kids at play,
Noises in our ears all day!
Ice cream, pickles, pumpkin, cheese,
Give me more for my taste buds please!
My eyes help me see all things clear,
My five senses I hold dear.
Now that you have heard my jive,
Let's all cheer for our senses five!

If you are a classroom teacher with limited space, these lessons may proceed as described.

If you have paraprofessionals or other adults assisting in your classroom, have them help pass bags around without having students see inside the bags. During the music portion of the lesson, have them help students who have trouble keeping a steady beat.

Five Senses Jive

R. Hamik and C. Wilson

1   2   3   4   5,   This   is   the   sen - ses   jive!

Lis - ten   loud   and   clear,   So   ev - ery   one   will   hear.   Your

skin   and   fin - gers   feel   and   touch,   Hot   and   cold   it's   just   too   much!

Sweet   and   spi - cy   is   the   thing   That   your   sense   of   smell   will   bring.

Whist - les,   laugh - ter,   kids   at   play,   Noi - ses   in   our   ears   all   day!

Ice - cream,   pick - les,   pump - kin,   cheese,   Give   me   more   for   my

taste   buds   please!   My   eyes   help   me   see

all   things   clear,   My   five   sen - ses_____

I   hold   dear.   Now   that   you   have   heard   my   jive,

Let's   all   cheer   for   our   sen - ses   five!

Lesson 11

Five Senses: Smelling and Singing

National Standards for Physical Education: 5, Exhibits responsible personal and social behavior that respects self and others in physical activity settings.

National Standards for Music Education: 1, Singing, alone and with others, a varied repertoire of music.

Equipment: None.

Lesson Focus:

- Sense of smell, playing a game while respecting others in PE.
- Singing in music.

Related Literature: *What Your Nose Knows!* by Jane Belk Moncure.

READ THE STORY

Read the story aloud to the class.

PE ACTIVITY

Take the students for a walk. Outside is best, but if the weather is not cooperating, inside will work. Tell them that they are going to see how many different smells they can identify on their walk.

Walk slowly and show them how to take a deep sniff. Try to walk past areas that are going to have a distinct smell. For instance, trees, bushes, a kitchen, and the teachers' workroom would all be places that have distinctive smells. When your walk is finished, have the students gather in a circle and describe some of the smells they remember.

MUSIC ACTIVITY

Tell the children how important it is to respect each other while playing games. Teach the children the song "Looby Loo." Teach the children how they can easily identify their right and left hands. If you hold your hands in the air, your left hand forms an "L" with your index finger and thumb at a ninety-degree angle. Your right hand does not. Have the students form a circle. Sing the song "Looby Loo" while doing the actions with the song. On the refrain, all join hands and circle to the left. On each verse, stop circling and do the actions that correspond with the words. Conclude the lesson by discussing how to treat each other with respect while playing games. Ask the students if they felt like they were respectful to each other while playing "Looby Loo" (hopefully, the answer is a resounding *yes*).

If you are a classroom teacher with limited space, the walk may proceed as described. You will probably want to find a larger space for Looby Loo.

If you have paraprofessionals or other adults assisting in your classroom, have them walk behind the class and encourage students to keep up with you. During the game Looby Loo, have them play with a smaller group of students.

Lesson 12

Five Senses: Hearing and Instrument Sounds

National Standards for Physical Education: 5, Exhibits responsible personal and social behavior that respects self and others in physical activity settings.
National Standards for Music Education: 6, Listening to, analyzing, and describing music.
Equipment: Sports equipment for PE, Musical instruments for music.
Lesson Focus:

- The sense of hearing in PE.
- Instrument sounds in music.

Related Literature: *Mickey McGuffin's Ear* by John Hall.

READ THE STORY

Read the story aloud to the class.

PE ACTIVITY

During this lesson your students will focus totally on their hearing. Have them sit in a large circle and close their eyes and focus on the sounds they hear. They will most likely be able to identify many sounds.

Get out a piece of sports equipment and with their eyes closed, have the students listen to the sound that the equipment produces. See if they can identify the sport by the sound. Begin with something simple such as dribbling a basketball. You could swing a bat and hit a ball, jump a rope, and so on.

Next do the "Sound Effects Song" on the Jim Gill CD, *Make it Noisy in Boise.*

MUSIC ACTIVITY

Discuss with the students their sense of hearing. Play different musical instruments for the children, introducing the instrument and letting them see how it works and sounds. Next, have the children cover their eyes. Play the different instruments for them, and have them tell you which instruments they hear.

Review the "Five Senses Jive" with the students. Once again, conclude by talking about the importance of hearing and letting the students hear the instruments one more time. Ask the students if they hear high, low, long, and short sounds. If time allows, have the students play some of the instruments.

Have the students listen to *Peter and the Wolf.* Show them pictures of the instruments that they hear. Have them describe the sounds of the different instruments (e.g., high, low, brass, percussion, and string). Have them also describe the movement of the different themes (e.g., loud, soft, staccato, legato, scary, happy, and so on).

If you are a classroom teacher with limited space, these lessons may proceed as described. If you have no classroom instruments, have the students create shakers using containers with lids and various common small items (i.e., beans, rice, rocks, sand, and such). With their eyes closed, have the students try to guess which small item is in each shaker.

If you have paraprofessionals or other adults assisting in your classroom, have them also invent sounds for the students to hear and try to guess what they are. They can also help students to play instruments correctly.

NOTE

Peter and the Wolf will be taught in greater depth in Unit 2 Lesson 18. This lesson prepares the students to learn more about instruments and instrument families.

Five Senses: Tasting and Instruments

—◄◄◄ɔɔɔ ᴎ ᴍᴍᴍ►—

National Standards for Physical Education: 5, Exhibits responsible personal and social behavior that respects self and others.

National Standards for Music Education: 1, Singing, alone and with others, a varied repertoire of music; 2, Performing on instruments, alone and with others, a varied repertoire of music.

Equipment: Variety of foods for tasting for PE, Orff instruments or pitched instruments for music.

Lesson Focus:

• Sense of taste in PE.
• Playing instruments, singing, and creating in music.

Related Literature: *A Tasting Party* by Jane Belk Moncure.

READ THE STORY

Read the story aloud to the class.

PE ACTIVITY

Students at this age do not often try new foods. This lesson will help them to distinguish different tastes as well as give them the opportunity to try new things. Hopefully they will discover something they might like.

Divide your students into groups of about four students each. Have food selections sitting on paper plates in tasting stations. Give each child a plastic glove. Choose foods that are easy to obtain: M&Ms for sweet, dill pickles for sour, pretzels for salty, jalapeño crackers for spicy, and a coffee bean for bitter are good choices. (Tell them just to put the coffee bean in their mouth but do not chew it or swallow it.)

At each of the stations have the students decide how to describe the different flavors. After a few minutes of discussion, have them rotate to the next food station.

Bring the students back together after they have tasted everything and discuss the different flavors. Ask which flavor they preferred and which they did not care for. Ask them if they would be willing to try new foods at home or for school lunch.

MUSIC ACTIVITY

Review the song "Hot Cross Buns" from Unit 1 Lesson 9. Next, have the children play the melody of the song on the instruments one note at a time. Start by singing the name of the note, and have the children point to it. Once you see that all of them know where the notes are, sing one phrase and have them sing and play that phrase after you. Continue in this listen and repeat fashion until they know the instrumental part well. It might take several lessons of playing the song phrase by phrase before they can play the song from beginning to end.

Next, have the children invent new "food words" to the song "Hot Cross Buns" (e.g., chicken stew, beans and dogs, cheese and fruit). Use the words *one a penny, two a penny* for the third phrase as usual.

Again, it might take some time to finish this lesson. Take several days if necessary.

"Hot Cross Buns"

Hot cross buns!
Hot cross buns!
One a penny,
Two a penny,
Hot cross buns!

If you are a classroom teacher with limited space, these lessons may proceed as described. If you have no classroom instruments, use different homemade instruments from Unit 1 Lesson 10 while you play "Hot Cross Buns."

If you have paraprofessionals or other adults assisting in your classroom, have them help monitor the "tasting plates." During the music lesson, have them help students to play notes and instruments correctly.

Five Senses: Sight and Music Relating to Art

—⏤⎯⎯⎯—

National Standards for Physical Education: 5, Exhibits responsible personal and social behavior that respects self and others in physical activity settings.

National Standards for Music Education: 6, Listening to, analyzing, and describing music; 8, Understanding relationships between music, the other arts, and disciplines outside the arts.

Equipment: One white paper plate and one piece of drawing paper per student and crayons and items for decorating.

Lesson Focus:

* Sense of sight, relating music and art in PE and music.

Related Literature: *Spectacles* by Ellen Raskin.

READ THE STORY

Read the story aloud to the class.

PE ACTIVITY

This is an important lesson for young children. For many young students, this seems to be about the time they have their first eye examination. Some of them show up at school with new glasses. This activity gives them the chance to be creative and design some glasses of their own.

Give each child a paper plate. Have the student first try to draw their hair and face or glue on yarn for hair. Have them use their imaginations. Next, have them cut out where they drew their eyes. Have them color on a pair of glasses. They can be as simple or as wild as they would like. If you have access to a mirror in your room, give the students the opportunity to look at themselves with their new "glasses" on.

Discuss what would happen if they did not have the sense of sight. What other senses would they have to rely on?

MUSIC ACTIVITY

Have the children listen to "Beauty and the Beast" by Maurice Ravel while you tell them the story of "Beauty and the Beast." Have the children imagine the beautiful garden. Next, have them draw a picture of Beauty and Beast in the garden as they listen to the piece while you tell them the story again. Briefly teach them about the music and the art of the impressionistic era. Tell them that paintings during the impressionistic period looked "layered." Details were blurred, and the use of color and light were highlights of this era. From a distance, you see a vivid scene. Close up to the painting, it looks like little chunks of paint. Music was also layered with planning. Briefly show them some pictures painted by Claude Monet so that they can see what impressionism looks like. Finish the lesson by discussing how the music of "Beauty and the Beast" sounded and how it made them feel. Give the students a chance to show the class their pictures and describe what they drew.

If you are a classroom teacher with limited space, both lessons can proceed as described.

If you have paraprofessionals or other adults assisting in your classroom, have them help students decorate their "faces" and "glasses." During the music portion of the lesson, have them walk around and ask students questions about their artwork.

If you have paraprofessionals or other adults assisting in your classroom, have them supervise the students who are kicking, especially those who need extra help. During the music portion, have them assist students who are not sure when and how to strike their note or are unsure of their singing. Smiles of encouragement are always helpful.

Lesson 15

Review Dental Health and Singing

—◄▥▥∫▥▥►—

National Standards for Physical Education: 6, Values physical activity for health, enjoyment, challenge, self-expression, and social interaction.
National Standards for Music Education: 1, Singing, alone and with others, a varied repertoire of music.
Equipment: Short nerf noodle and beanbags for PE.
Lesson Focus:

• Review dental health in PE and music.

Related Literature: *Berenstain Bears Visit the Dentist* by Stan and Jan Berenstain or *Tabitha's Terrifically Tough Tooth* by Charlotte Middleton.

READ THE STORY

Read one of the selected stories aloud to the class.

PE ACTIVITY

Review all of the tooth songs that were taught previously. Start with the music activity so you have time to sing all of the songs several times.

Have the students play the Tooth Fairy Tag game as taught in Unit 2 Lesson 8.

MUSIC ACTIVITY

Review the songs "The Tooth Hop," "Ouch, I Have a Sore Tooth," and "I Lost My Tooth Today." Review concepts of good singing, such as breathing like you are sniffing a rose or a yummy roast, singing on the correct pitch, supporting the sound (like calling across the playground), relaxing the shoulders and neck, and pronouncing the words as clearly as possible.

If you are a classroom teacher with limited space, find a larger space to play Tooth Fairy Tag. The music lesson may proceed as described.

If you have paraprofessionals or other adults assisting in your classroom, have them encourage students to sing. Have them also help monitor Tooth Fairy Tag.

Lesson 16

Nutrition and the Musical Alphabet

National Standards for Physical Education: 5, Exhibits responsible personal and social behavior that respects self and others; 4, Achieves and maintains a health-enhancing level of physical fitness.

National Standards for Music Education: 3, Reading and notating music.

Equipment: Food ads from your local newspaper for PE, pitched instruments for music.

Lesson Focus:

• Food groups in PE.
• The musical alphabet in music.

Related literature: *Eating the Alphabet* by Lois Ehlert.

READ THE STORY

Read the story aloud to the class.

PE ACTIVITY

This lesson will focus on food groups. To make it easy for the students to understand, divide the food groups into the following: meat, dairy, fruits, vegetables, grains, and other. Take the ads of foods from the local newspaper and cut them apart, mounting each picture on construction paper. If possible laminate them. This will keep your pictures nice for years.

Next, play Food Group Relay. Put the food pictures in the middle of the gym face up. Divide your class into small groups of no more than four each; they will function as a relay team. Call out a food group. Send the first student in each group to the middle relay-style to bring back a food from the group that you specify. When they take a food picture back to their group, the group will decide if it matches the food group you called out by showing thumbs up or thumbs down. If the food does not fit into the group you called out, help the students to decide which group it belongs to. As soon as the first child has gone and the team has decided on the food group of their selection, the next child should go. Continue until time runs out attempting to cover all of the food groups.

MUSIC ACTIVITY

Ask the children if they know the alphabet song to the tune of "Twinkle, Twinkle, Little Star." Have them sing it for you. Tell them that music has a special alphabet, too. Tell them that the musical alphabet has the notes A, B, C, D, E, F, and

G. Sing the notes for them. Explain that the notes keep repeating themselves. After the note G, notes start all over again with A. Like numbers, notes are infinite; they go on forever and ever. Assign students to xylophones, metalophones, and other pitched instruments. Have the students point to each note as you sing it. Next, have the students play each note after you. If you do not have enough instruments for all of the students to play, or if there are too many students to monitor at one time, have the students divide into groups and take turns playing in their groups. Have the groups that are not playing sing the note names with you. Sing the notes moving up a scale and then back down. Some of the notes will be too high or too low for the students to sing well. As you sing, keep the notes in a child-friendly range (from middle C to C').

Review the Curwen hand signs and syllables from Unit 1 Lesson 5. Have the students sing a D-major scale with you using the hand signs. If you want the students to get to know the hand signs well, have them sing the scale with the hand signs as soon as they come into the room every day as a warm-up. After they sing the scale, start your new lesson.

If you are a classroom teacher with limited space, find a larger space (e.g., gymnasium or outside) for the Food Group Relay. If you have no pitched classroom instruments, ask some of your students if they can bring their small toy pianos or xylophones to school to share.

If you have paraprofessionals or other adults assisting in your classroom, have them help monitor the students while playing Food Group Relay. During the music lesson, have them help students play the correct notes.

Lesson 17

Nutrition and a Steady Beat

—ᚌᚋᚌ—

National Standards for Physical Education: 3, Participates regularly in physical activity.
National Standards for Music Education: 2, Performing on instruments, alone and with others, a varied repertoire of music.
Equipment: Soft ball for tagging for PE, Hand drums or rhythm sticks for music.
Lesson Focus:

• Grain group in PE.
• Keeping a steady beat in music.

Related Literature: *Bread, Bread, Bread* by Ann Morris.

READ THE STORY

Read the story aloud to the class.

PE ACTIVITY

Today the students are going to play Carbo Tag. You will need to explain that the nutrient we get when we eat bread and grains is carbohydrates. Choose two taggers for your game. Give the taggers something soft to tag with. When you say, *go*, the students will try to stay away from the taggers. If they get tagged, they must freeze. The teacher will go to the "frozen ones," and they must give an example of something in the bread group to be in the game again.

If they are getting tagged too quickly and you cannot keep up, have the frozen ones come to you to give an example of a food in the grains group once they are tagged. Change taggers every few minutes.

MUSIC ACTIVITY

Teach the children "The Bread Jam." Some of the students will already be reading well. Copy the words to a transparency so you can point to the words while saying them, or project it from your computer. Say "The Bread Jam" again, and have the students pat their laps softly to the steady beat while you say it. Discuss the different types of bread in the piece. Next, pass out the rhythm instruments and have the students play to the steady beat as they say "The Bread Jam."

Conclude the lesson by asking the students the difference between playing the steady beat and playing the rhythm of the words. Have them play the rhythm of the words while they chant the piece.

"The Bread Jam"

White bread, rye bread
Pumpernickel, wheat
These are grains
That are good to eat.

Tortillas, pitas
Bagels too
These are things
That are good for you.

Oodles of noodles
Cereal by the bowl
These are foods
That make us feel full.

So many choices
So many grains
They help to keep us healthy
And give energy for our brains.

If you are a classroom teacher with limited space, find a larger space to play Carbo Tag. If you have no classroom instruments, have your students use the homemade drums that you need while teaching Unit 2 Lesson 1.

If you have paraprofessionals or other adults assisting in your classroom, have them help you walk around to the frozen ones to get an example of a food from the grains group during Carbo Tag. During the music lesson, have them help students keep a steady beat.

The Bread Jam

R. Hamik and C. Wilson

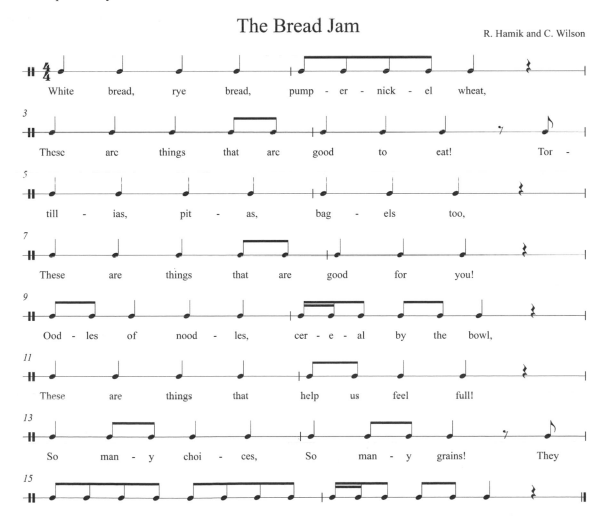

Lesson 18

Nutrition: Grouping and Instrument Families

National Standards for Physical Education: 3, Participates regularly in physical activity.
National Standards for Music Education: 6, Listening to, analyzing, and describing music.
Equipment: Food cards for PE, Instrument cards for music.
Lesson Focus:

- Food groups in PE.
- Instrument families in music.

Related Literature: *The Seven Silly Eaters* by Mary Ann Hoberman.

READ THE STORY

Read the story aloud to the class.

PE ACTIVITY

Review the food groups. Ask the students if they are trying to eat foods from all of the food groups. Have the students tell you if they have tried any new foods recently.

Today they are going to play Make-a-Meal Relay. The objective will be for the students to put together a meal containing a food from each of the food groups and something they would eat at one meal.

Do this activity relay-style with small groups of no more than four each. Place the food cards face up in the middle of the gym. Send the first person from each team to get a food card. Each team needs to decide what food group the selection belongs to before the next student goes to make another choice. If a team can tell they have two foods from the same group, have them take the food choice back and get a different one.

When each group has five food cards, go around and check them. If they need to make changes, tell them which group they are missing and give them clues of what they are looking for.

MUSIC ACTIVITY

Tell the children that types of animals, foods, books, and many other things are categorized into groups or families. Instruments are also categorized into groups or families. Teach the children characteristics of the different instrument families (e.g., brass, woodwinds, strings, percussion, and folk). Play *Peter and the Wolf* by Sergei Prokofiev for the students. Tell the children the story of Peter going into the woods against the wishes of his grandfather. Have them listen to the themes of each character while you tell them which instrument is playing, describing the characteristics of each instrument. Show them a picture of each instrument. Next, play *Peter and the Wolf* again. Have the students listen to the theme of each character and see if they can remember which instrument is playing.

Next, have the children find a self space in the room. Play *Peter and the Wolf* while having the students act out what they are hearing in the story. Some of the themes are long, such as the "Victory March" at the end. If the students are having a difficult time staying focused, stop the music and have them discuss what they are hearing, then move on to the next theme.

Have some instrumentalists from a local high school visit your class and play a song the children are familiar with on their instrument. Let the students ask the instrumentalist questions about the instrument being shown.

If you are a classroom teacher with limited space, find a larger space for the Make-a-Meal Relay. You may also want to find a larger space for the students as they act out the characters of *Peter and the Wolf*.

If you have paraprofessionals or other adults assisting in your classroom, have them help you monitor the Make-a-Meal Relay. They can also help you display the instruments cards in different instrument families and monitor the activity during *Peter and the Wolf*.

Lesson 19

Nutrition and Sounds

National Standards for Physical Education: 3, Participates regularly in physical activity.
National Standards for Music Education: 6, Listening to, analyzing, and describing music.
Equipment: Healthy and not healthy signs for PE, Instruments and other objects that make sounds for music.
Lesson Focus:

• Healthy and not healthy eating habits in PE.
• Musical and nonmusical sounds in music.

Related Literature: *Potluck* by Anne Shelby.

READ THE STORY

Read the story aloud to the class.

PE ACTIVITY

Hang the healthy and not healthy signs up on opposite walls of the gym. Have the students start in the middle of the gym. Tell them you are going to name a food or an eating habit, and they must decide if it is healthy or not healthy. This will be difficult at first as they will get confused between whether something is healthy or simply whether they like it. For example, if you say "eating broccoli," some students will run to the "not healthy" side because they do not care for broccoli, even though eating broccoli is healthy.

The students will move back and forth across the gym to the healthy or not healthy signs depending on what you call out. Remind them that they are to follow the general space rules and move safely.

Make sure when you are making up your list of foods and habits, you include things such as, do not eat breakfast (not healthy) and drink plenty of water (healthy).

MUSIC ACTIVITY

Have the children discuss what kinds of sounds are musical (e.g., someone singing, a piano playing, and so on) and which kinds of sounds are not usually considered musical (e.g., a dog barking, a train going by, someone speaking, and so on). Have the children listen to different sounds you make with instruments or other objects. Have them tell you if the sounds they hear are usually considered musical or nonmusical. Next, have individual students make some sounds that are musical or nonmusical. Have the class discuss the sounds.

Explain that sometimes musicians compose pieces of music using nonmusical types of sounds or that musicians sometimes try to imitate nonmusical sounds with instruments. Play the piece "The Little Train of the Caipira" by Heitor Villa-Lobos. Have the students tell you what they hear in the music (e.g., the train going slower or faster, the train whistle, or the train stopping). Next, play "The Train" by Quad City DJ for the students. They will notice that this is a contemporary sound. Have them tell you about the sounds and the instruments they hear, especially how this contemporary song imitates the rhythm of a train. Have the children find a self-space and dance to the music.

Play *Peter and the Wolf* for the students and have them tell you how the themes of the music are like the characters. Have them discuss how things that are considered nonmusical (e.g., grandfather's voice, the flight of the bird, and the gun blasts of the hunters) are incorporated into the music.

If you are a classroom teacher with limited space, find a larger space to play the healthy/not healthy game. The music lesson may proceed as described.

If you have paraprofessionals or other adults assisting in your classroom, have them help students decide during the game if the habits are healthy or not healthy. During the music lesson have the helpers create some musical and nonmusical sounds for the students to discuss.

Lesson 20

Health and Musical Review

—◁═◎═▷—

National Standards for Physical Education: 5, Exhibits responsible personal and social behavior that respects self and others.

National Standards for Music Education: 1, Singing, alone and with others, a varied repertoire of music; 2, Performing on instruments, alone and with others, a varied repertoire of music; 5, Reading and notating music; 6, Listening to, analyzing, and describing music.

Equipment: Any equipment or music needed for Unit 2 review.

Lesson Focus:

• Review of Unit 2 concepts and skills in PE and music.

Related Literature: *Cloudy With a Chance of Meatballs* by Judi Barrett.

────────────

READ THE STORY

Read the story aloud to the class.

PE ACTIVITY

This is the last lesson in Unit 2. This is a review day. Depending on the skills of your students, decide which part of the unit needs the most review.

Play plenty of games from the unit if time allows for it. Use any of the dance music or songs that the students have learned. Also try the "Banana Song" from the Jim Gill *Sneezing Song* CD just for some fun!

MUSIC ACTIVITY

Review all of the songs and concepts in Unit 2. Emphasize good singing, instrument playing, and listening. Have the students also review the instrumental pieces that they enjoyed. Review instrument families, high and low sounds, quarter notes, half notes, eighth notes, and quarter rests. See if the children remember how to say and clap the rhythms on the rhythm cards from Unit 2 Lessons 9 and 10. Enjoy seeing all of the things that your students can learn and remember!

If you are a classroom teacher with limited space, find a larger space for the tag games and relay games. If you do not have classroom instruments, use your homemade instruments that you used in Unit 2.

If you have paraprofessionals or other adults assisting in your classroom, have them help wherever you feel it is necessary.

Unit 3

POSITIVE PERSONALITY

Lesson 1

Respect Others

National Standards for Physical Education: 5, Exhibits responsible personal and social behavior that respects self and others in physical activity settings.
National Standards for Music Education: 1, Singing, alone and with others, a varied repertoire of music.
Equipment: None.
Lesson Focus:

• Respecting others in PE and music.

Related Literature: *The Pig Who Went Home on Sunday* by Donald Davis.

READ THE STORY

Read the story aloud to the class.

PE ACTIVITY

One of the hardest things to teach children is how to pick partners without hurting someone's feelings. This activity will help the students understand that when they pick a partner, it does not mean that they search for a friend. The goal of this activity is to get them in the habit of choosing someone who is close to them.

Tell the students to get back-to-back with any partner. (When the students get back-to-back with a partner, they stand with their back touching their partner's back.) Next, give them five seconds to find a new partner. Do this several times with the understanding that each time the students choose partners, their new partner must be a different person.

Include choices such as: find someone who is close to the same height that you are or find someone with a shirt close to the same colors as yours.

If time allows, play until most of the students have been partners with each other.

PE MUSIC

Learning Station CD, *Tony Chestnut*, "I Like Friends."

MUSIC ACTIVITY

Have the children tell you how they are all different (e.g., their hair, eyes, personalities, and so on). Teach the children that even though they all look and act different, they are similar in many ways. They all need food, sleep, shelter, and clothes. They all have a brain, blood, and a heart. They all want to be happy and accepted by others. They all have feelings and emotions. Teach them to be respectful of each other, and tell them that it is important to be kind to each other. Teach the students the song "If You Look Inside." Review good singing habits with the students.

"If You Look Inside"

I may not look like you.
I may be small, I may be tall.
I might not sound like you.
My voice is different, too.
But if you look inside of me,
You'll see I'm just like you.
We both have needs and feelings,
We both need kindness.

If you look inside,
You'll see my hopes and dreams.
If you look inside,
You'll see how hard I try.
If you look inside,
You'll see what I'm feeling.
You'll see all the good things,
Deep inside.

Conclude the lesson by talking about how important it is to be kind to each other, even though everyone has a different point of view. Discuss how our differences are gifts that can make us all stronger when we work together.

If you are a classroom teacher with limited space, find a larger area to do the partner activity. The music lesson may proceed as described.

If you have paraprofessionals or other adults assisting in your classroom, have them help monitor students as they find partners. They can also help the students sing.

Lesson 2

Respect Each Other

National Standards for Physical Education: 5, Exhibits responsible personal and social behavior that respects self and others in physical activity settings.
National Standards for Music Education: 1, Singing, alone and with others, a varied repertoire of music.
Equipment: None.
Lesson Focus:

• Respecting each other in PE and music.

Related Literature: *I Like Myself!* by Karen Beaumont.

READ THE STORY

Read the story aloud to the class.

PE ACTIVITY

This game is called I Like People Who. . . . It is a fun activity to get the students up and moving and learning things about themselves and others. Have them all line up on the same side of the gym. Give them a destination line on the other side of the gym. Begin by saying a phrase such as "I like people who say please." If this relates to them, they move to the other side of the gym. Continue with making statements and having students move from one side of the gym to the other.

By the nature of the game, the students will be moving in different directions because the statements will not apply to everyone. This is a good time to review general space rules so that students are not bumping each other as they cross paths.

This lesson also can be used to review healthy habits. You could make statements such as "I like people who brush their teeth every day."

MUSIC ACTIVITY

Have the children discuss what good manners are and why it is so important to have good manners. Explain that good manners keep everyone safe and comfortable. In certain situations, good manners and efficiency can save countless lives. That is why we practice fire drills and tornado drills in school.

Conclude the lesson by singing "Mind Your Manners" and "If You Look Inside" again. Emphasize good singing and especially good manners.

If you are a classroom teacher with limited space, find a larger space for the game I Like People Who. . . . The music activity may proceed as described.

If you have paraprofessionals or other adults assisting in your classroom, have them monitor students during the I Like People Who. . . . Helpers may also lead student singing.

Lesson 3

Respect: Helping Others

National Standards for Physical Education: 5, Exhibits responsible personal and social behavior that respects self and others in physical activity settings.

National Standards for Music Education: 1, Singing, alone and with others, a varied repertoire of music.

Equipment: Beanbags for PE.

Lesson Focus:

• Helping others in PE and music.

Related Literature: *The Ant Bully* by John Nickle.

READ THE STORY

Read the story aloud to the class.

PE ACTIVITY

This game is called Happy Helpers. It teaches not only respect but also manners.

Begin by discussing good manners. Next, have the students spread out in general space. Have them each place a beanbag on the top of their head. The objective is to try to move around the gym without the beanbag falling off.

If the beanbag falls off, a student must freeze and wait for a friend to rescue him. The friend will come over to him and ask, "Can I help you?" The reply should be, "Please." The friend should then put the beanbag back on the head of the child who requested help. After the beanbag is placed back on his head he needs to answer by saying, "Thank you."

If the helper drops his own beanbag while helping a friend, he is also frozen. Now they must wait for someone to come rescue them both.

Circulate around the gym checking to see that the students are using good manners.

MUSIC ACTIVITY

Review the songs "Mind Your Manners" and "If You Look Inside." Discuss with the students the importance of good manners. Talk about the importance of being a good friend. Teach the students the song "I'll Be There" (K–8 Music). Emphasize good singing and pronunciation. Conclude the lesson by discussing good manners toward each other.

If you are a classroom teacher with limited space, find a larger space to play the game Happy Helpers. The music lesson may proceed as described.

If you have paraprofessionals or other adults assisting in your classroom, have them help monitor the game. Also have the helpers lead student singing.

90

Lesson 4

Respect: Sharing and Cleaning Up

—◅◌◌◌◌◌▻—

National Standards for Physical Education: 5, Exhibits responsible personal and social behavior that respects self and others in physical activity settings.

National Standards for Music Education: 2, Performing on instruments, alone and with others, a varied repertoire of music; 4, Composing and arranging music within specified guidelines.

Equipment: Assorted equipment to play catch for PE, Rhythm band percussion instruments for music.

Lesson Focus:

• Sharing and cleaning up in PE and music.

Related Literature: *All the Colors of the Earth* by Sheila Hamanaka or *Too Many Pears!* by Jackie French.

READ THE STORY

Read the story aloud to the class.

PE ACTIVITY

This is a difficult age for children to learn how to share. Discuss sharing. Set out equipment that the students can use for the Catching Game. Emphasize that the students need to take turns choosing a piece of equipment to play catch with.

Have the students choose partners and then stand back-to-back with their partner. Give them only five seconds to do this. Have the students in each pair decide between the two of them who gets to choose the first piece of equipment. Offer suggestions. Maybe the tallest chooses first, or the girl. Once that is decided, have them get the equipment and begin playing catch.

Use a whistle or music to trade who chooses the equipment and who begins the Catching Game first. Now, the other student will decide which piece of equipment to play catch with. Go back and forth. Have them find a new partner at some point and practice choosing who goes first to get equipment and begin the game.

MUSIC ACTIVITY

Teach the students the importance of sharing. Have the students pick characteristics of the book that they liked. Next, have the students divide into groups. Pick a rhythm band percussion instrument that the students feel would be a good sound for a characteristic of the book. List the characteristics from the book on a chart. Have each group of students play their instruments when you point to their specific characteristic on the chart. For example, if you chose the word *love* and triangles to represent the word love, have the students play when you point to that word. Have the students practice playing loud, soft, medium loud, medium soft, and medium (i.e., *f*, *mf*, *m*, *mp*, and *p*). Show the students the musical expression symbols for these words.

Have the students trade instruments with each other and play their composition again. Discuss the importance of enjoying each instrument that they play, even if it is not their favorite instrument.

Conclude the lesson by asking the students if there are other stories that they could compose a piece of music for.

If you are a classroom teacher with limited space, either find a larger space for the Catching Game, or choose items that will not ruin your classroom (e.g., rolled socks, rolled paper wads, or nerf balls). If you have no rhythm band instruments, use the homemade instruments from previous lessons.

If you have paraprofessionals or other adults assisting in your classroom, have them monitor the catching game. Have them also help the groups of children play at the appropriate time.

Lesson 5

Respect: Choosing the Right Thing to Do

National Standards for Physical Education: 5, Exhibits responsible personal and social behavior that respects self and others in physical activity settings.

National Standards for Music Education: 1, Singing, alone and with others, a varied repertoire of music; 2, Performing on instruments, alone and with others, a varied repertoire of music.

Equipment: Signs that say *Do* and *Do not* for PE, Handheld percussion instruments for music.

Lesson Focus:

• Making good decisions in PE and music.

Related Literature: *The Ugly Vegetables* by Grace Lin.

READ THE STORY

Read the story aloud to the class.

PE ACTIVITY

This activity emphasizes making good decisions. Place the "Do" and "Do not" signs on the opposite sides of the gym. Line up the students in the middle.

Begin by calling out a situation, such as "someone asks to play with you on the playground and you say 'No!'" Now the students must decide whether to go to the "Do" side or the "Do not" side.

Continue calling out situations for the students. The students should all be moving to the same side of the gym. If they do not, you will need to stop and discuss why the decision they are making is a good choice or a poor choice.

MUSIC ACTIVITY

Discuss good citizenship with the students. Tell the students how important it is to make good decisions. Teach the students the song "Upstanding Citizen" (K–8 Music). The students will enjoy the beat of the song. Pass out the handheld percussion instruments. Have the students play to the steady beat of the refrain. If time allows, choreograph the song. Conclude the lesson by discussing citizenship and having the students play and sing "Upstanding Citizen" again.

Choreograph the song "Upstanding Citizen." Perform it for another class or for a group of teachers.

If you are a classroom teacher with limited space, find a larger area for the Do and Do not game. If this is not possible, make sure that the students remember how to move safely in your classroom. If you have no classroom instruments, use your homemade instruments from previous lessons.

If you have paraprofessionals or other adults assisting in your classroom, have them help monitor the Do and Do not game. They can also help you choreograph "Upstanding Citizen."

Lesson 6

Responsibility: Permission

National Standards for Physical Education: 3, Participates regularly in physical activity; 5, Exhibits responsible personal and social behavior that respects self and others in physical activity settings.
National Standards for Music Education: 1, Singing, alone and with others, a varied repertoire of music.
Equipment: None.
Lesson Focus:

• Asking permission and making good decisions in PE and music.

Related Literature: *Fat Cat* by Margaret MacDonald.

READ THE STORY

Read the story aloud to the class.

PE MUSIC

Dr. Jean, "Mother Gooney Bird."

PE ACTIVITY

The students are going to learn about responsibility. Getting permission is a huge responsibility. Start this day with the song "Mother Gooney Bird." The CD gives verbal directions. Follow the directions.

Next, play the game Mother May I? If you have a large group, you may want to have two games going on at the same time. You should be the first one to stand up front and be the mother. Have the students stand on a line across the gym from you.

Have one of the students ask, "Mother (or Father) May I take . . . " *(fill this in with a number and a type of step, for example, five baby steps)*. Then mother (or father) replies either "yes, you may" or "no, you may not." When a student reaches the mother (or father), he or she becomes the next mother (or father).

Continue to play until several students have had a chance to be the mother or father.

MUSIC ACTIVITY

Teach the children the importance of asking permission when they would like to go somewhere, borrow something, or do something special. Also teach the students the importance of making good decisions. Teach the children the finger play "Three Little Monkeys." Show the students how to do the hand actions with the play.

Review the songs "I'll Be There," "If You Look Inside," and "Upstanding Citizen." Conclude the lesson by talking about the importance of asking permission and making good decisions.

If you are a classroom teacher with limited space, find a larger space for Mother May I? The music lesson may proceed as described.

If you have paraprofessionals or other adults assisting in your classroom have them help monitor the game Mother May I? They can also help lead student singing.

Lesson 7

Responsibility: Sorting and Cleaning

National Standards for Physical Education: 5, Exhibits responsible personal and social behavior that respects self and others in physical activity settings.

National Standards for Music Education: 1, Singing, alone and with others, a varied repertoire of music.

Equipment: A lot of small PE equipment that the students can sort for PE, Rhythm band instruments for music.

Lesson Focus:

• Sorting and cleaning up in PE and music.

Related Literature: *It's Up to You, Griffin!* by Susan T. Pickford or *Stink Soup* by Jill Esbaum.

READ THE STORY

Read one of the selected stories aloud to the class.

PE ACTIVITY

Probably the most realistic responsibility of young children is for them to clean up after themselves. Take a mixture of PE equipment and dump it in a heap in the middle of the gym. Have several of the same or similar items. Now tell the students that you need help getting equipment put away and you need to have it sorted.

You can decide how you want it sorted. Have them put balls in one pile, cones in another, and so on. Do this relay-style with small teams of about four students each. They may only take one piece of equipment at a time to sort. After all the equipment is sorted, have them put it away. You could have boxes available for this or have them put it where you usually store it.

Children like to feel that they have been helpful. Make sure you emphasize how thankful you are for the help.

MUSIC ACTIVITY

Discuss the importance of keeping things organized. Teach the children the "Clean Up!" song. Pass out the rhythm band instruments. Have the children play to the steady beat as they sing the "Clean Up!" song. Show the children how to put each type of instrument into a separate container when they are finished using it. Have the children play and sing the song several times so that they get a chance to play and organize other instruments. Conclude the lesson by talking once more about the importance of organization.

If you are a classroom teacher with limited space, have the students organize classroom supplies. If you do not have rhythm band instruments, use your homemade instruments from previous lessons.

If you have paraprofessionals or other adults assisting in your class have them help direct the students as they play the "Clean Up" game. They can also help students organize the rhythm band instruments.

Clean Up!

C. Wilson

Responsibility: Clean Your Room

—⁓⁓〰〰⁓⁓—

National Standards for Physical Education: 4, Achieves and maintains a health-enhancing level of physical fitness.
National Standards for Music Education: 1, Singing, alone and with others, a varied repertoire of music; 2, Performing on instruments, alone and with others, a varied repertoire of music.
Equipment: Fleece balls for PE, Rhythm band instruments for music.
Lesson Focus:

• Clean up your room in PE and music.

Related Literature: *Pedrito's Day* by Luis Garay or *"It's Not My Job!"* by Ted Lish.

READ THE STORY

Read one of the selected stories aloud to the class.

PE ACTIVITY

There are two different names for this activity. It is often called Snowballs, but for the purpose of this unit, it is called Clean Your Room.

Divide your students into two groups. Position them on each half of the gym. Dump a box of fleece balls in the middle of the gym. Explain that on the signal *go*, the students are to pick up fleece balls and throw them to the other side of the gym. They are trying to keep their side clean by throwing balls to the other side. Of course, the students on the other side are doing the same thing. When the *stop* signal is given, they must freeze. Look at the two sides to see which one is cleaner. Declare a winner. Gather the balls back to the middle and start again.

Remind students that they are not throwing the balls at each other. Also, they should not kick the balls across the centerline. Ask students how many of them clean their own room.

Ask what chores they do around the house. Hopefully all of your students have some responsibilities at home.

MUSIC ACTIVITY

Review the "Clean Up!" song. Ask the children how they clean their room. Answers will vary. Teach the children the song "I'm Gonna Clean My Bedroom." Show the children the hand motions with the song. Pass out the rhythm band instruments and have them play to the steady beat as they sing. Have them sing the song and play the rhythm of the words. Have the students return the instruments to the appropriate containers. If you have time, let the students try playing several kinds of instruments. Conclude the lesson by discussing the importance of keeping your room picked up for both comfort and safety.

"I'm Gonna Clean My Bedroom"

I'm gonna clean my bedroom,
(point to self)
I'll make it nice and neat!
(spread hand out waist high)
I'm gonna clean my bedroom,
(point to self)
My mom will think I'm sweet!
(cup face in hands)

First, I'll make my bed,
Straighten blankets, fluff my pillows.
(pretend to smooth blankets, fluff pillows)
I'll put away my toys,
They give me lots of joy.
(pretend to put toys in a box)
Next I'll sort my laundry,
It will go to the machine.
(pretend to sort laundry)
My room looks nice and neat, now,
(point to self)
I'm proud that it's all clean!
(wave hand in the air above head)

If you are a classroom teacher with limited space and no fleece balls, find a larger or appropriate space for the activity. Use rolled sock balls in place of fleece balls. If you have no classroom instruments, use the homemade instruments from previous lessons.

If you have paraprofessionals or other adults assisting in your classroom, have them help monitor the activity. They can also help the children play rhythm band instruments.

Lesson 9

Responsibility: Keeping Others Involved

National Standards for Physical Education: 4, Achieves and maintains a health-enhancing level of physical fitness.
National Standards for Music Education: 1, Singing, alone and with others, a varied repertoire of music.
Equipment: Something soft to tag with for PE.
Lesson Focus:

• Keeping everyone in the game in PE and music.

Related Literature: *Ruby and the Muddy Dog* by Helen Stephens.

READ THE STORY

Read the story aloud to the class.

PE ACTIVITY

The focus of this Freeze Tag game is to keep everyone in the game. Emphasize that the students should try their hardest to get those who are tagged back in the game. Choose two students to be taggers, and give them something soft for tagging. When you call *go*, the tag game will begin.

   If you see a student who was tagged and has been waiting to be rescued for more than five seconds, begin pointing and reminding the others that someone needs to be rescued. Have the students *freeze* to find new taggers. Change taggers often.

   In closing, ask the students what their main responsibility was during the game. Have them raise their hands if they feel that they fulfilled that responsibility.

MUSIC ACTIVITY

Teach the children the song "The Mulberry Bush." Teach them how to play the song as a circle game. During the chorus, they walk around in a circle. During the verse, they stop to do the actions in the verse. Next, have the children play cooperative musical chairs while they sing the song. Count the number of students you have. Set out one chair fewer than your number of students. Have the students walk around the chairs and sing "The Mulberry Bush." They start to sing, and when you hold up a scarf, they quickly find a seat. If they see someone without a seat, they make room for that student. Once they have found a spot for all students, you take out another chair and continue the game. Continue until you see that there really is not enough room for all students. If the students get too excited trying to fit everyone in the circle, it is time to put back all of the chairs in the circle and start the game again.

If you are a classroom teacher with limited space, find a larger space to play Freeze Tag. To play cooperative musical chairs while singing "The Mulberry Bush," you will need a space that is a little bit larger.

If you have paraprofessionals or other adults assisting in your classroom, have them help monitor Freeze Tag, "The Mulberry Bush," and cooperative musical chairs.

Lesson 10

Responsibility: Chores

National Standards for Physical Education: 5, Exhibits responsible personal and social behavior that respects self and others in physical activity settings.
National Standards for Music Education: 1, Singing, alone and with others, a varied repertoire of music.
Equipment: Magazines that the students can cut pictures from, glue sticks, and poster paper for PE.
Lesson Focus:

• Chores in PE and music.

Related Literature: *The Firekeeper's Son* by Linda Sue Park.

READ THE STORY

Read the story aloud to the class.

PE ACTIVITY

This activity is to provide students with ideas of how they can help at home. Many students this age do not have designated chores at home. It is important that they start contributing their skills at home to help their families. It is good for children to realize that they can help and be responsible.

Have the students sit in small groups of no more than four each. Give them a piece of poster size paper and several magazines. Have them search for pictures of people doing things around the house that they are already doing or that they think that they could do. Cut out the pictures and glue them to the paper, creating a collage.

When the artwork is done have each group get up and show its poster. This will give students an idea of ways to help at home that they may not have thought of.

MUSIC ACTIVITY

Review the song "The Mulberry Bush." Have the students brainstorm how they can help their family around the house. Write their ideas on your dry-erase board or on a large piece of paper. Sing the song "The Mulberry Bush," and use words and actions for the tasks that they suggested (e.g., this is the way we feed the dog, or this is the way we pick up toys). Review the other songs learned in Unit 3.

If you are a classroom teacher with limited space, these activities may proceed as described.

If you have paraprofessionals or other adults assisting in your classroom, have them help students cut and paste pictures of household tasks. They can also choreograph the new verses of "The Mulberry Bush."

Lesson 11

Citizenship: Keep the Environment Clean

National Standards for Physical Education: 5, Exhibits responsible personal and social behavior that respects self and others; 6, Values physical activity for health, enjoyment, challenge, self-expression, and social interaction.

National Standards for Music Education: 1, Singing, alone and with others, a varied repertoire of music; 2, Performing on instruments, alone and with others, a varied repertoire of music.

Equipment: One garbage bag per student for PE.

Lesson Focus:

• Keeping our environment clean in PE.
• Steady beat in music.

Related Literature: *Eagle Boy* by Richard Lee Vaughan.

READ THE STORY

Read the story aloud to the class.

PE ACTIVITY

This activity needs to be done on a nice day. The students are going outside of the building and gather trash. You will need to set some boundaries so that students do not go someplace that is not safe. Also caution students about things they should not pick up such as glass. If the students find something that is suspect, have them talk to you before touching it.

The students will actually be racing each other to see who gets the most trash in their bag. This is a good time to remind them that twigs and rocks are not trash. They are a natural part of the environment and should not be put in the trash bags.

Have the students take their bags to the dumpster to properly dispose of the trash. Remind them that when they have trash they need to put it in the trashcan to keep our world clean.

MUSIC ACTIVITY

Discuss the importance of protecting the environment and keeping the Earth clean. Talk about the beauty of the Earth and all of the animals that live on this planet. Teach the students the song "Big Beautiful Planet." When the students are comfortable with the song, pass out the rhythm band instruments and have them play to the steady beat during the refrain. Students this age need a lot of steady beat and singing activities! Choreograph the song so that the students can perform the song at a chosen time and location. Conclude the lesson by talking about the importance of protecting the Earth and singing "Big Beautiful Planet."

If you are a classroom teacher with limited space, these activities may proceed as described. If you have no classroom instruments, use the homemade instruments from previous lessons.

If you have paraprofessionals or other adults assisting in your classroom, have them help students as they gather trash. They can also help pass out rhythm band instruments and model how to play to the steady beat.

Lesson 12

Citizenship: Taking Care of Those in Need

National Standards for Physical Education: 5, Exhibits responsible personal and social behavior that respects self and others in physical activity settings.

National Standards for Music Education: 1, Singing, alone and with others, a varied repertoire of music.

Equipment: Letter to parents and items for the food pantry and boxes for PE.

Lesson Focus:

• Taking care of those in need in PE and music.

Related Literature: *Uncle Willie and the Soup Kitchen* by DyAnne DiSalvo-Ryan.

READ THE STORY

Read the story aloud to the class.

PE ACTIVITY

This activity will require some preplanning. A week before you do this you will want to send a letter home with the students explaining what your objective for this activity is. Tell parents that the class is trying to help those less fortunate. (Some of your students may actually fit in this category.) Give them a list of items that the local food pantry is in need of. Ask each student to bring one item.

On the day you do this activity, have the students bring their items to class. The students could sort them into categories. You may have some toiletry items in one pile, drinks in another pile, and boxed food in another. Ask the students if they know why they are giving these items away. Let the students spend some time discussing why it is important to be generous. Have the student help carry the items to a car or van that will deliver the boxes to the pantry.

You may want to make this a school-wide project that your students are in charge of. They will have a lot of donated items to carry, but it will be exciting to see how much they collect.

MUSIC ACTIVITY

Talk to the children about the needs of people. People every day do not get enough to eat, do not have a nice place to live, warm clothes to wear, or even someone to take care of them. Teach them to be generous to others who are not so fortunate. Teach the students the song "It Starts With Me."

Have the students discuss how they can make the world a better place. There are many things that young persons can do to help others. They do not even need money! They can visit a neighbor who is old and lonely or get the mail for a neighbor who has been injured and has difficulty getting from place to place. Helping with chores at home and entertaining a younger brother or sister are also ways that they can help.

If you are a classroom teacher with limited space, these lessons may proceed as described.

If you have paraprofessionals or other adults assisting in your classroom, have them help sort items that the students have brought to donate. They can also help lead student singing.

Lesson 13

Citizenship: The Right to Vote

National Standards for Physical Education: 5, Exhibits responsible personal and social behavior that respects self and others in physical activity settings.

National Standards for Music Education: 1, Singing, alone and with others, a varied repertoire of music.

Equipment: Premade ballots and pencils for PE.

Lesson Focus:

• The right to vote in PE and music.

Related Literature: *Duck for President* by Doreen Cronin.

READ THE STORY

Read the story aloud to the class.

PE ACTIVITY

The students are going to learn the importance of voting to make a decision. Discuss how adults vote to decide on laws and leaders for our country. Emphasize that it is the duty of citizens to vote.

Give the students a chance to vote. Tell them that you are getting ready to paint your living room. Explain the color of your furniture and carpet. Next show the students two color samples. Pass the samples around. Now tell the students that they are going to help you decide on the color by voting.

Pass out a ballot with the two color choices and a pencil to each student. Remind them that they can only vote for one color. Have them pass the ballots back to you when they are finished voting. Tally the votes out loud so that the students can hear the results coming in. Announce the winner and tell them you now know what color paint to purchase.

MUSIC ACTIVITY

Teach the children the term *democracy*. Tell them that in a democratic society, all citizens have a right and a responsibility to vote. Teach the children about the Bill of Rights. Talk about some important local decisions that have been determined by a vote of the people. Sing the song "My Country, 'Tis of Thee," also known as "America," for the students. Teach them the first verse of the song. Introduce the children to other patriotic songs. "The Star-Spangled Banner" and "You're a Grand Old Flag" are both songs they should be familiar with. Conclude the lesson by having the students cover their eyes and then vote on a favorite song to sing.

If you are a classroom teacher with limited space, both lessons may proceed as described.

If you have paraprofessionals or other adults assisting in your classroom, have them help the students vote. They can also help lead students singing and think of other patriotic songs.

Citizenship: The Flag

National Standards for Physical Education: 4, Achieves and maintains a health-enhancing level of physical fitness.
National Standards for Music Education: 1, Singing, alone and with others, a varied repertoire of music.
Equipment: A coloring page of the flag for each student, one red crayon and one blue crayon for each student for PE; Percussion instruments for music.
Lesson Focus:

• The flag in PE and music.

Related Literature: *My Teacher for President* by Kay Winters.

READ THE STORY

Read the story aloud to the class.

PE ACTIVITY

Discuss the U.S. flag (or the flag of your country) and give a brief description of how it was determined. Tell the students that they are going to make their own flag. For more information about the flag of the United States, go to www .ushistory.org for the history and Google images for flag pictures.

Have the students divide into relay teams of four students each. Have each team find a self-space on the floor. Explain that the crayons to color their flag have been hidden around the gym. Each child will need to find one red crayon and one blue crayon. Only one person at a time can leave the group to search; once a crayon is found, he or she brings it back to the group and the next child in line goes to find a crayon. When all of the crayons have been found, students may color their flag on the floor in their self-space.

Have a model for the students to see of what the flag should look like when it is complete. Have a flag parade. They may take their flags home when you are finished with this activity.

MUSIC ACTIVITY

Teach the children the song "You're a Grand Old Flag." Have the students discuss patriotic days and celebrations. Usually sometime during a parade, they will see soldiers or scouts carrying the flag. Have the students play percussion instruments to the steady beat of the song. Have the children form a line with percussion instruments and have a parade in your music room. Conclude the lesson by having them sing patriotic songs.

If you are a classroom teacher with limited space, give the students the crayons to color their flags at their tables or desks. If you have no rhythm band instruments, use your homemade instruments from previous lessons.

If you have paraprofessionals or other adults assisting in your classroom, have them help students find crayons. They can also help organize the parade.

Lesson 15

Citizenship: Pollution

—◁░◁∫∩░▷—

National Standards for Physical Education: 3, Participates regularly in physical activity.
National Standards for Music Education: 1, Singing, alone and with others, a varied repertoire of music; 2, Performing on instruments, alone and with others, a varied repertoire of music.
Equipment: Resonator bells or boom whackers for music.
Lesson Focus:

• Pollution in PE and music.

Related Literature: *We the Kids* by David Catrow.

READ THE STORY

Read the story aloud to the class.

PE ACTIVITY

Keeping the world clean is part of being a citizen. Talk to the students about things that pollute our Earth. Emphasize how exhaust fumes from cars, buses, and factories pollute the environment. Explain that if everyone would walk to places that are close instead of driving, they could help make the air we breathe healthier.

Have the students tell you places they could walk to instead of riding in a car. Make sure they know that walking is great exercise and can help them stay healthy.

Have the students find a partner and line up behind you. Tell them that they are going on a walk to save the Earth and air they breathe. For safety reasons, stay close to the school. Determine how long your walk will be with the amount of class time you have and the attention span of your students.

MUSIC ACTIVITY

Teach the children how important it is to keep the Earth beautiful. Talk to them about conserving the Earth's resources. Teach the students the song "I Love the Mountains." When the students are comfortable with the song, teach them how to sing the song in a two-part round. If you have another adult who can help sing part one while you sing part two, it will give the students a better idea of how a round sounds. If you are alone trying to teach the students how to sing a round, have them speak the words in the round first and then add the notes. If your students do not sing well in a round yet, remember that education is a layering process. Young students need a lot of exposure and practice of various musical forms and styles.

Next, use resonator bells to have half of the students play an ostinato while the other half of the students sing "I Love the Mountains." You can use the notes F, D, G, and C in that order. Have the students who are playing divide into four groups. Have the first group play F, the second group play D, the third group play G, and the fourth group play C. Point to each group when they should play during the song. Make sure that they are standing in the order that they play. First, practice the song slowly, and then play the song at the regular tempo. Switch roles and let the singers play the ostinato and the players sing. Conclude the lesson by singing and playing "I Love the Mountains." Discuss ways to save the resources of the Earth.

If you are a classroom teacher with limited space, both lessons may proceed as described. If you have no resonator bells or boom whackers, use your homemade instruments from previous lessons to play to the steady beat of "I Love the Mountains."

If you have paraprofessionals or other adults assisting in your classroom, have them monitor the students as they take a walk. They can also help lead group two during round singing.

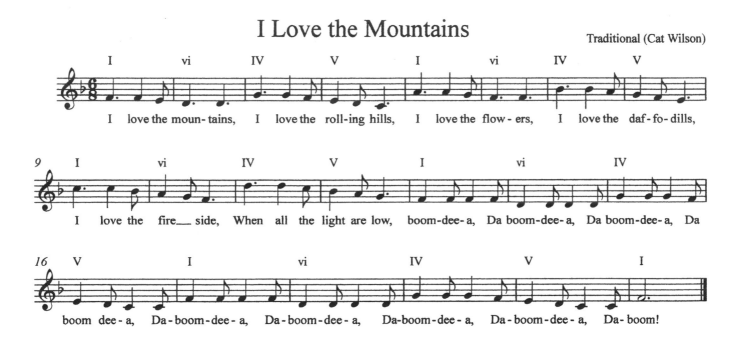

I Love the Mountains

Traditional (Cat Wilson)

Lesson 16

Fairness: Picking Teams

National Standards for Physical Education: 5, Exhibits responsible personal and social behavior that respects self and others in physical activity settings.

National Standards for Music Education: 1, Singing, alone and with others, a varied repertoire of music; 9, Understanding music in relation to history and culture.

Equipment: None.

Lesson Focus:

• Picking teams in PE and music.

Related Literature: *The Farmer* by Mark Ludy.

READ THE STORY

Read the story aloud to the class.

PE ACTIVITY

Picking teams is difficult at any age. Talk to the students about what makes a fair team and what does not. Is it fair if all of the tall people are on the same basketball team? Remind them that when picking teams you also don't want to hurt anyone's feelings. Tell them what happens when you have two captains choosing sides and how that makes others feel. The last people to get chosen often get their feelings hurt.

See if they can come up with a fair and respectful way to organize teams. Try out a few of their ideas to see if they work. Hold up two thumbs and say *two thumbs up*. The students should form two lines in front of you that are even in length as quickly as possible. See if those teams would be fair.

Have the students brainstorm for ideas that make fair teams. Maybe they would think it is fair to have the same number of boys or girls on a team. Tell your students that it is important for them to keep these things in mind when they are choosing teams on the playground or in their neighborhood.

MUSIC ACTIVITY

Tell the students that long ago people played games and sang songs without the use of any electronic devices for entertainment. Explain that long ago, people used to travel in wagons when they were settling the country. Teach the students the song "Old Brass Wagon" (K–8 Music). Talk about being fair when picking out teams or dance circles. Find a fair way to assign students to small circles with six students in each circle. (You could have the students number off from one to six, and then have them find their respective circles; ones form a small circle, twos form a circle, and so on. or have the students draw numbers to find their circle.) Teach the students the choreography to "Old Brass Wagon." Discuss the historical value of songs and games, especially in times before television, radio, and electricity were invented. Conclude the lesson by talking about being fair when choosing groups or partners and why it is important to be fair.

If you are a classroom teacher with limited space, these lessons may proceed as described.

If you have paraprofessionals or other adults assisting in your classroom, have them help the students come up with fair ways for choosing teams. Have them also help the students move to the song "Old Brass Wagon."

Lesson 17

Fairness: Rules and Organization

National Standards for Physical Education: 5, Exhibits responsible personal and social behavior that respects self and others.

National Standards for Music Education: 1, Singing, alone and with others, a varied repertoire of music; 2, Performing on instruments, alone and with others, a varied repertoire of music.

Equipment: Two small pieces of equipment per group for PE, Rhythm band instruments.

Lesson Focus:

- The importance of rules in PE.
- The importance of organization in music.

Related Literature: *Tops & Bottoms* by Janet Stevens.

READ THE STORY

Read the story aloud to the class.

PE ACTIVITY

This activity emphasizes the importance of rules and organization. The students are going to try to play a game without rules. Put them in small groups sitting around the gym. Give each group two small pieces of equipment. Simply tell them they are going to play a game with the two things you gave them and say, *go*.

The confusion on their faces will be amazing. Let them discuss and struggle for a while. Rotate among the groups and see what the discussion is all about. Stay close because some groups will be prone to argue.

After a time ask the students about their game. Some groups may have cooperated enough to make up their own game. Hopefully they will tell you they could not play because they did not have any rules. If they did not come up with this on their own, lead them into trying to play a game without rules. If they do not invent rules for their group, everyone will be confused.

Close by talking about situations in life that require rules. Do they have rules at home, school, and day care?

MUSIC ACTIVITY

Discuss the importance of rules and organization with the students. Talk about the ways things are organized in our society and culture. When you order food in a restaurant or wait for a cab, you wait in line for your turn. When people drive down the street, they follow traffic rules. Review the song "Old Brass Wagon." Have the students form several small circles. Put rhythm band instruments in the middle of each circle. Tell the students to play the instruments, and see what they do if they are not given rules. See if they start to figure out how to proceed and be fair to everyone. After they struggle for a few minutes (or seconds), ask the students to brainstorm to come up with procedures to play the instruments during the song. Write down their ideas on the board. Have the class decide the best way to proceed. How will they all get a turn?

Conclude the lesson by discussing the importance of rules in your classroom, on the playground, and in society. Have the students play the instruments and sing "Old Brass Wagon" one more time with the rules they decided on.

If you are a classroom teacher with limited space, these lessons may proceed as described. If you have no rhythm band instruments, use your homemade instruments from previous lessons.

If you have paraprofessionals or other adults assisting in your classroom, have them monitor the small groups as they attempt to play a game without rules. They can also help monitor student groups as they attempt to play the rhythm band instruments.

Lesson 18

Fairness: Making Games

National Standards for Physical Education: 5, Exhibits responsible personal and social behavior that respects self and others in physical activity settings; 6, Values physical activity for health, enjoyment, challenge, self-expression, and social interaction.

National Standards for Music Education: 1, Singing, alone and with others, a varied repertoire of music; 9, Understanding music in relation to history and culture.

Equipment: Small pieces of equipment for PE, A small rock for music.

Lesson Focus:

- Making games in PE.
- Keeping a steady beat and games around the world in music.

Related Literature: *The Old Woman Who Lived in a Vinegar Bottle* by Margaret Read MacDonald.

READ THE STORY

Read the story aloud to the class.

PE ACTIVITY

Review the importance of having rules. Ask the students what happened in the activity from Unit 3 Lesson 17 of trying to play a game without rules. Today, they are going to make up their own game and rules. Put the students into small groups.

Give each group two or three pieces of equipment. Have each group make up their game. Set a limit that they must have three rules for their game. If they are having trouble getting started, you might want to give them some suggestions for rules or one rule to start with.

Give the students time to play their new game. Have the students share their games with each other and explain the rules. Are the games that they invented similar to games they have played before?

MUSIC ACTIVITY

Talk to the students about musical games. Tell the students that children all over the world play different musical games. Ask them about some of the musical or rhyming games that they play when they are on the playground. Maybe they play "Cinderella" or "Miss Suzy Had A Baby" with a jump rope (i.e., students jump to the beat and say the rhyme). Teach the children the song "Obwisana," from Ghana. Teach them the rock passing game that goes with the song. The children sit in a circle and pass a stone on the beat. Have the students start by putting their right hand in the circle, and moving their hand to the right on the strong beat (beat one), and then back in front of them on the weak beat (beat one). When they are comfortable with the right-hand motion, have them pass the rock counterclockwise to the steady beat of the song. Children this age may have some difficulty passing the rock on the beat or passing with their right hand. Give them the experience, and keep trying. They will remember that children all over the world have fun playing musical games.

Conclude the lesson by discussing musical games from around the world.

If you are a classroom teacher with limited space, these lessons may proceed as described.

If you have paraprofessionals or other adults assisting in your classroom, have them help monitor students as they invent new games. They can also help students who are having trouble moving their right hand to the steady beat.

Lesson 19

Fairness: Taking Turns and Singing

National Standards for Physical Education: 5, Exhibits responsible personal and social behavior that respects self and others in physical activity settings.
National Standards for Music Education: 1, Singing, alone and with others, a varied repertoire of music.
Equipment: Balls for PE.
Lesson Focus:

• Taking turns in PE.
• Singing in music.

Related Literature: *The King of the Birds* by Helen Ward.

READ THE STORY

Read the story aloud to the class.

PE ACTIVITY

The students are going to do an activity that requires taking turns. Lay several balls of all kinds in the middle of the gym. Have the students find a partner to play catch with and get back-to-back.

The first step is for each pair of students to decide who is going to go first. Start off with the tallest one picking a ball from the center. After several minutes, signal for the students to put the balls back in the center of the gym. Ask the students who should get to pick the ball this time. Play the game several times, signaling for the students to exchange balls every few minutes. Emphasize being fair as the students work in pairs.

Close by talking to the students about the importance of taking turns.

MUSIC ACTIVITY

Talk to the children about the importance of taking turns. Teach the children the song "Roll That Red Ball." Have the children sit in a circle. Have the children sing the song "Roll That Red Ball." Each time they sing the phrase "roll that red ball," have them roll the ball to another child. Be sure that all children get a turn to roll the ball. Tell the children to try to remember who has not had a turn so that they can roll the ball accordingly.

Conclude the lesson by asking the children what other games they know where they roll a ball. Discuss taking turns.

If you are a classroom teacher with limited space, find a larger space for the catching game. The music lesson requires enough space for the students to sit in a large circle.

If you have paraprofessionals or other adults assisting in your classroom, have them monitor the pairs of students as they play catch. During "Roll That Red Ball," you can also have helpers monitor another circle of students by dividing the students between yourself and your helpers; this way each student can have more turns.

Lesson 20

Fairness: Playing by the Rules

National Standards for Physical Education: 4, Achieves and maintains a health-enhancing level of physical fitness; 5, Exhibits responsible personal and social behavior that respects self and others in physical activity settings.
National Standards for Music Education: 1, Singing, alone and with others, a varied repertoire of music.
Equipment: Soft objects to tag with for PE.
Lesson Focus:

• Playing by the rules in PE and music.

Related Literature: *The True Story of the 3 Little Pigs!* by Jon Scieszka.

READ THE STORY

Read the story aloud to the class.

PE ACTIVITY

The students are going to play a game directly related to the story. This activity is called "Three Little Pigs" Tag. Choose a student to be the wolf. Divide the class into three groups. Designate three areas in the gym. The first area will be the house of straw, the second will be the house of sticks, and the third the house of bricks. Each group of students has its own area.

When you say *run little pigs*, all of the students run through the gym trying not to get tagged by the wolf. While they are running, take away the boundaries of the first house (the one made of straw). Now the pigs can return to safety only in the house of sticks and the house of bricks.

If a student gets tagged she becomes a wolf. If you eventually have too many taggers, the others caught could remain stationary and tag only if someone comes in their path. Continue the game by eventually taking away the house of sticks.

Change the wolf often. Start over if you need to with all three houses intact.

MUSIC ACTIVITY

Discuss the importance of following the rules of a game. Emphasize the safety and comfort of all participants. Teach the students the song "We Are Playing in the Forest." Teach the children the rules of the game. A child is chosen to be the wolf. The children play as they sing the song. The wolf hides behind a "tree" (the tree could be the piano or another large thing). When the song is finished, the children should freeze. The wolf looks at them. If the wolf sees a child moving, that child becomes the new wolf.

Conclude the lesson by discussing the importance of following rules.

If you are a classroom teacher with limited space, find a larger area for "Three Little Pigs" Tag.

If you have paraprofessionals or other adults assisting in your classroom, have them help monitor "Three Little Pigs" Tag and "We Are Playing in the Forest."

Lesson 21

Trustworthy: Gossip and Listening

National Standards for Physical Education: 5, Exhibits responsible personal and social behavior that respects self and others.
National Standards for Physical Education: 2, Performing on instruments, alone and with others, a varied repertoire of music. 6, Listening to, analyzing, and describing music.
Equipment: Lummi sticks for music.
Lesson Focus:

• Gossip and listening in PE and music.

Related Literature: *What's So Terrible about Swallowing an Apple Seed?* by Harriet Lerner and Susan Goldhor.

READ THE STORY

Read the story aloud to the class.

PE ACTIVITY

This activity is known as Pass It On or Gossip. You will probably need to explain what it means to gossip. People should not repeat what they hear about others, especially if it is hurtful or not necessarily true. Tell the students that they are going to play a game that will show how gossip can be interpreted in ways that are silly or are no longer true.

Have the students sit in a line. If your group is big, have them sit in two lines. Always have an adult begin the game. Tell the first student sitting in line a short phrase. He will then whisper what he heard to the next student in line. Have them keep passing the message down the line. When the phrase reaches the last person, have her say out loud what she heard. It most likely will be comical.

Play the game several times. After the students understand the game, they should be able to start their own phrase. If you have a student who cannot whisper, have him sit and watch the game the first time you play.

MUSIC ACTIVITY

Tell the children how important it is to listen carefully. Have the children sit in a circle. Teach them to play the game "I Like. . . ." It is a cumulative rhythm game. You start the game by saying who you are and what you like that begins with the same letter as your name. For example, "I'm Mrs. Wilson, and I like waffles." Then the class repeats what you said ("She's Mrs. Wilson, and she likes waffles"). Then the class plays the rhythm of the words that they just said on the Lummi sticks. The next person starts (i.e., "My name is Marcus, and I like Mars bars"), the class repeats what he said, and then plays the rhythm of what he said. Then they also say and play what you said. Keep going around the circle until each student has had a turn. If the game gets too complicated with too many people to remember, repeat the phrases of four students and then start over. At this age it may be difficult for students to come up with something they like that begins with the same letter as their name. You may want them to think of their phrase before you begin the game. If the students are really good at the game, have the student sing their phrase on the pitches *sol-mi-la-sol-mi-fa sol-mi-la-sol-mi.*

Conclude the lesson by discussing with the children the importance of good listening.

If you are a classroom teacher with limited space, these lessons may proceed as described.

If you have paraprofessionals or other adults assisting in your classroom, have them monitor a group of students playing Gossip. You can also divide your students into smaller groups and have each helper play "I Like . . ." with a group of students.

Lesson 22

Trustworthy: Friends

⟨⟨⟨⟩⟩⟩

National Standards for Physical Education: 5, Exhibits responsible personal and social behavior that respects self and others in physical activity settings.

National Standards for Music Education: 1, Singing, alone and with others, a varied repertoire of music.

Equipment: None.

Lesson Focus:

• Trusting friends in PE and music.

Related Literature: *Believing Sophie* by Hazel Hutchins.

READ THE STORY

Read the story aloud to the class.

PE ACTIVITY

This activity is called a Trust Walk. Have the students find a partner. Explain or have the students discuss what trusting someone means. Tell them that in this activity it will be important that they take care of their partner and not let him get hurt. One student in each pair will close his eyes while his partner leads him around the gym.

If you do not think the students can keep his eyes closed, you may want to use blindfolds. Have the tallest student be the first leader. The leader will lead the "blind" student around the gym by holding his hand or arm and giving verbal directions. Have the leader take the blind student through some kind of obstacle course. Folding chairs set out and cones make a great obstacle course for the Trust Walk.

After a few minutes, have the students switch roles. The shorter one now becomes the leader. Repeat the activity.

Discuss what it felt like to be blind and have to trust someone else to lead you around the gym.

MUSIC ACTIVITY

Discuss the importance of friendship. Talk about the ways to be a good friend. Teach the students the songs "You Could Be My Friend" and "I'll Be There" (K–8 Music). Conclude the lesson by discussing the ways that friends make life easier and better.

If you are a classroom teacher with limited space, find a larger space to set up your obstacle course and complete the Trust Walk. The music lesson may proceed as described.

If you have paraprofessionals or other adults assisting in your classroom, have them help pairs of students who are having trouble communicating during the Trust Walk. During the songs have the assistants help lead the student singing.

Lesson 23

Trustworthiness and Working Together

National Standards for Physical Education: 3, Participates regularly in physical activity.

National Standards for Music Education: 2, Performing on instruments, alone and with others, a varied repertoire of music; 4, Composing and arranging music within specified guidelines.

Equipment: Orff instruments or other pitched instruments (boom whackers or resonator bells) and rhythm band percussion instruments for music.

Lesson Focus:

- Trusting others in PE.
- Working together in music.

Related Literature: *King Bob's New Clothes* by Dom DeLuise.

READ THE STORY

Read the story aloud to the class.

PE ACTIVITY

The students will play an old-fashioned game of Follow the Leader. This is a great way to learn to trust others.

Have the children form groups of four or fewer students. Choose who will be the first leader in each group. Make sure the leaders understand that they are to do fun activities to lead the group around the gym, but they need to be sure to go slowly enough so that they do not leave anyone behind. Give the start signal.

After a few minutes, switch leaders. Keep repeating the activity until every student has had the opportunity to be the leader.

MUSIC ACTIVITY

Tell the students how important it is to work together. Explain how musicians work together in different ensembles. Explain the role of the conductor and the roles of musicians. Have Orff instruments or other pitched instruments set up with the notes G, A, and B. Divide the children into small groups of four to five students each. Have instrument stations set up that include different types of instruments for each group of students to use. Stations could include hand drums, triangles, wood blocks, and Orff instruments. Have the children work together to compose a piece of music using the notes G, A, and B. Have them compose a melodic section eight beats long and then a rhythmic section eight beats long.

Give them a piece of paper to write down their composition. They do not have to be sophisticated when writing down their composition. They can use the letters for the notes and draw pictures for the rhythm instruments in the sequence that they play. Walk around and monitor the students. Some will have trouble coming up with ideas. Encourage them to come up with something that they can easily repeat. Some groups of students might even compare a piece of music using a steady beat. Musical development will vary widely among the students. Some children may still be in rhythmic and melodic babble. These students will enjoy the experimental process. Other students will already be thinking of melodies and forms. Conclude the lesson by having each group play their composition for the class.

Some of the compositions will have good structure. Have the students write lyrics for their simple compositions. Have them sing and play their compositions for another group of students. This lesson will take shape depending on the ability levels of your students.

If you are a classroom teacher with limited space, find a larger space for Follow the Leader. If you have no classroom instruments, have the students compose their pieces using their voices on the notes *sol-mi-la*. They can use body percussion for the rhythmic section of the music. Different types of pats, claps, and stomps can be quite effective. You can also use homemade instruments from previous lessons.

If you have paraprofessionals or other adults assisting in your classroom, have them help monitor the groups playing Follow the Leader. During the composition lesson, have the helpers monitor groups and make sure that all students have a chance to contribute their ideas.

Lesson 24

Trustworthy: The Meaning of Trust

—⟪⟫—

National Standards for Physical Education: 3, Participates regularly in physical activity; 5, Exhibits responsible personal and social behavior that respects self and others in physical activity settings.

National Standards for Music Education: 1, Singing, alone and with others, a varied repertoire of music.

Equipment: Colored scarves or crepe paper strips that are the colors of the rainbow for music and PE.

Lesson Focus:

• The meaning of trust in PE and music.

Related Literature: *My Big Lie* by Bill Cosby or *Edwurd Fudwupper Fibbed Big* by Berkeley Breathed.

READ THE STORY

Read one of the selected stories aloud to the class.

PE ACTIVITY

This lesson teaches the students to be trustworthy. When someone says she is going to do something, she should get it done. Historically, the rainbow has been a symbol of trust. When the students see a rainbow it can remind them of people they love and depend on.

A great way to teach the colors of the rainbow is to use the acronym *Roy G. Biv*. The colors of the rainbow are: red, orange, yellow, green, blue, indigo, and violet. Use crepe paper or scarves and give each student one color. Have them identify the color they are holding. Tell them they are making a rainbow. When their color is called they should come to a certain section of the gym. You could mark these sections ahead with color-coded paper or simply place students in the correct spot. Practice putting the students and colors in order. You can do this as one big group or have several small rainbows.

Now mix up the students again and have them stand on a starting line. On the signal *go*, have them jog back to their spot in the rainbow and wave their streamer. If you have fun music about the rainbow to play while doing this activity, the students will appreciate it (e.g., "Somewhere Over the Rainbow"). Take pictures with a digital camera and display them for the students to see.

MUSIC ACTIVITY

Talk to the children about trust, and ask them which friends or adults they are safe trusting. Tell the children that a rainbow is formed when the sun shines even though it is raining. Teach the children the song "Follow the Rainbow"

(K–8 Music). Pass out scarves that are the same colors you would see in a rainbow. Give one scarf to each child. On the refrain, have the children wave all of their scarves in the air. On the verse, have the children wave their scarves as their color of scarf is sung.

Conclude the lesson by talking about trust and about rainbows.

If you have extra time tell the children that it takes two chords to accompany the song "Follow the Rainbow." Show them the D minor chord using resonator bells. Show them the C major chord using resonator bells. Give half of your class a bell for the D minor chord (i.e., d, f, or a). Give the other half of your class a bell for the C Major chord (i.e., c, e, or g). Play the CD of "Follow the Rainbow." When the D minor chord is being used, point to that group of children and have them play each time you signal (half notes work best; direct each note). When the C major chord is used, have that group play each time you signal (again, half notes are best; direct each chord).

If you are a classroom teacher with limited space, make sure you have enough space to enjoy making rainbows with the students. The music lesson may proceed as described.

If you have paraprofessionals or other adults assisting in your classroom, have them help place students in the rainbow formation. They can also help students identify the color of their scarves and wave them at the appropriate times during the song "Follow the Rainbow."

Lesson 25

Trustworthy: Trusting Friends to Help

National Standards for Physical Education: 4, Achieves and maintains a health-enhancing level of physical fitness.
National Standards for Music Education: 1, Singing, alone and with others, a varied repertoire of music.
Equipment: Something soft to tag with for PE.
Lesson Focus:

• Trusting friends to help in PE and music.

Related Literature: *A Day's Work* by Eve Bunting or *A Big Fat Enormous Lie* by Marjorie Weinman.

READ THE STORY

Read one of the selected stories aloud to the class.

PE ACTIVITY

The students are going to play High-Five Tag. Choose two people to be "it" and give them a soft object to tag with. Tell the students that if they get tagged, they must freeze and raise one arm up in the air. The tagged student must remain frozen until another student gives him a high-five. Change the students who are "it" every few minutes.

Explain to the students that they were placing trust in their friends to set them free. Ask them how they would have felt if their friends had passed them by and left them out of the game. It is important for all of the students to feel they can trust someone.

MUSIC ACTIVITY

Talk to the children about the people they trust. Talk about how a baby trusts the people who take care of him or her for everything. Teach the children the lullaby "Hush Little Baby." Tell them that if they have a baby brother or sister, they can sit with the baby and sing the song for the baby. Teach them the song "Sleep Baby Sleep." Ask them how they can help care for younger brothers and sisters.

Conclude the lesson by asking the children what other lullabies they know or what songs their parents or others may have sung for them when they were little.

If you are a classroom teacher with limited space, find a larger space for High-Five Tag. The music lesson may proceed as described.

If you have paraprofessionals or other adults assisting in your classroom, have them help monitor High-Five Tag. During the lullabies have the helpers lead student singing.

Lesson 26

Caring: Giving Compliments

National Standards for Physical Education: 5, Exhibits responsible personal and social behavior that respects self and others in physical activity settings.
National Standards for Music Education: 1, Singing, alone and with others, a varied repertoire of music.
Equipment: None.
Lesson Focus:

• Giving compliments in PE and music.

Related Literature: *Alexander and the Wind-Up Mouse* by Leo Lionni.

READ THE STORY

Read the story aloud to the class.

PE ACTIVITY

Learning how to give compliments is difficult for children. It is important that they begin the learning process of giving compliments as well as receiving them.

Place the students is small groups of three or four each for this activity. Give examples of what an appropriate compliment sounds like by giving several students compliments. Suggest subjects that make good compliments. It is easiest to have the students begin by complimenting each other's clothing.

You may have to direct a lot of this activity. Continue to let the students give compliments to each other. Give helpful examples. Remind them that it is also important to say *thank you* after receiving the compliment.

MUSIC ACTIVITY

Teach the children how to give a sincere compliment. Teach the children the song "Skip to My Lou." Have the children sit in a circle. Choose a child or several children to skip around the circle to the song "Skip to My Lou." During the verse (*Lost my partner*), have the children who are "it" skip around the circle. Just before the refrain, have those children stop and choose a partner by giving that person a compliment. During the refrain, the pairs link arms and skip around the circle. When the refrain is over, the children who got to choose a partner go back into the circle, and the children who were most recently chosen continue the game. Continue until all children have had a turn.

"Skip to My Lou"

(A child or several children skip around the circle)
Lost my partner, what will I do?
Lost my partner, what will I do?
Lost my partner, what will I do?
Skip to My Lou, my darling!

(Children skipping choose a partner by stopping to give another child a compliment. Children then link arms with their partner and skip around the circle)
Lou, Lou, skip to My Lou,
Lou, Lou, skip to My Lou,
Lou, Lou, skip to My Lou,
Skip to My Lou, my darling.

Conclude the lesson by discussing how to give and how to receive a compliment and how good it feels to receive a compliment.

If you are a classroom teacher with limited space, the PE lesson may proceed as described. Make sure you have sufficient space to enjoy the game "Skip to My Lou."

If you have paraprofessionals or other adults assisting in your classroom, have them assist students giving compliments. You may also have them monitor half of the group in another circle during the game "Skip to My Lou." This way the students can have more compliments and more turns.

Lesson 27

Caring for the Sick and Those Far Away

—————

National Standards for Physical Education: 5, Exhibits responsible personal and social behavior that respects self and others in physical activity settings.
National Standards for Music Education: 1, Singing, alone and with others, a varied repertoire of music.
Equipment: Construction paper, scissors, and crayons for PE, Camera and recording device for music.
Lesson Focus:

• Caring for those who are sick or far away in PE and music.

Related Literature: *Tico and the Golden Wings* by Leo Lionni.

———

READ THE STORY

Read the story aloud to the class.

PE ACTIVITY

It is so important to teach children compassion at an early age. Ask the students what makes them feel better when they are sick. Discuss why the things they suggest make them feel better. If it is not mentioned, ask them if they have ever received a get-well card. Tell them that they are going to make get-well cards for some special people. Plan to take the cards to a local hospital or nursing home where they will be appreciated. Pediatric wards and cancer care facilities are appreciative of cards from young children.

Fold the construction paper the wide way. Make a verse on white paper and copy it for the students to glue into their cards. "Thinking of you" or other simple sentences are usually appropriate. Give the students things they can use to decorate the card. Stickers, colors, or markers are good choices.

Students love to hear back from people who receive their cards. People who do not feel well are grateful for the thoughtfulness of the children.

MUSIC ACTIVITY

Discuss how important it is to care for people who are sick, infirm, or are far away. Teach the children the song "If You're Happy." Review some other songs you have learned. Take pictures of the children performing. Record their singing and have them wish their audience well by waving and saying hello. Send your pictures and recordings to a local hospital, a nursing home, or troops overseas on duty. You may need permission from the children's parents or guardians to send pictures, depending on your school district. If possible, visit a local hospital or nursing home for a performance.

Conclude the lesson by talking about the importance of compassion for others.

If you are a classroom teacher with limited space, these lessons may proceed as described.

If you have paraprofessionals or other adults assisting in your room, have them help students glue their verse to the inside of their cards. They can also help take pictures of the students to send to grateful audiences.

Lesson 28

Caring Words

National Standards for Physical Education: 5, Exhibits responsible personal and social behavior that respects self and others in physical activity settings.
National Standards for Music Education: 1, Singing, alone and with others, a varied repertoire of music.
Equipment: None.
Lesson Focus:

• Caring words in PE and music.

Related Literature: *Rosie and Michael* by Judith Viorst.

READ THE STORY

Read the story aloud to the class.

PE ACTIVITY

This activity will give the students a chance to practice giving compliments. Have the students spread out in general space. Play some upbeat music for the students. When the music starts, give them a locomotor movement to do (e.g., skipping, hopping, or jogging). When the music stops, the students must find a partner as quickly as possible.

Instruct the students to give their partner a compliment. If the students need some coaxing, give them examples to get started. An example could be, "What nice thing could you say about your partner's smile"?

Continue changing locomotor movements each time you start the music. Play for several minutes so that the students get a chance to interact with each other.

MUSIC ACTIVITY

Discuss how good it feels when someone says something nice to you. Teach the children the song "What Are You Wearing?" Next, have the children insert a compliment in the song. Instead of singing "Sally wore a red dress," sing the compliment (e.g., *I like Michael's haircut, haircut, haircut. I like Michael's haircut all day long.*). Take turns asking the children to give compliments. Sing about each child until all children have heard something nice about themselves.

Conclude the lesson by talking about how nice it feels to hear a compliment.

If you are a classroom teacher with limited space, find a larger space to enjoy giving compliments while enjoying locomotor movements. The music activity may proceed as described.

If you have paraprofessionals or other adults assisting in your classroom, have them help monitor the PE activity by assisting students with compliments and locomotor movements. During the music activity the helpers can also suggest compliments to sing about and lead another circle in the "What Are You Wearing?" song and game.

Lesson 29

Caring: Symbol of Caring

National Standards for Physical Education: 3, Participates regularly in physical activity; 4, Achieves and maintains a health-enhancing level of physical fitness.
National Standards for Music Education: 1, Singing, alone and with others, a varied repertoire of music.
Equipment: Poly spots or dome markers for PE, Rhythm band instruments for music.
Lesson Focus:

• Symbol of caring in PE and music.

• **Related Literature:** *The Wednesday Surprise* by Eve Bunting.

READ THE STORY

Read the story aloud to the class.

PE ACTIVITY

This game is similar to Go Fish. Set the poly spots or dome markers on the floor all over the gym. Make hearts to place under the spots or markers. Put hearts under half of them. Have the students find a partner. Have the partners line up behind one of the end lines in the gym.

On a *go* signal, the first child in each pair of the partners runs out to turn over a marker. If there is a heart, they keep it and bring it back to their partner. If there is no heart they return to their partner and tap their hand. Then the partner goes out to find a heart.

Continue playing until all of the hearts are found. You can then do counting activities to see which group found the most hearts. You could also change locomotor movements each time they go out.

Talk to the students about why hearts are a symbol of caring. What holiday makes us think about hearts?

MUSIC ACTIVITY

Discuss how the heart is a symbol of caring. Teach the children the song "Skidamarink." Teach the children the actions to the song. Next, pass each child a rhythm band instrument (or have them take turns playing in groups). While the children sing the song, have them play their instrument to the steady beat. Have the children tell you which people they feel love them. Give them more chances to sing and play "Skidamarink."

Conclude the lesson by having them perform the song for their other teachers or other special people. Tell them to perform the song for their mom, dad, or babysitter tonight.

If you are a classroom teacher with limited space, these lessons may proceed as described. Emphasize moving safely when searching for hearts in the classroom. If you have no rhythm band instruments, use your homemade instruments from previous lessons.

If you have paraprofessionals or others assisting in your classroom, have them help hide hearts ahead of class. They will also be helpful when handing out and using instruments.

Lesson 30

Caring: Showing You Care

—◆◆◆—

National Standards for Physical Education: 3, Participates regularly in physical activity; 4, Achieves and maintains a health-enhancing level of physical fitness.
National Standards for Music Education: 1, Singing, alone and with others, a varied repertoire of music.
Equipment: Something soft for tagging for PE.
Lesson Focus:

• Showing you care in PE and music.

Related Literature: *The Grump* by Mark Ludy.*

READ THE STORY

Read one of the selected stories aloud to the class.

PE ACTIVITY

The students have been learning about caring for one another. Tell them that they are going to play a game that shows others that they care. This is called HHH Tag (i.e., *H* for hug, for handshake, and for high five).

Choose two students to be "it." They will tag as many students as they can. If a student is tagged, she must freeze and wait until another student gives her an H (i.e., hug, handshake, or high five). Play several rounds; switch the students who are "it" often. Give the students some safety reminders on safe hugging, handshaking, and high-fiving.

If you see a student who is frozen for a long time, remind the students to show their friends they care by setting them free.

MUSIC ACTIVITY

Teach the importance of caring for each other. Discuss how important it is that all of the students get along well and play nicely with each other. Teach them a song about some animals that play together nicely called "One Little Elephant." Pick a child to walk around the room and be the elephant and have that child pick another elephant. Keep going until all of the children have had a chance to be an elephant. If you have a jump rope, use the jump rope as the spider's web.

Conclude the lesson by discussing the importance of playing well together.

If you are a classroom teacher with limited space, find a larger space for HHH Tag. The music lesson may proceed as described.

If you have paraprofessionals or other adults assisting in your classroom, have them monitor students playing HHH Tag. They can also work separately with half of the students to play and sing "One Little Elephant"; this way the students can have more opportunities to be elephants.

NOTE

The Grump by Mark Ludy is a long book, but the kids love the story. If your students have a difficult time sitting for long, you may want to edit the story and make it shorter.

Unit 4

SKILLS AND THRILLS

Lesson 1

Jumping, Landing, and Playing

National Standards for Physical Education: 1, Demonstrates competency in motor skills and movement patterns needed to perform a variety of physical activities.

National Standards for Music Education: 1, Singing, alone and with others, a varied repertoire of music; 2, Performing on instruments, alone and with others, a varied repertoire of music.

Equipment: Orff instruments or resonator bells for music.

Lesson Focus:

• Jumping and landing safely in PE.
• Playing instruments in music.

Related Literature: *One, Two, Three, Jump!* by Penelope Lively.

READ THE STORY

Read the story aloud to the class.

PE ACTIVITY

The first motor skill you will teach the students is jumping and landing safely. They need to understand that a jump is taking off of two feet. When they land, it should be on the balls of their feet with their knees bent.

Have the students practice jumping and landing from their personal space. Listen for soft landings and make sure no one is landing on body parts other than feet.

Next, see if the students can tell you what a hop is. They need to tell you that you take off of one foot and land on the same foot. Most of your students will not have the muscle strength or coordination to do this more than a few times in a row. Have them practice hopping holding on to something for support. Make sure they practice with both the right and left legs.

Now bring them back to personal space and have them jump or hop according to your instruction. Continue practicing.

MUSIC ACTIVITY

Tell the children that chords are often used for song accompaniments. Chords are three or more different notes played at the same time. Teach the children to sing the song "Hey Diddle Diddle." Review correct instrument playing technique (i.e., strike the bar or bell in the middle). Have the children divide into three groups to play the three chords that are used to accompany the song. Assign a group of children to play the D major chord (i.e., D, F#, A), another group to play the G major chord (i.e., G, B, D), and a group to play the A major chord (i.e., A, C#, E). Give each child one note of the chord to play. Have the children play the accompaniment while you sing the song for them. Point to each group when they are to play. Signal with your fingers the chord structure as they play (i.e., I, D chord; IV, G chord; and V, A chord). Follow the chord letters in the music. When they are comfortable playing the song while you sing it, have them try to sing and play at the same time.

Conclude the lesson by discussing how chords are the framework for accompaniment. Play some other simple songs the children know that involve the use of the three chords I, IV, and V (e.g., "Happy Birthday," "Hush Little Baby," and "Twinkle, Twinkle, Little Star").

If you are a classroom teacher with limited space, find larger spaces for jumping, hopping, and landing. If you have no pitched instruments in the classroom, have the students bring their xylophones from home. Most of these xylophones will be diatonic (i.e., have no flat or sharp keys). Play the root (i.e., the lowest note) of each chord because playing the F# and the C# will not be possible.

If you have paraprofessionals or other adults assisting in your classroom, have them help students who are having trouble jumping and hopping correctly. The helpers can also assist the students play the xylophone correctly.

Lesson 2

Jumping, Hopping, Staccato, and Legato

National Standards for Physical Education: 1, Demonstrates competency in motor skills and movement patterns needed to perform a variety of physical activities.

National Standards for Music Education: 1, Singing, alone and with others, a varied repertoire of music; 6, Listening to, analyzing, and describing music.

Equipment: Poly spots for PE.

Lesson Focus:

• Difference between a jump and a hop in PE.
• Staccato and legato in music.

Related Literature: *Jumpers* by Jillian Powell or *Bounce* by Doreen Cronin.

READ THE STORY

Read one of the selected stories aloud to the class.

PE ACTIVITY

Give each student a poly spot. Have the student take the poly spot to a personal space and stand over it. Give the students several tasks to do that include both jumping and hopping with the poly spot. Examples:

Jump over the poly spot.
Jump as high as you can on the poly spot.
Jump sideway off and on the spot.
Jump forward and backward off and on the spot.
Hop with your left foot on the spot.
Hop with your right foot on the spot.
Hop over the spot.
Hop sideway off and on the spot.

You may still have some students who cannot hop without support. Let these students use the wall or a chair for support.

In closing, have the students tell you the difference between a jump and a hop. Ask them how they should land safely.

MUSIC ACTIVITY

Discuss the terms *staccato* and *legato* with the students. It will be a review from a lesson in Unit 1 Lesson 7. Staccato is bouncy, like a ball. Legato is smooth, like waving a scarf in the air. Teach the children the song "Pop Goes the Weasel." Ask them which part of the song is staccato. Make sure to emphasize the word *pop*. Review the song "Hush Little Baby." Have them sing it legato. Ask them how staccato and legato are different.

Have the students review the rhythm cards from Unit 1 Lesson 9 (i.e., quarter notes, eighth notes, half notes, and quarter rests). Have them clap and speak the notes staccato and legato using the syllables *ta*, *ta-a*, *tee-tee*, and *rest*. Play "Pop Goes the Weasel" "Duck Duck Goose" style. Have a "monkey" choose a "weasel." Modify this game by having the weasel be the next monkey even if he or she is caught. Do not put anyone in the middle of the circle. Keep the game moving and make sure that everyone gets a turn. If necessary, have two monkeys choose two weasels. The children sing the song as the monkeys walk around the circle. On the word *pop*, the monkeys each pick a weasel and chase them.

Conclude the lesson by having them describe staccato and legato. Ask them about other songs they know that are staccato or legato.

If you are a classroom teacher with limited space, find a larger space for these activities.

If you have paraprofessionals or other adults assisting in your classroom, have them help children jump and hop on their poly spots. They can also work with another circle of students to play "Pop Goes the Weasel."

Lesson 3

Jumping and Songs with Scales

National Standards for Physical Education: 1, Demonstrates competency in motor skills and movement patterns needed to perform a variety of physical activities.

National Standards for Music Education: 1, Singing, alone and with others, a varied repertoire of music; 2, Performing on instruments, alone and with others, a varied repertoire of music.

Equipment: Yardstick, balloon, and colored tape for PE, Xylophones (or another instrument that can play a diatonic scale) for music.

Lesson Focus:

* Jumping for height and distance in PE.
* Playing and singing songs with scales in music.

Related Literature: *Dancing in the Wings* by Debbie Allen.

READ THE STORY

Read the story aloud to the class.

PE ACTIVITY

This activity will help your students understand the difference between jumping for height and jumping for distance. They have already learned about how to land safely on their feet and land quietly on the balls of the feet. Now you want to emphasize the arm swing (i.e., drive the arms up for height and out for distance). Have them practice the different arm swings in a personal space several times.

Set up this activity in stations. Have four different stations, two different stations for height and two different stations for distance. The two height stations will be jumping to hit a balloon that is suspended from a yardstick and jumping to touch a piece of tape on the wall marking the height of a famous athlete. Students will try to hit the balloon at the first station and touch the tape mark at the second station. The two distance stations will be doing a standing broad jump from a starting line and measuring the jump and standing behind a line and jumping to preselected lines labeled with animals. For instance two feet could be a cat, three feet a frog, and four feet a kangaroo. Give your students fun marks to aim for.

Let each child spend about three to five minutes at each station and rotate. When you are ready to have the students switch station, have them stop the activity and point to the station they are going to next on your signal. When closing this lesson, make sure the children understand how to swing their arms when jumping high and how to swing their arms when jumping long.

MUSIC ACTIVITY

Teach the children that a scale has eight notes. Have them sing a scale using Curwen syllables and hand signs. Teach the children the song "One, Two, Buckle My Shoe." Teach them to play the song on the xylophones. Tell them which notes to play as you sing them. Sing each note change and have them repeat the notes using the xylophones. Have them play small sections at first. Give them the experience of playing in small segments so they can be successful. When you feel like they can put the whole song together, try it slowly. Once they are comfortable playing the song, have them sing the words as they play. It may take several class sessions for them to be able to play the song without repeating after you.

Conclude the lesson by having them sing a scale using syllables or numbers and telling you how many notes are in a scale.

If you are a classroom teacher with limited space, find a larger space for the jumping activity. If you do not have classroom instruments, have your students bring diatonic xylophones from home.

If you have paraprofessionals or other adults assisting in your classroom, have them monitor jumping stations. They can also assist the students with the instruments.

Lesson 4

Balance

National Standards for Physical Education: 1, Demonstrates competency in motor skills and movement patterns needed to perform a variety of physical activities.

National Standards for Music Education: 1, Singing, alone and with others, a varied repertoire of music; 6, Listening to, analyzing, and describing music.

Equipment: None.

Lesson Focus:

• Balance criteria in PE and music.

Related Literature: *Madeline and the Gypsies* by Ludwig Bemelmans.

READ THE STORY

Read the story aloud to the class.

PE ACTIVITY

Begin the lesson with an explanation of balance. Ask the students if any of them have a baby brother or sister at home. Continue discussing why the babies cannot sit up without help or walk until they get older. Let them know that balance comes with muscle growth and strength.

Have the students try to stand on one leg. Point out to them if anyone is wobbling or falling over. Tell them that for a position to be considered a balance, it must be held for three seconds. It should be still enough to take a picture. Now try the one-leg balance again, checking for the two criteria.

Have the students begin with a one-leg balance. After one second tell them to close their eyes. You will notice that many of the students will begin to fall over. Explain that this is because with their eyes closed they do not know if they are straight up or leaning. Have them pick an object in the room and stare at it. Have them try the balance again, focusing on this specific spot. Let them know that balancing is easier when their eyes are focused on something.

Try the one-leg balance again, letting the students count with you to three seconds. Now have them try it using the other leg.

MUSIC ACTIVITY

Tell the children that music has balance and form. Teach the students the song "All the Pretty Little Horses." Have the students identify which parts of the song are the same and which parts of the song are different. In the beginning and at the end of the song, the words and the notes are the same. The middle of the song is different.

Conclude the lesson by discussing other songs the children know. Ask them if there are repeated phrases or notes that help the music to feel balanced or give it symmetry.

If you are a classroom teacher with limited space, these lessons may proceed as described.

If you have paraprofessionals or other adults assisting in your classroom, have them help students with their balancing activities. Have them help lead the student singing during "All the Pretty Little Horses."

Lesson 5

Balance and ABA Form

National Standards for Physical Education: 1, Demonstrates competency in motor skills and movement patterns needed to perform a variety of physical activities.

National Standards for Music Education: 1, Singing, alone and with others, a varied repertoire of music; 6, Listening to, analyzing, and describing music.

Equipment: None.

Lesson Focus:

- Points of balance for PE.
- ABA form for music.

Related literature: *Clifford at the Circus* by Norman Bridwell.

READ THE STORY

Read the story aloud to the class.

PE ACTIVITY

Review the balance criteria from Unit 4 Lesson 4. The students should understand that a balance must be held still for at least three seconds. In this lesson they will learn about points of balance. Explain that a point of balance is the part of their body that is supporting their weight. If they are sitting down, the point of balance is their bottom. When standing up the points of balance are their feet.

Have them try a few different one-point balances. This could be on the left or right foot or if possible on their bottom with their feet up. See if they can figure out several two-point balances. Try the balances and remind them again of the criteria. Continue working on balance, going up to four-point balances.

A good way to assess this activity is to have the students share a balance with the class and tell them what the point of balance is.

MUSIC ACTIVITY

Tell the students that many songs have form. Teach the students the song "Fiddle-Dee-Dee." Have the students tell you which parts of the song are the same. Call those parts the *A* part. Call the part in the middle the *B* part. The end of the song goes back to the *A* part. Sing the song several times. Conclude the lesson by having the students discuss form and tell you about the form of other songs they know. See if they can tell you the form of "All the Pretty Little Horses" (ABA); "Fiddle-Dee-Dee" is also ABA form.

If you are a classroom teacher with limited space, these lessons may proceed as described.

If you have paraprofessionals or other adults assisting in your classroom, have them help students with balancing, singing, and identifying form.

Lesson 6

Weight Transfer and Singing

National Standards for Physical Education: 1, Demonstrates competency in motor skills and movement patterns needed to perform a variety of physical activities.

National Standards for Music Education: 1, Singing, alone and with others, a varied repertoire of music.

Equipment: Tumbling mat for PE.

Lesson Focus:

- Rolling for PE.
- Number songs for music.

Related Literature: *Silly Sally* by Audrey Wood.

READ THE STORY

Read the story aloud to the class.

PE ACTIVITY

Explain the word *transfer*. Transfer is moving from one place to another. Weight transfer is the same. The students are going to learn how to move their weight from one part of their body to another. Give them the example of walking. When walking, you move your weight from one foot to the other foot. When they stand up and sit down, the weight moves from the feet to their bottom. Have the students practice a few simple weight transfers.

Tell the students that they are going to learn how to do a forward roll. The weight is going to transfer from the feet to the head. Then it will transfer to the back and then back to the feet again. Give the students the cues, tuck their chin to their chest, and round their back. Have a student give a demonstration of a simple forward roll. The students need to practice several of these. Make sure that only one student is on the tumbling mat at a time.

The other two rolls to teach at this time are the log roll and the egg roll. The log roll is a simple roll that does not require a tuck. Have the students lie on their side on the mat as straight as possible. Roll like a log down the mat trying to keep the legs together. The egg roll starts from a sitting position with the arms in between the legs holding the ankles outside of knees are up near the chest and slightly apart. Feet should be together. They should roll to their back and rock from side to side.

Give the students several practice attempts emphasizing safety at all times. For their last turn on the mat, let the students do the favorite roll they learned.

MUSIC ACTIVITY

Tell the children that many songs have a number pattern. Give some examples of songs with number patterns (e.g., "This Old Man," "Five Little Ducks," and "One Little Elephant"). Teach the children the song "The Ants Go Marching." Have the children sing the song with you. Make up gestures for the song. Sing the entire song. Have the children march in a circle and play rhythm band instruments to the steady beat as they sing the song. If they are really good at singing and playing to the steady beat, have them play on the words *the ants go marching . . . hurrah, hurrah* and have them do the gestures on the verse.

Conclude the lesson by having the children name for you some "number songs" they know.

If you are a classroom teacher with limited space, teach the log roll and the egg roll on a carpet. If you have mats for resting you may teach the forward roll using these mats. The music lesson may proceed as described.

If you have paraprofessionals or other adults assisting in your classroom, have them assist students with various rolls. During "The Ants Go Marching," thcy can lead a circle of students in singing and playing.

Weight Transfer and Cooperative Game Playing for Music

—⊷⋙∫⋘⊷—

National Standards for Physical Education: 1, Demonstrates competency in motor skills and movement patterns needed to perform a variety of physical activities.

National Standards for Music Education: 1, Singing, alone and with others, a varied repertoire of music; 9, Understanding music in relation to history and culture.

Equipment: Tumbling mats for PE.

Lesson Focus:

• Rolling backward for PE.
• Singing and cooperative game playing for music.

Related Literature: *The Catspring Somersault Flying One Handed Flip-Flop* by Suann Kiser.

READ THE STORY

Read the story aloud to the class.

PE ACTIVITY

The students learned three front roll variations of weight transfer in Unit 4 Lesson 6. In this lesson, they are going to learn some of the same ideas, only backward. Review the concept of weight transfer. Practice the forward roll, log roll, and egg roll before trying anything new.

The first back roll to teach is the backward roll. Explain that tucking the chin and rounding the back are still going to be important. The students will start on their feet in a low tucked position with their hands close to their ears, palms facing backward. They will roll back and flatten hands on the mat beside their head helping to push themselves over. If a student is small, help him over by placing your hand behind the neck and knee. Do not try to do this with a larger student or one who does not stay tucked.

Some students may need to start with a back rocker. This is just starting on the feet and tucking the body and rocking back and then forward to the feet again. Encourage the student to get a strong rock back and forth going on before attempting the back roll.

The last backward roll to try is the back straddle roll. Have the student sit on the mat with legs apart in a straddle position. Roll backward tucking the chin and pulling the legs over the head. The idea is to land on the feet, legs still in a straddle position. If the student only accomplishes a straddle back rocker, that is a good start.

To conclude the lesson, see if the students can tell you how the weight transfers during a backward roll (i.e., it should go from feet to back to head to feet).

MUSIC ACTIVITY

Tell your students that children all over the world enjoy playing games. One old, popular singing game from England is called London Bridge. First teach the students the song. Next, teach the children how to play the game. Two children are chosen to be the "bridge." They form the bridge by facing each other, joining hands, and raising their arms. The bridge children secretly decide which one of them is silver and which one of them is gold. The other children form a line and go under the bridge during the song. On the words *my fair lady* (or *my fair laddie* for a boy), the bridge falls. The bridge children put their joined arms around the student who is "it." The child in the bridge is gently swayed back and forth during the chorus. At the end of the song, the child who is it is asked how he or she would like to pay. The child responds with either silver or gold. He or she then takes the place of either the child who chose silver or gold as a part of the bridge, and the game continues.

Conclude the lesson by having the children tell you about some singing games that they play. Can they name another old singing game (e.g., "Old Brass Wagon")?

"London Bridge"

London Bridge is falling down,
Falling down,
Falling down.
London Bridge is falling down,
My fair lady!
Take the keys and lock her up,
Lock her up,
Lock her up!
Take the keys and lock her up,
My fair lady!

If you are a classroom teacher with limited space and no mats, teach the backward rolls on mats that are used for resting placed on top of a carpet. The music lesson may proceed as described.

If you have paraprofessionals or other adults assisting in your classroom, have them help students with their backward rolls. During the game London Bridge have them either watch a separate group of students playing the game or have them help you start the game by being a side of the bridge.

Lesson 8

Catching and a Steady Beat

National Standards for Physical Education: 1, Demonstrates competency in motor skills and movements patterns needed to perform a variety of physical activities.
National Standards for Music Education: 1, Singing, alone and with others, a varied repertoire of music.
Equipment: Colorful scarves for PE.
Lesson Focus:

- Catching alone and with a partner for PE.
- Keeping a steady beat with a partner and hand coordination for music.

Related Literature: *Hey Batta Batta Swing!* by Sally Cook and James Charlton.*

READ THE STORY

Read the story aloud to the class.

PE ACTIVITY

Go through the important tips of catching. When catching, the students need to keep their eyes on the object and reach their hands toward it. I like starting with scarves when catching because the students have plenty of time to react to it.

Begin by having the students toss the scarf in the air and catch it with two hands. If they are successful, they need to try to toss with one hand and catch with the other. From there have them toss the scarf and catch with other parts of the body (i.e., the head, shoulder, knee, and so on).

As you scan the class, move those students who are ready to a partner. Now they can begin tossing and catching with a partner. Encourage them to try using both the right and the left hand.

MUSIC ACTIVITY

Tell the children that keeping a steady beat is an important part of music. Teach the students the rhyme "Peas Porridge Hot." Pick a partner or another adult helper who can demonstrate the hand patterns with you. Slowly demonstrate the hand patterns for the children with your partner. Have the students choose a partner. Teach the students the hand patterns for "Peas Porridge Hot" by going through the patterns slowly with your partner as they work with their partner. Have the students try the song with the hand patterns several times with their partner. Have the children switch partners and do the song and hand patterns again.

Conclude the lesson by asking the children what other rhymes with hand patterns they know. Their answers will vary. Watch the children on the playground to see what kinds of rhymes and hand patterns they use as games.

If you are a classroom teacher with limited space, have the students stand in place and toss a scarf, rolled up sock, or grocery bag. Have them work alone first. When they are ready to toss and catch with a partner, have them stand close together (about three feet apart).

If you have paraprofessionals or other adults assisting in your classroom, have them toss and catch with students who need extra help. During "Peas Porridge Hot," have extra helpers work slowly with students who need extra assistance.

"Peas Porridge Hot"

Peas porridge hot,
Peas porridge cold,
Peas porridge in the pot
Nine days old.
Some like it hot,
Some like it cold.
Some like it in a pot
Nine days old.

On the word *porridge*, clap your hands together.
On the word *hot*, clap your partner's hands.
Repeat this action on the phrase *peas porridge cold.*
On the word *peas*, slap your knees again.
On the word *porridge*, clap your hands together.
On the words *in the*, clap your right hand with your partner's right hand.
On the word *pot*, clap your hands.
On the word *nine*, clap left hand with your partner's left hand.
On the word *days*, clap your hands.
On the word *old*, clap your partner's hands.

NOTE

*This book is long, so choose the most interesting and important sections to read.

Lesson 9

Catching and Singing

—◦•〜••◦—

National Standards for Physical Education: 1, Demonstrates competency in motor skills and movement patterns needed to perform a variety of physical activities.

National Standards for Music Education: 1, Singing, alone and with others, a varied repertoire of music.

Equipment: Beanbags for PE, Playground ball for music.

Lesson Focus:

* Catching alone and with others for PE.
* Singing and keeping a steady beat for music.

Related Literature: *Stop that Ball!* by Mike McClintock, *Balls!* by Michael J. Rosen, or *Out of the Ballpark* by Alex Rodriguez.

READ THE STORY

Read one of the selected stories aloud to the class.

PE ACTIVITY

Review the tips for catching. The students need to reach for the object and keep their eyes on the object they are trying to catch. Explain that today it may be harder to catch because the equipment will be heavier. Have each student get a beanbag.

From a personal space, have the students toss the beanbag up and try to catch it with two hands. If they have success, have them try to toss the beanbag with one hand and catch it with the other. Remind them that they will have more success if they are not trying to toss higher than they can reach.

Scan the room and if you have students who are ready to work with a partner, have them work in pairs and toss and catch to each other. Have them start about four or five feet apart. By the end of the class, try to get most of the students with a partner to play catch. Remind them to keep their eyes on the beanbag.

MUSIC ACTIVITY

Ask the students what they learned in PE about catching and throwing. Show the children how to gently roll a playground ball. Teach the children the song "One Two Three O'Leary." Have the students form a circle and sing the song. On each number, the child with the ball bounces it to the next child on his or her right. On the name "O'Leary," the child with the ball tosses it to another child in the circle. The traditional game has the child passing the ball under his or her leg. In a regular-sized classroom it is probably best just to toss it with hands. Keep playing until each child has had a chance to toss the ball.

If you need to simplify the game, have the children sit pretzel-style in a circle while they pass the ball to the right on each number. Have them roll the ball on the floor on the name "O'Leary." Many of your students might not be able to pass the ball to the steady beat of the music yet. Just keep the game going by telling them that the ball is "hot," so they do not want to keep it.

If you are a classroom teacher with limited space, have the students stand closer together when learning how to catch and toss. The sitting circle version of "One Two Three O'Leary" might work best depending on the space you have in your classroom.

If you have paraprofessionals or other adults assisting in your classroom, have them catch and toss with students who need extra help. During the musical game, you might consider having the children make smaller circles with each adult so that they get more chances to handle the ball. Decide if you want the various circles to sing as a class or independently.

Conclude the lesson by having the children sing the song. Have them tell you about another game song that they played that used a rolling ball (e.g., "Roll That Red Ball").

"One, Two, Three O'Leary" *(to the tune of "Ten Little Indians")*

One, two, three O'Leary,
Four, Five, Six O'Leary,
Seven, Eight, Nine O'Leary,
Ten, O'Leary caught it!

Lesson 10

Catching, Lines, and Spaces

National Standards for Physical Education: 1, Demonstrates competency in motor skills and movement patterns needed to perform a variety of physical activities.

National Standards for Music Education: 5, Reading and notating music.

Equipment: Plastic grocery bags for PE, Poster board with a staff drawn on it and beanbag animals in music.

Lesson Focus:

• Catching for PE.

• The music staff, line notes, and space notes for music.

Related Literature: *Mouse Practice* by Emily Arnold McCully.

READ THE STORY

Read the story aloud to the class.

PE ACTIVITY

Young children really enjoy tossing plastic grocery sacks. It is fun for them to use items in a way that is out of the ordinary. The grocery sacks are a novelty and fun to catch. Hand each child a grocery bag and put them in a personal space.

You can do many of the same catching ideas that you tried with the scarves. The children can catch one- or-two handed, catch with other body parts, and maybe even try some tricks such as toss clap and catch. Let the students experiment with the bags and come up with their own unique way to catch.

Make sure you emphasize to the students to keep the bags off of their heads.

MUSIC ACTIVITY

Teach the children that music is written on a staff. The staff has five lines and four spaces. Have the children look at their hands. Each hand has five fingers and four spaces. Show the students that notes are written either on a line or in a space. Show them some line notes and space notes on your dry-erase board or blackboard.* Draw several examples of line notes and space notes. Have the children identify if the note you are drawing is a line note or a space note. Have the children gather around a staff on a poster board or large paper. Make sure that the lines are about five inches apart. You may want to have several poster boards with the staff on them and have four or five children gather around each one.

Give a beanbag animal to each group of students. Make sure that the animal is small enough to fit between the lines on the staff. Have the students take turns tossing the animal on the staff. Have them say if the animal lands on a line or in a space. If you want to keep your music staffs for a long time, laminate them.

Conclude the lesson by putting or tossing an animal on a line or a space. Have the children tell you if the animal landed on a line or in a space. Show the students on your dry-erase board or blackboard how notes are written in lines or in spaces.

If you are a classroom teacher with limited space, both the PE and music lessons can proceed as described. Remind children of classroom furniture, and if possible, have the students push what furniture they can back out of the way.

If you have paraprofessionals or other adults assisting in your classroom, they can move about the room and work with students who are having difficulty.

NOTE

*A line note has a line of the staff going through the center of it. A space note is written between the lines with no line going through it.

Lesson 11

Throwing Underhand and Line and Space Notes

—⟶⟨♪⟩⟵—

National Standards for Physical Education: 1, Demonstrates competency in motor skills and movement patterns needed to perform a variety of physical activities.

National Standards for Music Education: 5, Reading and notating music.

Equipment: Clothespins for PE, Copies of large staff on paper and a marker for each student for music.

Lesson Focus:

• Opposition with underhand throw for PE.
• Line notes and space notes for music.

Related Literature: *H Is for Home Run* by Brad Herzog.

READ THE STORY

Read the story aloud to the class.

PE ACTIVITY

It is hard for young students to tell you if they are right- or left-handed. Have them pretend several times that they are throwing a ball before determining which hand is truly dominant.

As you go around the gym watching the students pretend to throw, determine if they are right- or left-handed and place a clothespin on the opposite pant leg or sock. Explain to them that the leg with the clothespin is the leg they will step forward with.

The three cue words *up, up*, and *away* work well for teaching underhand throwing. Have the students step forward with the opposite foot on the first *up*. Next, they draw back the throwing arm on the second *up*. On the word *away*, they will release the object and follow through to the sky.

Have the students practice several times using the cue words and pretending to throw an object.

Now ask the students when an underhand throw might be used. They should give you answers such as bowling, softball, and kickball.

MUSIC ACTIVITY

Review Unit 4 Lesson 10 with the students on line and space notes, (i.e., line notes have a line running through the center of them; space notes have no line running through the center of them). Review that the staff has five lines and four spaces. Using whole notes, show the children how notes are written on your dry-erase board. Pass a paper with a large staff on it and a water-based marker to each student. Have the students draw some whole notes on their staff for you. Have them put an *L* inside a line note, and an *S* inside a space note. Have the children color their notes with crayons if you want to see some beautiful color.

Conclude the lesson by reviewing line notes and space notes. Let the children take their papers with them. Some of the students will have difficulty drawing notes and making the letters *L* and *S* at this point in their lives. The important thing is to remember that education is a layering process and to keep exposing the students to new and musical things!

If you are a regular classroom teacher with limited space, make sure your students are not too close to desks, chairs, or other obstacles that could cause injury during the PE portion of this lesson. The music lesson can proceed as described. If you are unclear about the staff or line notes and space notes, ask someone in your building who reads music to show you what these terms are.

If you have paraprofessionals or other adults assisting, have them help monitor the students to make sure they are stepping with the opposite leg as they are pretending to throw during the PE portion of the lesson. Have other adults monitor the students while they draw line and space notes. Have them help children who need extra assistance and cheer on students who have great-looking notes. Smiley faces and stickers always help little ones to feel good about their hard work and new knowledge of music and PE.

Lesson 12

Throwing Underhand and Time Signatures

—◁◁◁◖◗▷▷▷—

National Standards for Physical Education: 1, Demonstrates competency in motor skills and movement patterns needed to perform a variety of physical activities.

National Standards for Music Education: 4, Composing and arranging music within specified guidelines; 5, Reading and notating music.

Equipment: Beanbags for PE, Paper with two lines on it (like the staff, but simplified), washable markers for each child, and xylophones or resonator bells for music (or ordinary items if you do not have instruments).

Lesson Focus:

- Underhand throw a beanbag for PE.
- Line notes, space notes, and composing for music.

Related Literature: *J is for Jump Shot* by Michael Ulmer.

READ THE STORY

Read the story aloud to the class.

PE ACTIVITY

Review the underhand throwing cues that were taught in Unit 4 Lesson 11. Have the students practice a few pretend throws.

Give each student a beanbag. Put the students all on the same starting line facing the same direction. Have them hold the beanbag in their throwing hand and put the opposite foot in front of the line. Do a quick visual check to see if all of the students have their opposite foot forward.

When the students are first beginning to practice, give them a target to aim at. Have all of the students say *up, up, and away* together as they throw. After practicing this way a few times, let them throw on their own. Walk back and forth, assessing that they are using opposition (opposite foot comes forward from throwing hand).

MUSIC ACTIVITY

Review with the children line notes and space notes from Unit 4 Lessons 10 and 11 (i.e., a line note is written on a line, and a space note is written in a space). Have each child write a piece of music by putting eight whole notes on the paper with the simplified (two line, one space) staff. The top line will be B, the space note will be A, and the bottom line note will be G. Tell them that the top line will be the highest note, the space note will be the middle note, and the bottom line will be the lowest note. You may want to have them label inside their notes using the letters B, A, and G. Tell them to draw their notes across their staff, just like when they write their name. Tell them not to stack their notes on top of each other because they will not be able to read their music. Have them make their notes big so they are easy to see. This will make the playing portion of this lesson easier. After they have drawn the eight notes, show them some xylophones or resonator bells with the notes B, A, and G on them. Make sure that bars other than B, A, and G have been removed from the instruments or it will be too hard for the children to play their musical compositions. Depending on how many instruments you have available, divide the children into small groups. Show them how to play one of their compositions by playing their high note on B, their middle note on A, and their low note on G. Give each child a turn in their small group to play the music each composed. Have another child hold the "performer's" music and tell the performer to play the high, medium, or low pitch so that the performer only has to concentrate on hitting the right note. If the children have labeled their notes with letter names, the "assistant" can tell the performer the letter names of the notes to play.

Conclude the lesson by reviewing the staff, line notes, and space notes and the words *high*, *medium*, and *low*. Teach the students that the notes written high on the staff have a higher pitch than notes written lower on the staff.

If you are a regular classroom teacher with limited space, have your students practice throwing by using paper wads. If you do not have instruments, find some cans, buckets, metal trays, or pots and pans from the lunchroom or home. Have the students label the top line on their staff with an *h* for high, their space with an *m* for medium, and their lowest line note with an *l* for low. Use wooden spoons or other items as mallets. Make sure you give three things to each group, one with a high sound, one with a medium sound, and one with a low sound. Have them play their compositions on the everyday items.

If you have paraprofessionals or other adults assisting in your classroom, have them help monitor the students while they practice throwing and check for the use of opposite foot from the throwing hand. During music have them monitor the small groups and make sure that the students understand which item or note to play for the B, A, and G (or the high-pitched, medium-pitched, and low-pitched sounds).

Name_____

The Simplified Staff

Lesson 13

Throwing Overhand and Duets

—⬛〰⬛—

National Standards for Physical Education: 1, Demonstrates competency in motor skills and movement patterns needed to perform a variety of physical activities.
National Standards for Music Education: 1, Singing, alone and with others, a varied repertoire of music.
Equipment: Clothespins for PE.
Lesson Focus:

- Overhand throwing cues.
- Duets and singing together for music.

Related Literature: *By My Brother's Side* by Tiki Barber and Ronde Barber.

READ THE STORY

Read the story aloud to the class.

PE ACTIVITY

You will teach the overhand cues for throwing just like you did the underhand cues. This time the words will be, *I want you.*

Have the students face the same way (unless you have figured out from the last time which ones are left-handed). Tell them that instead of facing the target, this time their non-throwing side will be to the target. When you say the word *I*, the students should point to the target with the non-throwing hand and their opposite foot. On the word *want*, the students will draw back their throwing arm behind their head. The word *you* will be used to actually throw the object and follow through to the floor reaching to the opposite pocket.

This can be a really difficult concept for young children. The key points at this age are side to the target (i.e., non-throwing side faces the target) and opposition (i.e., use the opposite foot from the throwing hand when stepping forward).

Have the students practice overhand throwing with a pretend ball. If a student is still struggling with opposition, get the clothespins out and put one on the pant leg or sock. It works best to have all of the students practice at the same time. This will give you a chance to circulate and watch for those needing extra help. It will also help you pick out the left-handed students and turn them to make sure their non-throwing side is facing the target.

MUSIC ACTIVITY

Tell the children that a duet is when two people sing together. Sometimes their musical parts are different and that makes beautiful harmony. Teach the children to sing "Row, Row, Row Your Boat." Review the song "Hot Cross Buns." Tell the children that singing the songs together can make a duet or a partner song. Have all of the children speak "Hot Cross Buns" while you speak "Row, Row, Row Your Boat." Next, have them sing "Hot Cross Buns" while you sing "Row, Row, Row Your Boat." If they have trouble singing their song while you sing yours, tell them to plug up their ears and try again! If that does not work, play "Hot Cross Buns" on the piano while you sing "Row, Row, Row Your Boat." They will think that singing duets is fun!

Conclude the lesson by discussing duets and partner songs. "Three Blind Mice" and "Frère Jacques" are fun partner songs, too.

If you are a classroom teacher with limited space, have students practice overhand throwing by using paper wads. The paper wads will not travel as far. If you have a difficult time singing duets, play the songs along from the *Wee Sing* CD for the children.

If you have paraprofessionals or other adults assisting in your classroom, have them help the students who are having trouble with overhand throwing. If your paraprofessionals are good singers, have them sing "Row, Row, Row, Your Boat" with half of the students while you sing "Hot Cross Buns" with the remaining students.

Lesson 14

Throwing Overhand and Treble Clef

National Standards for Physical Education: 1, Demonstrates competency in motor skills and movement patterns needed to perform a variety of physical activities.

National Standards for Music Education: 5, Reading and notating music.

Equipment: Shuttlecocks for PE, Paper, crayons, and a paper clip for each student and a pretend goalpost made from chairs for music.

Lesson Focus:

- Overhand throwing with strong force in PE.
- Treble clef for music.

Related Literature: *T is for Touchdown* by Brad Herzog.

READ THE STORY

Read the story aloud to the class.

PE ACTIVITY

Review the cues for overhand throwing from the Unit 4 Lesson 13. Have the students pretend to throw an object as hard as they can several times. Give each student an area or target to throw toward.

Have the students try the throw with a shuttlecock. It is light and will take a lot of force to get to the target. If the students are throwing with strong force, chances are they are making the step to the target useful.

Have students stand close to the target or far away depending on their success. You will still have to check for opposition (i.e., using the opposite foot from their throwing hand when they step forward) and may even need to put clothespins on some students having difficulties. Encourage the students to say the words *I want you* to themselves each time they throw.

MUSIC ACTIVITY

Show the children how to draw a treble clef on your dry-erase board. First make the J, then the loop like half of an oval to the right, and then the swirl like a "snailed" circle that ends on the G line. Have them make a treble clef on their paper as you show them again how it is done. If a student needs help, draw the treble clef with him or her. Let the child hold onto the pencil as you draw. Have the children color their paper with their crayons. Next, show the children how to make a paper airplane. Attach a paper clip to the nose of each plane. Give each child a chance to fly a plane through your goalpost. Explain that the treble clef is used for notes that sound higher.

Conclude the lesson by talking about the treble clef. Tell the students again that the treble clef is used for notes that sound higher. Have them remember that goalposts are high, and they sent their treble clef high in an airplane.

If you are a classroom teacher with limited space, have the students throw the shuttlecocks at a designated empty wall. The shuttlecocks are light, so they will not go far. If you do not have shuttlecocks, use paper wads. If you are unsure of how to draw a treble clef, ask someone in your building who reads music to show you how. It will not take long to learn.

If you have paraprofessionals or other adults assisting, have them watch students and make sure they are stepping off with the opposite foot from the throwing hand as they aim at the target. During the music portion of the lesson, have them help students need assistance drawing the treble clef and making the paper airplane.

Lesson 15

Throwing and Echo Singing

National Standards for Physical Education: 1, Demonstrates competency in motor skills and movement patterns needed to perform a variety of physical activities.

National Standards for Music Education: 1, Singing, alone and with others, a varied repertoire of music.

Equipment: Beanbags for PE.

Lesson Focus:

- Switching from one throw to another in PE.
- Singing a story and echo singing in music.

Related Literature: *Miss Nelson Has a Field Day* by Harry Allard.

READ THE STORY

Read the story aloud to the class.

PE ACTIVITY

By now students have learned how to do an underhand and an overhand throw. Give students a beanbag and tell them to find a personal space. Have them throw their beanbags at a wall. Watch them as they perform two overhand throws and two underhand throws. Ask them to tell you what the differences are between the two.

Watch the students to make sure their opposite shoulder from their throwing hand is facing the target while performing an overhand throw. Be sure they are facing their target when performing an underhand throw. Make sure that they are stepping with the opposite foot from their throwing hand and following through with their throwing hand (i.e., hand to the ceiling on an underhand and hand to the opposite hip pocket on an overhand).

MUSIC ACTIVITY

Teach the children that some songs tell a story as they progress. Songs that tell stories as they progress accumulate. Some songs use an echo or call-and-response-style. Teach the children the song "The Green Grass Grows All Around." Make up hand movements for the song as you sing. Sing the song several times so that the students understand the story of the song. Ask the students to tell you about what was in the wood. Ask them if they remember which things are on the tree.

Conclude the lesson by telling the children that some songs tell a story. Ask them if they know other songs that tell stories.

If you are a classroom teacher with limited space, use a clear wall in the hallway to practice throwing the beanbags. The music lesson can proceed as described.

If you have paraprofessionals or other adults assisting in your classroom, have them monitor the students while they perform their overhand and underhand throws. During the music portion of the lesson, have the assistants help you choreograph the song.

Lesson 16

Kicking and Playing Accompaniments

National Standards for Physical Education: 1, Demonstrates competency in motor skills and movement patterns needed to perform a variety of physical activities.

National Standards for Music Education: 1, Singing, alone and with others, a varied repertoire of music; 2, Performing on instruments, alone and with others, a varied repertoire of music.

Equipment: Balls for kicking, Orff instruments or resonator bells for music.

Lesson Focus:

• Kicking a stationary ball in PE.
• Playing an accompaniment with two chords in music.

Related Literature: *K is for Kicking* by Brad Herzog.

READ THE STORY

Read the story aloud to the class.

PE ACTIVITY

Teach the students how to kick a stationary ball. The cues that will be taught for kicking will be:

Eyes on the ball.

Weight on the non-kicking foot.

Kick using the inside of the shoelaces.

When your children begin working on kicking skills, have them do a one-step approach. The non-kicking foot should step even with the ball as they bring the kicking foot forward. Have the students practice this skill before you give them a ball.

Have the students point to what they feel is the inside of the shoelaces. Give every child a ball and have them stand about five feet from a wall. Have them kick the ball toward the wall trying to keep the ball on the ground. Tell the students to pretend that their ball is a smiley face. If they kick the ball in the nose, the ball will stay on the ground.

Have the students practice several times using the one-step approach. Make sure they place the ball back on the ground each time they kick to assure the ball is stationary.

MUSIC ACTIVITY

Review the song "The Green Grass Grows All Around." Divide the children into two groups. Review how to play instruments correctly. Remind the students that they can make an accompaniment for a song with chords and that chords are made up of three notes. Have one group of students play notes on the I chord (i.e., D, F#, A). Have the other group of students play notes for the A7 chord (i.e., A, C#, E, G). Assign students to one note only. Have the D chord students play when you signal one with your finger. Have the A7 students play when you signal vee with your fingers. Make sure that they strike their note only once each time you give them a signal. It will be easier if you face the group that is supposed to play at the appropriate time. Sing the song while you have the children play the accompaniment. Next, have them sing and play at the same time. Some students will be able to do this; for others it will be difficult.

Conclude the lesson by telling the children that they can use chords to accompany singing. Tell them there are three notes in a chord.

If you are a classroom teacher with limited space, have the students stand close to an empty wall (about five feet away) to practice kicking. Consider using the hallway, gym, or an outside wall. If you have no instruments, have the children do their movements from the previous day for "The Green Grass Grows All Around." You can also have the students pat their legs to the steady beat of the song.

If you have paraprofessionals or other adults assisting in your classroom, have them supervise the students who are kicking, especially those who need extra help. During the music portion, have them assist students who are not sure when and how to strike their note or are unsure of their singing. Smiles of encouragement are always helpful.

NOTE

This activity uses D major chords to correspond with the *Wee Sing* music book. This key may be too low for your students to sing comfortably. You can move the tonic to F major by spelling the I chord (i.e., F, A, and C), and V7 chord (i.e., C, E, G, B *flat*). Simply mark on your music if the chord is I or V7 above the chord symbols for conducting purposes.

Lesson 17

Soccer Dribble and Singing

National Standards for Physical Education: 1, Demonstrates competency in motor skills and movement patterns needed to perform a variety of physical activities.

National Standards for Music Education: 1, Singing, alone and with others, a varied repertoire of music.

Equipment: Balls to kick in PE.

Lesson Focus:

• Soccer dribble in PE.
• Singing and days of the week in music.

Related Literature: *Winners Never Quit!* by Mia Hamm.

READ THE STORY

Read the story aloud to the class.

PE ACTIVITY

When teaching children how to dribble a soccer ball with their feet, it is easiest to use two cues. The first cue to tell them is *gentle taps* so that they keep the ball within their reach and do not have to chase after it. The second cue is *feet like a duck* because they should dribble the ball with the insides of their feet with their toes turned out. Explain to the students that when they are dribbling a soccer ball, they want the ball to stay close to their feet so the other team does not take it away.

Give every student a ball. Have them spread out in general space. Make sure they each have a ball between their feet and that they understand that they cannot use their hands to move or stop the ball. Direct them to use gentle taps with their toes pointing out and to move the ball in front of them.

For some students, this will take a lot of practice, and for others who have been playing soccer, it will be simple. When asking the students to freeze, make sure they are stopping the ball with their feet. Encourage them to go slowly and concentrate on controlling the ball. Tell them not to go fast.

When students get to a general space boundary, instruct them to change directions using their feet, not their hands. Tell them to keep their eyes up to avoid running into someone.

MUSIC ACTIVITY

Review good singing habits with the students. Tell the students to pronounce their words well. Have them sing clearly. Tell them to try their best to sing on the pitch, not just chant words to songs. Sometimes telling young children that melodies have high and low sounds called notes is all it takes to get them singing rather than chanting. Teach the students the song "Today Is Monday." Feel free to choreograph the song. Ask them to tell you if they have certain things they do on certain days of the week. Have them sing the song several times until they are comfortable with the song. Have them review other songs they know.

Conclude the lesson by reviewing with the students how to sing well.

If you are a classroom teacher with limited space, go to the gym or to the playground to practice dribbling the soccer balls. The music portion of the lesson can proceed as described.

If you have paraprofessionals or other adults assisting in your classroom, have them watch the students dribble the soccer ball and remind them not to touch the ball with their hands. During the music lesson, have the assistants stand by students who need help singing and sing beside them.

Lesson 18

Kicking in the Air and Singing

—⊸∙⊶—

National Standards for Physical Education: 1, Demonstrates competency in motor skills and movement patterns needed to perform a variety of physical activities.

National Standards for Music Education: 1, Singing, alone and with others, a varied repertoire of music; 9, Understanding music in relation to history and culture.

Equipment: Balls for kicking in PE.

Lesson Focus:

* Kicking the ball in the air in PE.
* Singing in music.

Related Literature: *Froggy Plays Soccer* by Jonathan London.

READ THE STORY

Read the story aloud to the class.

PE ACTIVITY

Refer back to the kicking lesson you taught in Unit 4 Lesson 17. The children were to imagine a smiley face on the ball they are going to kick. When the students kicked the ball to stay on the ground, they kicked the "face" in the nose. Now the students are going to try to kick the ball in the air so they will need to kick the face under the chin.

Give each student a ball and place him or her about five feet away from the wall. Have them practice the one-step approach again where their non-kicking foot steps beside the ball. When they bring the kicking foot into contact with the ball, they need to get their toe under the bottom of the ball to lift it in the air. If some students have more experience kicking a ball into the air, they may move back farther and take an approach toward the ball before making contact with their kicking foot.

Let the students continue to practice. Emphasize that it is not kicking as hard as you can but getting proper foot placement.

MUSIC ACTIVITY

Review good singing technique with the students. Review some of the songs they have learned. Tell the students the history of sea chanteys. Long ago when sailors traveled on big clipper ships, they would sing to set the tempo or speed of the work they would have to get done. A chantey man knew exactly which song to choose to match the tempo of the work they had to do. Usually leading the singing was the chantey man's only responsibility. There was no radio, TV, or Internet long ago. When the work was finished for the day, the crew often sang for entertainment. Teach the students the song "Oh Shenandoah." Shenandoah was a famous American Indian chief long ago, and a river is named after him. Sing the song until the students are comfortable with the melody.

Conclude the lesson by asking the students why sailors long ago sang sea chanteys.

If you are a classroom teacher with limited space, have the students practice kicking the ball into the air in the gym or outside. The music lesson can proceed as described.

If you have paraprofessionals or other adults assisting in your classroom, have them supervise students as they kick the ball into the air. Make sure that they notice whether the students are getting their kicking foot under the ball to send it into the air. During the music portion of the lesson, have them sing near students who need encouragement and assistance singing.

Kicking a Rolling Ball and Singing

—◂◖◗▸—

National Standards for Physical Education: 1, Demonstrates competency in motor skills and movement patterns needed to perform a variety of physical activities.
National Standards for Music Education: 1, Singing, alone and with others, a varied repertoire of music.
Equipment: Balls for kicking in PE.
Lesson Focus:

- Kicking a rolling ball in PE.
- Singing in music.

Related Literature: *The Dog That Stole Football Plays* by Matt Christopher.

READ THE STORY

Read the story aloud to the class.

PE ACTIVITY

The students have already learned how to kick a stationary ball and kick on the ground or in the air; now they will learn how to kick a ball that is rolling to them. The approach is not any different; they just have to develop a sense of timing.

Tell them that they are still going to use a one-step approach, but they will want to step before the ball gets to them. As they step into the kick, they will still need to kick using the inside of their shoelaces.

Have the students get back-to-back with a partner. Give each pair a ball. Have each pair of students decide which one will roll (pitch) the ball first so that the other student can kick it. Make sure that the students who are rolling the ball know to roll it as smoothly as possible. They should also understand not to roll the ball too fast.

Have the students who are pitching roll five balls to their partner and then switch. The student who was the kicker is now the pitcher. Do not put too much emphasis today on whether they are kicking on the ground or in the air. Focus on the timing of the kick with a moving ball. Continue practicing. More advanced students will be able to kick a ball from a faster pitch.

MUSIC ACTIVITY

Review "Oh Shenandoah" with the students. Teach the students the song "Michael Row the Boat Ashore." Make sure that they sit up tall when they sing. Have them row, sway, or pat to the steady beat of the song. Sing it until the students are comfortable with it.

Conclude the lesson by reviewing other songs they have learned.

If you are a classroom teacher with limited space, practice kicking the rolling balls in the gym or on the playground. The music lesson can proceed as described.

If you have paraprofessionals or other adults assisting in your classroom, have them help students who need to develop a sense of timing regarding when to kick the ball. During the music portion of the lesson, have them sing near students who need encouragement singing.

Lesson 20

Dribbling with Hands and Practicing

⸺◁░░░⫘░░░▷⸺

National Standards for Physical Education: 1, Demonstrates competency in motor skills and movement patterns needed to perform a variety of physical activities.

National Standards for Music Education: 1, Singing, alone and with others, a varied repertoire of music; 2, Performing on instruments, alone and with others, a varied repertoire of music; 7, Evaluating music and music performances.

Equipment: Basketballs for PE, Resonator bells or Orff instruments for music.

Lesson Focus:

- Dribble or two-handed bounce in PE.
- Singing and playing practice in music.

Related Literature: *Salt in His Shoes* by Delores Jordan.

———————

READ THE STORY

Read the story aloud to the class.

PE ACTIVITY

In this lesson, do not spend a great deal of time focusing on proper dribbling skills. Young students need the chance to explore with the ball before things get technical. If you have students who have played basketball with older siblings, you will see better skills in these students; but for most of the students, assume that this may be their first experience with a basketball.

Give each child an appropriate ball. This simply means that the ball will bounce and is not too heavy for them to manipulate. Have them find a self-space and put the ball between their feet. Remind the students to stay in their self-space while practicing. Tell them that they are going to push the ball to the floor using both hands, preferably their finger pads, and when the ball comes up to them, they are going to push it down again.

Allow a lot of practice time. You may need to switch to a different ball with some children until you find out what works for them. If a child is more advanced and is able to dribble one-handed, just let him continue to practice that skill.

Have many different sizes and weights of balls, and you can find one that works for each child. Tell the students this is a skill that requires a lot of practice and maybe they could even work on it at home.

183

MUSIC ACTIVITY

Teach the students the importance of practicing. Tell them that their hard work when they practice music or sports will result in small gains in performance each time they practice. Over time, all of that practice will make them much better at things they would like to do. Consistent practice usually reaps rewards. Review the song "Michael Row the Boat Ashore." Next, teach the children to play an accompaniment to it on instruments.

Divide the students into three groups. Make group 1 the I chord (or root chord) of the song. Give them each two bells and mallets of any combination of C, E, or G. When you hold up the number one with your finger, have them strike their bells once with their mallets. Next, make group 2 the IV chord (subdominant). Give them two bells each, any combination of B flat, D, or F. Have them play when you hold up the number four with your hand. Have group 3 be the V (dominant) chord. Give them two notes of any of the dominant chord members (i.e., G, B, D). Have the students play the accompaniment of the song using chords while you show them which chords to play with your hands by using the numbers I, IV, and V.

Have the students play the song while you sing the melody. When they are used to following your hand signs, have them try to sing and play at the same time. It will be difficult at first. It might be hard for you to look at the chords on your paper while trying to conduct your students at first. Practice makes perfect.

Conclude the lesson by discussing what went well and what still needs work. Talk about the importance of practice.

If you are a regular classroom teacher with limited space, take your students to the gym or outside to practice dribbling. If you do not have instruments for the music portion of the lesson, have the children sit in a circle while they sing and pretend to row the boat to the steady beat of the song. They can also pat their legs to the steady beat of the song. The students can also come up with other movements for other verses of the song.

If you have paraprofessionals or other adults assisting in your classroom, have them assist students who need extra help dribbling. For the music portion of the lesson, have the paraprofessionals sit next to the children who need help figuring out when to strike the bell. If your paraprofessionals are good singers, have them stand next to the children who are not confident singers to encourage them to participate.

Lesson 21

Dribbling and Singing

National Standards for Physical Education: 1, Demonstrates competency in motor skills and movement patterns needed to perform a variety of physical activities.

National Standards for Music Education: 1, Singing, alone and with others, a varied repertoire of music; 2, Performing on instruments, alone and with others, a varied repertoire of music; 7, evaluating music and music performances.

Equipment: Basketballs for PE, Instruments for music (e.g., resonator bells, two triangles, and two drums).

Lesson Focus:

• Dribbling cues in PE.
• Practicing in music.

Related Literature: *Gus and Grandpa at Basketball* by Claudia Mills.

READ THE STORY

Read the story aloud to the class.

PE ACTIVITY

Today you are going to teach the students the important cues to know when learning how to dribble a basketball properly with one hand. The cues are:

1. Eyes over the ball.
2. Dribble waist high.
3. Keep the ball at your side.
4. Use your finger pads.

You should have a pretty good idea of which balls work best from Unit 4 Lesson 20. Give each student a ball and ask him or her to find a self-space. Demonstrate each of the cues and explain why it is important. If they do not keep their eyes over the ball, they will trip over something. If you dribble higher or lower than waist high, you could lose control of the ball. Keeping the ball at your side ensures that you will not bounce it off of your toes. You have better control over the ball if you dribble it with you fingertips, similar to the way you would pet a puppy.

Give them time to practice. Some of the students may revert to a two-handed bounce and that is OK; just encourage them to continue to try using one hand.

MUSIC ACTIVITY

Once again, discuss the importance of practicing the things you would like to learn how to do. Sing the song "Michael Row the Boat Ashore." Hopefully the students will remember it from previous lessons. Have the students review their instrumental parts. It will take them a few minutes to remember how to play and get the best sound out of the instrument. Have the students play and sing "Michael Row the Boat Ashore." Have them do it several times. Ask them if it was easier today than it was yesterday. Ask them if it sounded better. Their answers will vary, but hopefully it will sound better with more practice. Have the children help you clean up the instruments. Teach the students to sing the song "Down in the Valley."

Conclude the lesson by telling the students that they will practice more songs tomorrow and that they are going to be fine musicians.

If you are a classroom teacher with limited space, have the students practice dribbling in the gym or on a hard surface such as asphalt. The music portion can proceed as described. If you have no instruments, have the students pat their legs to the steady beat of the song and make up hand motions.

If you have paraprofessionals or other adults assisting in your classroom, have them watch the students to see if they are dribbling using the four cues. During the music portion of the lesson, have the paraprofessionals help children who are having trouble playing their instrument on the conducting cue or have them sing with the students.

Lesson 22

Dribbling and Practicing

—◁◁◁◁◁◁ ◁ ◁▷▷▷▷▷▷—

National Standards for Physical Education: 1, Demonstrates competency in motor skills and movement patterns needed to perform a variety of physical activities.

National Standards for Music Education: 1, Singing, alone and with others, a varied repertoire of music; 7, Evaluating music and music performances.

Equipment: Basketballs for PE.

Lesson Focus:

- Dribbling practice in PE.
- Singing practice in music.

Related Literature: *The Princesses Have a Ball* by Teresa Bateman.

READ THE STORY

Read the story aloud to the class.

PE ACTIVITY

Today is a review day. Give each student a ball. Practice the dribbling cues from Unit 4 Lesson 21 and start off with the students staying in their personal space.

If you have some students who are ready to practice a more advanced skill, let them try to walk and dribble. Encourage them to move slowly and not to disrupt those still standing in their self-spaces.

Continue to allow a lot of practice time. This is a skill that takes time and effort.

MUSIC ACTIVITY

Talk about the importance of practice. Tell the children that good singing requires a lot of practice, just like good reading or writing. They need to sing often if they want to be good singers, and they need to listen so that they match pitches and sing with a pleasing tone. Teach the children to sing the song "Sarasponda." It is a fun song that children have sung for many years, and it is a fast song. Sing the song several times. They will enjoy clapping to the steady beat of the song. Next have the children sing "Down in the Valley," "Michael Row the Boat Ashore," and "Oh Shenandoah."

Conclude the lesson by asking them if they feel more comfortable singing the songs after all of the practice they have had. Ask them if the songs sound better and why. Ask them what they could improve.

187

If you are a classroom teacher with limited space, have the students practice dribbling in the gym or outside on asphalt or another hard surface. The music lesson can proceed as described.

If you have paraprofessionals or other adults assisting in your classroom, have them check to see that students are using the four cues when they dribble a ball. During the music portion of the lesson, have the paraprofessionals stand by children who need help and encouragement singing.

Lesson 23

Volleying and Singing

National Standards for Physical Education: 1, Demonstrates competency in motor skills and movement patterns needed to perform a variety of physical activities.

National Standards for Music Education: 1, Singing, alone and with others, a varied repertoire of music; 2, Performing on instruments, alone and with others, a varied repertoire of music. 9, Understanding music in relation to history and culture.

Equipment: Balloons for PE, Lummi sticks for music.

Lesson Focus:

- Volleying in the air in PE.
- Singing and keeping a steady beat.

Related Literature: *Play Ball, Joey Kangaroo!* by Donna Lugg Pape or *Play Ball* by Margaret Hillert.

READ THE STORY

Read one of the selected stories aloud to the class.

PE ACTIVITY

The students are going to learn how to volley today. Discuss what volleying is. Explain that volleying is striking something with your body. There are two kinds of volleying: one is for foursquare and the other for volleyball. Today they are going to try to keep a balloon in the air, so this would be a volleyball skill. (A hacky sack would also be considered volleying, but volleying with the feet might be too complicated for this age.)

Begin by having the students find a self-space. Give every student a balloon. Tell the students they are going to use their hands to keep the balloon in the air as long as they can without it touching the floor. Give them time to practice. Have them practice with other body parts. If the balloon looks like it is going to get out of control, have them try using elbows, head, knees, or other body parts.

To close the lesson, have the students count how many volleys they have in a row. Ask the students how many were able to get at least ten in a row. Celebrate success with a class pat on the back.

MUSIC ACTIVITY

Review the songs "Sarasponda" and "Oh Shenandoah." Discuss good singing. Be sure to talk about breathing, pronunciation, and matching the pitch. Using a lighter sound that you can feel in your head helps high notes sound better and makes them easier to sing. Help the students learn to sing notes using their head voice. Review other songs that the children know from Unit 4. Pass a pair of Lummi sticks to every student. As they sing the song "Sarasponda," have them play to the steady beat with the Lummi sticks.

Conclude the lesson by singing other songs while keeping a steady beat. Listen for students who are matching pitches!

If you are a classroom teacher with limited space, balloons will work in your situation. The music lesson may proceed as described. If you do not have Lummi sticks, have the students pat their legs to the steady beat of the song.

If you have paraprofessionals or other adults assisting in your classroom, have them monitor students as they practice volleying. During the music portion of the lesson, have them help students who need assistance finding the steady beat by patting the beat beside them.

Lesson 24

Volleying and Matching Pitch

—◄꜀꜀ꜱ꜀ꜱꜱ►—

National Standards for Physical Education: 1, Demonstrates competency in motor skills and movement patterns needed to perform a variety of physical activities.
National Standards for Music Education: 1, Singing, alone and with others, a varied repertoire of music.
Equipment: Balloons for PE. A penny and a pin (one that you might wear) for music.
Lesson Focus:

* Volleying with a partner in PE.
* Matching pitch in music.

Related Literature: *Clifford The Big Red Dog: The Missing Beach Ball* by Sonali Fry.

READ THE STORY

Read the story aloud to the class.

PE ACTIVITY

Review with the students the skill of volleying. In Unit 4 Lesson 23, they had the opportunity to volley a balloon by themselves and with different body parts. In this lesson, they are going to volley to a partner.

Have each pair spread out in general space. Have them volley to their partner, trying not to let the balloon touch the floor. Emphasize that they want to let their partner hit every other volley. If the balloon gets too far away, they may have to volley twice to get it to their partner, but the goal is to have each student volley every other hit.

To conclude the lesson, ask the students which was easier, volleying with a partner or doing it by themselves. Ask them if they had ten volleys in a row.

MUSIC ACTIVITY

Teach the students to play the game Who Has the Penny? Who Has the Pin? Begin by telling them they are going to play a game. You start by telling them, close your eyes and open your hands. No peeking! Give the penny to one child and the pin to another. Sing the phrase *Who has the penny?* The child who has the penny should sing back to you, *I have the penny.* Next sing the phrase *Who has the pin?* The child who has the pin should sing back to you, *I have the pin.* Have all of the children open their eyes and guess who had the penny and who had the pin. If you have many students, you may want to use two pennies and two pins at the same time. This game gives you a good opportunity to see who is already matching the pitches. At this age, only a few might be able to match pitch well, unless their teacher sings with them often or you have a talented group of students.

Conclude the activity by having the students tell you which notes are higher or lower in the song.

If you are a classroom teacher with limited space, make sure that the pairs of students stand close together when they practice volleying. The music lesson may proceed as described.

If you have paraprofessionals or other adults assisting in your classroom, have them help children who need assistance volleying. During the music lesson, you may consider having other adults take a group of students and play the game with them. That way more students can have more turns.

Who Has the Penny?

traditional, arranged by C. Wilson

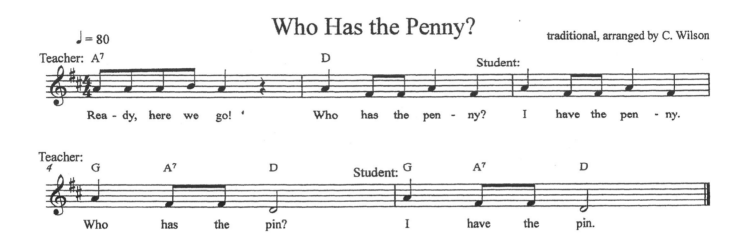

Lesson 25

Volleying and Singing

National Standards for Physical Education: 1, Demonstrates competency in motor skills and movement patterns needed to perform a variety of physical activities.

National Standards for Music Education: 1, Singing, alone and with others, a varied repertoire of music. 9, Understanding music in relation to history and culture.

Equipment: Balls that bounce for PE.

Lesson Focus:

• Volleying to the wall in PE.
• Singing in music.

Related Literature: *Volleyball for Fun!* by Darcy Lockman.*

READ THE STORY

Read the story aloud to the class.

PE ACTIVITY

The volleying that the students will learn today is normally used for foursquare. It is done by making a scooping motion with your hands.

Have the students stand in their self-space facing a wall. Stand with one foot slightly in front of the other, knees bent, and hands pointed down with palms facing forward. Drop the ball in front of the back foot and use both palms to scoop it toward the wall.

This is a difficult skill and will require a lot of practice. The students may have to practice just dropping the ball over and over. If they do not have a difficult time, have them volley it continuously toward the wall. Start with drop, scoop, drop, and catch. Try to move to drop scoop, drop scoop, and soon.

Have the students explain the difference between this type of volleying and what they were doing with the balloons in Unit 4 Lesson 23.

MUSIC ACTIVITY

Teach the children to sing the song "I've Been Working On the Railroad." Tell the students that long ago, trains were the only mode of transportation besides horse-drawn wagons to get mail and other things across the country. People worked hard to build the railroad system in the United States. Building the train tracks across the country was hard, grueling work. Laborers sang to pass the time as they worked. They used to swing their hammers to the steady beat of the song. Sing the song again. Have the students stand and pretend to swing their large hammers as they sing.

Conclude the lesson by asking the children what other piece they learned about included a train (e.g., "The Little Train of Caipira"). Have them tell you about other people who sang to help make their job easier (e.g., the sailors on clipper ships long ago).

If you are a classroom teacher with limited space, find a larger space with a wall for the volleying activity. A clear hallway or an outside wall without windows will work nicely. The music lesson may proceed as described.

If you have paraprofessionals or other adults assisting in your classroom, have them help students volleying. They can also help lead student singing.

NOTE

*This book is long, so choose the most important parts to read.

Volleying, Singing, and Playing Instruments

—◦◦◦◦◦◦◦—

National Standards for Physical Education: 1, Demonstrates competency in motor skills and movement patterns needed to perform a variety of physical activities.

National Standards for Music Education: 1, Singing, alone and with others, a varied repertoire of music; 2, Performing on instruments, alone and with others, a varied repertoire of music.

Equipment: Balls that bounce for PE, Bass xylophone, alto xylophone, and finger cymbals (or other pitched instruments) for music.

Lesson Focus:

• Volleying with a partner for PE.
• Singing and playing for music.

Related Literature: *Bump! Set! Spike!* by Nick Fauchald.

READ THE STORY

Read the story aloud to the class.

PE ACTIVITY

Review the volleying to the wall skill that was taught in the Unit 4 Lesson 25. Remind the students that their palms are forming a scoop to push the ball toward the wall.

Not all of your students may be ready to work with a partner. If you have some students who are not ready to work on volleying with a partner, have them practice volleying alone using the wall as in the previous lesson.

Have the rest of the students find a partner. They will need to stand about five feet apart. Start the ball with a drop and volley or scoop the ball toward the partner. The partner will want to let the ball drop in front of her before trying to volley it back. Continue practicing.

Let your students know this is the skill that they will need to play foursquare; however, foursquare takes four people to play.

MUSIC ACTIVITY

Teach the students the song "Sweetly Sings the Donkey." Explain that they will learn to play an ostinato to accompany the song. An ostinato is a pattern that keeps repeating throughout the song. The pattern that you will be teaching them is two quarter notes followed by a half note on the pitches D and A. The D and the A will be played at the same time.

After the children have learned to sing the song, teach the rhythm of the pitched instrument parts by having the children pat their legs with both hands while saying *ta, ta, hold it.* Next have them say it again as *quarter, quarter, half note.* Assign the children to the pitched instruments. Show them how to hold the mallets and how to play the part. To keep the children from playing out of turn, have them cross their arms with their mallets under their arms when they are not playing the instruments. Finally, show the finger cymbal players how to play their part. They will play their instruments on beat one at the beginning of every measure. Have them all play together and see what happens. They will probably need to practice before the song starts to sound good.

The children might have some difficulty singing and playing at the same time. If you do not have a lot of instruments, have a few of your students play while the others sing. They can take turns playing and singing. Keep practicing.

Conclude the lesson by having the students tell you what an ostinato is.

If you are a classroom teacher with limited space, have the children practice volleying in the gym or outside. If this is not an option, have the children use a large paper wad to volley on a classroom wall. If you do not have pitched instruments, have the children play the ostinato on rhythm band instruments or with Lummi sticks. If you have no instruments or sticks, have them pat their legs for the pattern.

If you have paraprofessionals or other adults assisting in your classroom, have them help the students who need to practice volleying alone. They can also help students who are having difficulties volleying with a partner. During the music portion of the lesson, they can lead the singing or direct the ostinato for the students on instruments, whichever role they are more comfortable with.

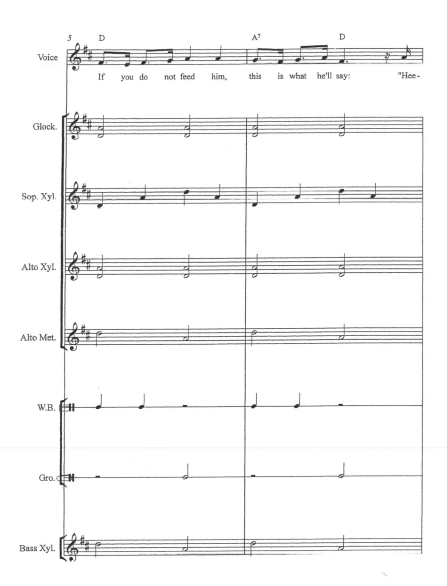

If   you   do   not   feed   him,   this   is   what   he'll   say: "Hee-

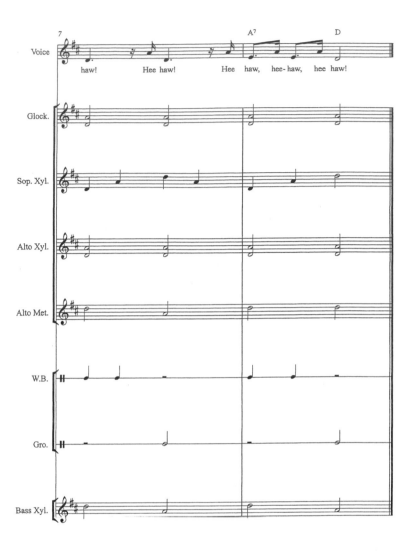

Lesson 27

Striking with Paddles and Singing

—⟁⟁—

National Standards for Physical Education: 1, Demonstrates competency in motor skills and movement patterns needed to perform a variety of physical activities.

National Standards for Music Education: 1, Singing, alone and with others, a varied repertoire of music; 2, Performing on instruments, alone and with others, a varied repertoire of music.

Equipment: Short-handled paddles and balloons for PE, Bass xylophone, alto xylophone, alto glockenspiel, and finger cymbals for music.

Lesson Focus:

- Striking with a short-handled object in PE.
- Singing and playing for music.

Related Literature: *The ABC's of Tennis* by Cheryl Lagunilla.

READ THE STORY

Read the story aloud to the class.

PE ACTIVITY

Ask the students to tell you what they know about tennis. Teach the students how to grasp the handle. Use the handshake grip. If the handle of the paddle were someone's hand, grasp it as if shaking it. Use the cues *stiff wrist* and *flat surface* (the paddle should be parallel to the target). Have the students practice gripping the paddle.

Next, have the students stand with their opposite foot from the side they are holding the paddle with forward. Swing the paddle underhand as if striking a ball to the wall.

Give each student a balloon. Students should hold the balloon in the hand without the paddle; they will strike the balloon with a paddle. Spread out with a lot of space between them. Tell them to swing the paddle underhand and strike the balloon toward the wall. The students will be hitting the balloon from the opposite hand that they swing the paddle with. After several practice attempts, they can throw the balloon up and strike it continuously with the paddle. Encourage them to keep the face of the paddle flat to the surface they are striking.

To close, have the students review the striking cues. They need to have a strong, straight wrist and flat paddle surface toward the target.

MUSIC ACTIVITY

Review singing and playing "Sweetly Sings the Donkey." Review other songs the children have learned. Give the students a lot of time to practice singing and playing songs they know. Review the terms forte (loud) and piano (soft). Have them sing or play forte or piano while you conduct them.

Conclude the lesson by asking the children which songs are their favorites.

If you are a classroom teacher with limited space, find a larger space for the striking activity. If you do not have paddles, make them by bending a clothes hanger in the shape of a triangle. Stretch one leg of panty hose over the hanger. Put duct tape around the handle to keep the stocking on and make the paddle safe.

If you have paraprofessionals or other adults assisting in your classroom, have them help make paddles (if you need them) and have them help students with striking. During the music portion of the lesson, have them help you set up instruments and assist students playing.

Lesson 28

Striking with a Bat and a Steady Beat

National Standards for Physical Education: 1, Demonstrates competency in motor skills and movement patterns needed to perform a variety of physical activities.

National Standards for Music Education: 1, Singing, alone and with others, a varied repertoire of music.

Equipment: Batting tees and soft bats and balls for PE, Lummi sticks for music.

Lesson Focus:

• Striking with a bat in PE.
• Singing and steady beat.

Related Literature: *Girl Wonder* by Deborah Hopkinson or *Batter Up* by Neil Johnson.

READ THE STORY

Read one of the selected stories aloud to the class.

PE ACTIVITY

Teach the batting stance first. Make sure that the students have a large self-space. The students will need to stand side to the target with feet shoulder-width apart. They need to be at medium level with knees bent. Levels were taught in Unit 1 Lesson 4. Have them pretend they are gripping a bat. The dominant hand should be on top with hands close together. Elbows should be out and the bat should be over the shoulder but not resting on it. Now have them pretend to swing a bat and strike a ball.

The number of groups you have will depend on how many tees you have. Demonstrate the swing of the bat striking the ball off of the tee. They should try to strike just the ball and not touch the tee. Practice swinging the bat several times away from the tee before actually trying to strike the ball off of the tee.

Go through safety rules with the students. The tees need to be far apart with the target area being toward the wall. Those waiting for their turn must be far enough back that they cannot be hit with the swing of the bat.

Let each student hit three or four balls before switching to the next student. Students need to get into a rhythm. Use several balls, or have them use one ball and place it back on the tee each time.

Encourage the students to use a level swing and to keep their feet on the ground. A baseball swing involves stepping slightly forward with the foot that is closest to the target and rotating the ball of the opposite foot toward the target as though a bug is being smashed with the opposite foot. The young children will be able to do this if they are experienced baseball players. If they have not played baseball, start teaching them to swing the bat by keeping the foot closest to the target stationary and the opposite foot doing the "smash the bug" rotation as they swing.

Close the lesson with some final practice swings with a pretend bat from their self-space. Ask them to remind you of some batting pointers taught in the lesson.

MUSIC ACTIVITY

Teach the children to sing the song "A Ram Sam Sam." Have them sing the song several times until they are comfortable singing it. Have them make fists. On the words *ram-sam-sam*, have them tap one fist on top of the other. On the words *guli guli*, have them "roll" their fists around each other. On the words *A rafi*, have them throw their arms up in the air. Next, pass out the Lummi sticks. Have the students play on the words *ram-sam-sam*. Review singing other songs the students know.

Conclude the lesson by having the students sing "A Ram Sam Sam" before they leave. Ask them what words are on the highest pitches in the song.

If you are a classroom teacher with limited space, make sure you have plenty of space for the swinging activity. If you do not have Lummi sticks, have the students clap on the words *ram-sam-sam*.

If you have paraprofessionals or other adults assisting in your classroom, have them help supervise students while batting. During "A Ram Sam Sam," they can help lead students singing and doing hand actions.

Lesson 29

Striking with a Club and Singing with a Steady Beat

—⟨⟩—

National Standards for Physical Education: 1, Demonstrates competency in motor skills and movement patterns needed to perform a variety of physical activities.
National Standards for Music Education: 1, Singing, alone and with others, a varied repertoire of music; 2, Playing instruments alone and with others.
Equipment: Croquet mallets or plastic golf clubs for PE, Rhythm band instruments for music.
Lesson Focus:

• Striking with a long-handled piece of equipment in PE.
• Singing and steady beat for music.

Related Literature: *P is for Putting* by Brad Herzog.

———

READ THE STORY

Read the story aloud to the class.

PE ACTIVITY

The students are going to learn the strike for golf or croquet. Teach only the putt at this level. You will not want your students doing a full swing to drive the ball yet.

Teach the thumbs down grip. The dominant hand will be on top of the nondominant hand. Put the stick between the feet and hold the hands palms out, fingers down. Now have them wrap their hands around the handle. Most children are going to want to move their hands as if sweeping with a broom. This is not correct. You will have to be diligent on keeping their hands in a proper grip. Show the students how to putt the ball. The feet should be shoulder-width apart. The arms will stay straight. The shoulders will move slightly away from the target and then toward it to strike it. The arms will naturally move with the shoulders.

Give them some sort of a target to shoot for that is not far away. You will want them using light force to get the ball there. A croquet gate or a carpet sample would work well. Help the students to understand that they will not lift the head of the club up higher than their knees.

Give the students plenty of room to practice. Reinforce the grip and the use of light force.

MUSIC ACTIVITY

Have the students tell you what they must do to sing well (i.e., listen and match the pitch, be expressive, pronounce the words very clearly). Review songs the students know well. Teach the children the song "*Viva la Compagnie*." Have the children sing the song several times until they are comfortable singing it. Next, have them stand in a circle. Have them clap to the steady beat on the verse and circle to the right on the chorus.

If time permits, have a "rhythm band parade." Give each child a rhythm band instrument. Form a line and march parade-style around the room as everyone joins in singing the song.

Conclude the lesson by asking the students how the song made them feel.

If you are a classroom teacher with limited space, make sure you have plenty of space when you do this striking activity. If you do not have croquet mallets or plastic golf clubs, consider using wrapping-paper tubes. Send a note home to parents and caregivers before the holidays to collect the tubes. Use soft foam balls or "sock balls" (rolled socks) as balls. The music lesson may proceed as described. Use your homemade percussion instruments for the parade if you do not have rhythm band instruments.

If you have paraprofessionals or other adults assisting in your classroom, have them help students with the striking activity. They can also help lead the parade and pass out instruments.

Lesson 30

Striking with a Hockey Stick and Vocal Sounds

—◁▥▥▯◁▥▥▷—

National Standards for Physical Education: 1, Demonstrates competency in motor skills and movement patterns needed to perform a variety of physical activities.

National Standards for Music Education: 1, Singing, alone and with others, a varied repertoire of music.

Equipment: Hockey sticks and balls for PE, Paper and crayons for each student and three voice-flexing cards that you have made for music.

Lesson Focus:

- Striking with a long-handled implement for PE.
- Vocal flexing for music.

Related Literature: *Hat Tricks Count* by Matt Napier.

READ THE STORY

Read the story aloud to the class.

PE ACTIVITY

You will have already taught the grip used for the hockey stick. It is the same grip used for a golf club or croquet mallet.

Begin by teaching the hockey dribble. This would involve short taps using each side of the stick to move the ball forward. Tell the students that they do not want the ball to get any further than they can reach. Give each student a stick and a ball and have them practice. Emphasize control, not speed.

After they can dribble, let them try a short hit to goal. They should only take easy shots. If the students take a high swing, they could hurt someone. Use cones or poly spots to mark the goal area. The students will dribble up close to the goal and try to shoot it in. The head of the stick should not go higher than their knees.

MUSIC ACTIVITY

Review singing the major scale on solfège syllables with the students. Ask them which pitches are high and which pitches are low. Have the students sing each pitch after you. Have the students make high and low sounds with their voices. Animal sounds make good vocal exploration exercises. Try some high and low animal sounds. Give several students an opportunity to show the class their high and low sounds. Keep discussing different vocal sounds (i.e., high, low, long, or short).

Next, show the students three different voice-flexing cards that you have made with paper and crayons. Choose a vowel sound and have the students flex their voices as you point to the vocal exercise on the card using a predetermined vowel sound. Discuss ways to represent the vocal sounds on paper (e.g., a smooth line for legato, a dot for staccato, and so on). Finally, have the students make their own voice-flexing card using paper and crayons. Have the students do the vocal exercises on their cards.

Conclude the lesson by having the students tell you different types of vocal sounds (e.g., high, low, long, or short). Let the students take their special musical work home.

If you are a classroom teacher with limited space, make sure that you have enough room for the striking activity. If you do not have hockey sticks, use the wrapping-paper tubes you collected for the striking lesson in Unit 4 Lesson 29. The music lesson may proceed as described.

If you have paraprofessionals or other adults assisting in your classroom, have them help the students learn to strike the ball with the hockey stick or tube. Helpers could even be goalies. During the music activity have them monitor students and vocalize some of the sounds they see on student cards.

Lesson 31

Striking with a Racket and a Song in a Minor Key

⸺◦◦◦⸺

National Standards for Physical Education: 1, Demonstrates competency in motor skills and movement patterns needed to perform a variety of physical activities.

National Standards for Music Education: 1, Singing, alone and with others, a varied repertoire of music; 2, Performing on instruments, alone and with others, a varied repertoire of music.

Equipment: Rackets and balloons for PE, Resonator bells and mallets for music.

Lesson Focus:

• Striking with long-handled equipment in PE.
• Playing chords in a minor key.

Related Literature: *I Want to Play Tennis* by Ann S. Bartek.

READ THE STORY

Read the story aloud to the class.

PE ACTIVITY

This activity will be similar to the activity you taught with paddles and balloons in Unit 4 Lesson 27. Students will grip the racket with the same handshake grip as used with the paddles. Because the racket handle is longer, the students will need to toss the balloon up with the non-striking hand before attempting to strike it.

Work mostly with the underhand or forehand hits. This will mean the students will toss the balloon either out in front of them or off to the dominant side and swing the paddle in an underhand motion. Give plenty of practice opportunities.

If a student is ready to move on, let him or her strike continuously to a wall or other flat surface.

MUSIC ACTIVITY

Tell the students that songs are written in major and minor keys. Play the song "Viva la Compagnie." Tell the students that it is in a major key. Play the song "Hey, Ho! Nobody Home." Tell the students that it is in a minor key. Play or sing a major and a minor scale for the children. Play major and minor chords for the children. Have them tell you how the chords sound different. Teach the students to sing the song "Hey, Ho! Nobody Home." Play other songs that are in major and minor keys. Have the students tell you if the song is in a major key or a minor key.

Next, divide your students into two groups. Pass out resonator bells for the E minor chord to one group of students (i.e., *E, G, B*), and pass out bells for the B minor chord to the second group of students (i.e., B, D, F#). Tell the first

207

group of students that you want them to strike their bell once when you hold up one finger. Tell the second group that you want them to play when you hold up five fingers (one finger for the I and five fingers for the V chord). Sing the song while you have the students accompany you. Use your finger signs to help them play the correct chords. As they get better at playing the song, have them sing the song with you. Remind them that they cannot all play at once, only when you hold up their number.

Conclude the lesson by playing chords and having students tell you which chords are major and which chords are minor.

If you are a classroom teacher with limited space, make sure you have plenty of room for the striking activity. Use the homemade panty-hose paddles for this lesson if you do not have rackets. If you have no pitched instruments, have the children bring xylophones from home. Assign each child to play one note. Omit the F# because it will not exist on a diatonic xylophone. The V triad will still sound minor because B and D are a minor third apart.

If you have paraprofessionals or other adults assisting in your classroom, have them help students during the striking activity. They can also help students play at the correct time while singing the song "Hey, Ho! Nobody Home."

Lesson 32

Many Ways of Making Music and Revisit Catching

National Standards for Physical Education: 1, Demonstrates competency in motor skills and movement patterns needed to perform a variety of physical activities; 5, Exhibits responsible personal and social behavior that respects self and others in physical activity settings.

National Standards for Music Education: 6, Listening to, analyzing, and describing music; 8, Understanding relationships between music, the other arts, and disciplines outside the arts; 9, Understanding music in relation to history and culture.

Equipment: Objects to catch for PE, Recording of *Carnival of the Animals* for music,

Lesson Focus:

- Catching with a partner in PE.
- Moving to music.

Related Literature: *M is for Melody* by Kathy-jo Wargin.

READ THE STORY

Read the story aloud to the class.

PE ACTIVITY

Have the students find a partner. Set out several different pieces of equipment that the students can play catch with. Vary the size of the equipment. Let the students work with equipment they feel comfortable with. Review the catching cues of *reach* and *pull it in*.

Emphasize to the students that they do not need to get far away from each other. Tell them that you are looking for accuracy. In other words, how many throws they can catch with their partner.

Allow plenty of time to practice and the opportunity to switch to a new piece of equipment.

MUSIC ACTIVITY

Discuss with the children the many ways of making music. You can sing, play instruments, and make instruments of your own. You can even use your body for percussion.

Next, show the students pictures of different orchestral instruments. Play *Carnival of the Animals* by Camille Saint-Saëns. Discuss the instruments that the children hear and the character of each animal. Have the students move to the music using animal gestures. Tell the students how Saint-Saëns intended to amuse and entertain his friends by having an "animal carnival."

Many of Saint-Saëns's friends were musicians and pianists. When he included pianists in the animal themes, he wanted his friends to laugh.

Discuss how music is used in celebrations such as carnivals, birthdays, and special occasions. Conclude the lesson by discussing the many ways to make music and the many ways that music can help us to express how we feel.

If you are a classroom teacher with limited space, use soft objects such as sponges or rolled-up socks for the catching activities. The music activity may proceed as described.

If you have paraprofessionals or other adults assisting in your classroom, have them help students with the catching activities. They can also help students move creatively during *Carnival of the Animals*.

NOTE

Music Smart by Gwen Hotchkiss includes *Carnival of the Animals*, as well as other helpful teaching notes.

Many Ways of Making Music
Continued and Revisit Kicking

National Standards for Physical Education: 1, Demonstrates competency in motor skills and movement patterns needed to perform a variety of physical activities.

National Standards for Music Education: 6, Listening to, analyzing, and describing music; 8, Understanding relationships between music, the other arts, and disciplines outside the arts; 9, Understanding music in relation to history and culture.

Equipment: Soccer balls for PE, Recording of *Carnival of the Animals* for music.

Lesson Focus:

• Soccer dribble in PE.
• Different ways to make music in music.

Related Literature: *Berlioz the Bear* by Jan Brett.

READ THE STORY

Read the story aloud to the class.

PE ACTIVITY

Review the cues for dribbling a soccer ball. These cues work well: (1) *feet like a duck* and (2) *gentle taps*. Remind everyone that they are to stay inside the general space area and that you are looking for control, not speed.

Have each student get a soccer ball and begin dribbling. Use a drum or whistle to have the students stop dribbling. Check to see that when they stop dribbling they are using their feet to stop the ball, not their hands. (Have them put the bottom of their foot on top of the ball to stop it.)

After several minutes of practice, have the students do a time test. When you give the start signal, have them begin dribbling. Every time they touch another student or their ball does, they give themselves a point. Tell them that this is a game in which you do not want to get points. Go for one minute and then try again. Have the students compare their scores between the first game and the second game. Ask how many of the students were able to lower their score from the first try.

MUSIC ACTIVITY

Discuss the story. Ask the students how a bee stuck in a double bass might sound. Talk about how instruments can imitate animal sounds. Listen to the themes of *Carnival of the Animals* again. Discuss how each theme suits each animal.

Talk about the instruments used in each theme, and show the students pictures of the instruments. Have the students move dramatically to the themes in *Carnival of the Animals*.

Conclude the lesson by having students tell you which animal theme they enjoyed the most.

If you are a classroom teacher with limited space, try to go outside or to the gymnasium to dribble the soccer balls. The music lesson may proceed as described.

If you have paraprofessionals or other adults assisting in your classroom, have them help students with the dribbling activities. Helpers can also suggest creative ways to move to *Carnival of the Animals*.

Lesson 34

Many Ways to Make Music and Revisit Dribbling

National Standards for Physical Education: 1, Demonstrates competency in motor skills and movement patterns needed to perform a variety of physical activities; 5, Exhibits responsible personal and social behavior that respects self and others in physical activity settings.
National Standards for Music Education: 6, Listening to, analyzing, and describing music; 8, Understanding relationships between music, the other arts, and disciplines outside the arts; 9, Understanding music in relation to history and culture.
Equipment: Basketballs for PE, Recording of *Carnival of the Animals* in music.
Lesson Focus:

- Dribbling with hands in PE.
- Instruments and moving dramatically for music.

Related Literature: *Zin! Zin! Zin! a Violin* by Lloyd Moss.

READ THE STORY

Read the story aloud to the class.

PE ACTIVITY

Review the dribbling cues for basketball.

1. Eyes up.
2. Ball no higher than the waist.
3. Ball at the side.
4. Use finger pads.

Give students a basketball and have them warm up by dribbling in their self-space. They can dribble with either hand or both hands if needed.

Have the students find a partner. Tell them it is "short day," so the shorter partner is the first leader. They are going to play Follow the Leader while dribbling the ball. Tell the leaders to take it slow so that they do not lose their partner. After several minutes of practice, switch and let the other partner be the leader.

MUSIC ACTIVITY

Play the main themes of *Carnival of the Animals* again. Discuss the themes and the instruments used with the students. Have the students move dramatically to the themes. Discuss how music can tell a story without using words.

Conclude the lesson by having the students tell you which themes and animals they enjoyed the most. Ask them if they had to choose an instrument to represent an animal, which instrument would they choose for a particular animal and why.

If you are a classroom teacher with limited space, try to find a gymnasium or other suitable space for dribbling. The music activity may proceed as described.

If you have paraprofessionals or other adults assisting in your classroom, have them help their students with dribbling. They can also help students think of creative ways to move to *Carnival of the Animals.*

NOTE

Art connection: Have the students make a picture of their favorite *Carnival of the Animals* themes.

Singing a Song in Three-Quarter Time and Revisit Rhythms

—=⁓⁓⁓=—

National Standards for Physical Education: 1, Demonstrates competency in motor skills and movement patterns needed to perform a variety of physical activities.

National Standards for Music Education: 1, Singing, alone and with others, a varied repertoire of music; 5, Reading and notating music.

Equipment: CD player for PE.

Lesson Focus:

• Keeping a simple rhythm in PE.
• Learning about three-quarter time.

Related Literature: *Music Is* by Lloyd Moss or *Our Marching Band* by Lloyd Moss.

READ THE STORY

Read one of the selected stories aloud to the class.

PE ACTIVITY

This lesson is a review day for songs that were done previously in the year. Sing and move to the following songs:

"The Run Walk Song" (Unit 1 Lesson 1)
"A New Way to Walk" (Unit 1 Lesson 3)*
"Toe Leg Knee" (Unit 1 Lesson 5)
"Spaghetti Legs" (Unit 1 Lesson 6)
"Zig Zag" (Unit 1 Lesson 7)*
"Everything Has a Shape" (Unit 1 Lesson 9)
"Mr. Mirror" (Unit 1 Lesson 12)
"Wiggly Wiggly Wiggles" (Unit 2 Lesson 1)
"My Heart is a Muscle" (Unit 2 Lesson 1)
"Pump Pump Shuffle" (Unit 2 Lesson 4)
"The Shiny Clean Dance" (Unit 2 Lesson 5)
"The Sneezing Song" (Unit 2 Lesson 6)
"Sound Effects" (Unit 2 Lesson 12)

MUSIC ACTIVITY

Teach the students the song "Music Alone Shall Live." Ask the students if they can feel how many beats or pulses repeat over and over in a musical measure (three). Have the children sway to the beat as you sing the song. Show the students where the time signature is located on a piece of music. Tell them that the top number of a time signature tells the performer how many beats or pulses they will feel in each musical measure. Have the students sing the song several times until they are comfortable with it. Ask the students if there are other ways they can move to show you three beats in a measure. (An example of showing three beats in each measure would be to pat legs on beat one, clap on beat two, and snap fingers on beat three). Ask them if the song is staccato or legato (it is legato).

Conclude the lesson by asking the students if they know of any other songs that use three beats in a measure. Once again, tell them where a time signature is located on a piece of music.

If you are a classroom teacher with limited space, all of the PE songs may be done in a self-space unless the song has an asterisk beside it. Songs with an asterisk require more space. The music lesson may proceed as described.

If you have paraprofessionals or other adults assisting in your classroom, have them help lead the student dancing and singing. They can also help create ways to move to three-quarter meter.

NOTE

*All of the PE songs may be done in a self-space unless the song has an asterisk beside it. Songs with an asterisk require more space.

Lesson 36

Singing in a Round and Hula Hoops

National Standards for Physical Education: 1, Demonstrates competency in motor skills and movement patterns needed to perform a variety of physical activities.
National Standards for Music Education: 1, Singing, alone and with others, a varied repertoire of music.
Equipment: One hula hoop per student.
Lesson Focus:

- Manipulative (hula hoops) for PE.
- Singing in a round for music.

Related Literature: *The Remarkable Farkle McBride* by John Lithgow.

READ THE STORY

Read the story aloud to the class.

PE ACTIVITY

This lesson will depend on how much experience your students have had with hula hoops. Begin by letting the students experiment with the hoops. Offer suggestions for them to try, such as going around the legs or arms.

They could practice using the hoop beside their body and spin it or jump in and out of it. Have a short contest to see who can keep the hoop spinning the longest. Have the students invent a trick they can do with the hoop.

MUSIC ACTIVITY

Review the song "Music Alone Shall Live" with the students. Ask them if they remember how many beats were in each measure of the song. Explain how to sing in a round. A group of students starts singing, and they sing all the way through the song. Another group of students starts singing at the beginning of "Music Alone Shall Live" after the first group has sung through the first four measures of the song. The first group that started keeps singing the melody even after the new group starts. The groups starting at different times make harmony when they sing together. It is helpful to have another adult present who can sing so that you can show the students how to sing in a round. If this is not possible, record yourself singing the song, and then show the students a round by singing a round with your recording. Ask the students what other songs they learned that are good songs to sing in a round (e.g., "Hey, Ho! Nobody Home").

Conclude the lesson by singing the round one more time.

If you are a classroom teacher with limited space, make sure you have sufficient space for students using hula hoops. The music lesson may proceed as described.

If you have paraprofessionals or other adults assisting in your classroom, have them supervise students hula-hooping. They can offer creative suggestions. During the music portion of the lesson another adult will be invaluable for helping during round singing. Have him lead a group of students in singing a part of the round.

Lesson 37

Instrument Identification and Revisit Kicking

National Standards for Physical Education: 1, Demonstrates competency in motor skills and movement patterns needed to perform a variety of physical activities.

National Standards for Music Education: 6, Listening to, analyzing, and describing music.

Equipment: Poly spots and balls for kicking for PE, A recording of *Peter and the Wolf*, pictures of orchestral instruments for music.

Lesson Focus:

- Kicking a rolling ball in PE.
- Identifying instruments for music.

Related Literature: *I Know a Shy Fellow Who Swallowed a Cello* by Barbara S. Garriel.

READ THE STORY

Read the story aloud to the class.

PE ACTIVITY

Your students will have learned the kicking technique in previous lessons, so this lesson will be a review of kicking from a roll and putting it into a modified game situation.

Divide your class into small groups of three or four each. Give each group two poly spots and a ball. Set up one poly spot for home plate and one straight out in front of it about fifteen feet away. Place one student in the middle of the poly spots as the pitcher. One of the others will stand behind home plate to kick and the other student will stand beyond the other poly spot.

The pitcher rolls the ball to the kicker; the kicker kicks the ball and takes off running to the other poly spot. Meanwhile the third student chases the ball down to return it to the pitcher. Rotate after each pitch. Kicker goes to pitcher, pitcher to fielder, and fielder to kicker. Choose some students to help demonstrate this process. Show the process several times to be assured that the students will understand the rotation. Do not put an emphasis on scoring. Just enjoy the game.

If you see a student pitching too fast or not rolling smoothly, offer some advice so that the ball will be easier to kick. Students will need some prompting to remember to run after they kick. This activity can be played for more than one day. The students will not tire of it.

MUSIC ACTIVITY

Tell the students the story of *Peter and the Wolf*. Play the music for them. Show them pictures of the different instruments that play during each theme of the music. Ask them to tell you if the sound each instrument makes is high or low. Does the size of the instrument have anything to do with whether the instrument makes a high or a low sound? Does the size of each instrument have something to do with the animal it represents? Have the students move dramatically to each theme of *Peter and the Wolf*.

Conclude the lesson by showing the students the pictures of each instrument one more time. This lesson may be repeated so the students get to hear the instruments, think of the story, and move to the music.

If you are a classroom teacher with limited space, go outside to play the kicking game. The music lesson may proceed as described.

If you have paraprofessionals or other adults assisting in your classroom, have them help supervise the kicking game. They can also offer suggestions for creative movement during *Peter and the Wolf*.

Lesson 38

Instrument Families and Revisit Jump and Hop

—⁓⁓—

National Standards for Physical Education: 1, Demonstrates competency in motor skills and movement patterns needed to perform a variety of physical activities; 2, Demonstrates understanding of movement concepts, principles, strategies, and tactics as they apply to the learning and performance of physical activities.

National Standards for Music Education: 1, Singing, alone and with others, a varied repertoire of music; 2, Performing on instruments, alone and with others, a varied repertoire of music; 6, Listening to, analyzing, and describing music.

Equipment: Poly spots for PE, Xylophones and the *Moving with Mozart* CD for music.

Lesson Focus:

• Differentiate between jump and hop.
• Learning about Mozart.

Related Literature: *Mozart Finds a Melody* by Stephen Costanza.

———

READ THE STORY

Read the story aloud to the class.

PE ACTIVITY

Remind the students of the difference between a jump and a hop. A jump is taking off using two feet, and a hop is taking off using one foot and landing on the same foot. Scatter poly spots on the floor about three to four feet apart.

Turn on some music; if possible use something by Mozart. The CD called *Moving with Mozart* is a good choice for this lesson. Give the students prompts while the music is playing and have them freeze when the music stops. Use the following prompts:

1. Jump over as many poly spots as you can.
2. Jump on as many poly spots as you can.
3. Hop over as many poly spots as you can.
4. Hop on as many poly spots as you can.

You could use other prompts relating to colors or numbers. Conclude by asking the students which was harder, a jump or a hop. Ask them if their muscles were getting tired.

MUSIC ACTIVITY

Tell the children that Wolfgang Amadeus Mozart was a famous composer who lived many years ago. He was born in 1756, and he died in 1791. He was born in Salzburg, Austria. Mozart had amazing musical ability. He played the clavier at the age of three, and by age five he was composing complex musical works. He was a child protégé and a musical genius. Unfortunately, he had problems paying his bills on time even though he was well respected. He did not take good care of himself, and he never slept well. He died just before his thirty-sixth birthday and was buried in a pauper's grave in Vienna.

Mozart wrote the variations on the melody of "Twinkle, Twinkle, Little Star." Play or sing the song for the children, and have them sing it. Next, write the letter names of the notes of the first two phrases on the board (CCGGAAG, FFEE-DDC). Show the children where the notes are on the xylophones, and have them play and sing the notes of the first two phrases. Show the students how to play the song note by note. Most of them will not be able to play the song in tempo, but they will be able to play each note, and enjoy the musical experience.

Next, have the children listen to the "Minuet" (#4) on the *Moving with Mozart* CD. Have the students find a partner, and teach them how to dance the minuet by listening to the directions on the CD. Have the children dance the minuet several times.

Conclude the lesson by having the children tell you what they remember about Mozart.

If you are a classroom teacher with limited space, use the hallway, gymnasium, or other larger space for the poly spot activity. If you have no Orff instruments, have the students bring toy xylophones from home.

If you have paraprofessionals or other adults assisting in your room, have them help supervise the poly spot activity. During "Twinkle, Twinkle, Little Star" have helpers point to the right notes on the xylophones for the students as you sing the letter of the notes.

NOTE

"Twinkle, Twinkle, Little Star" is easier for the children to sing in the key of D. If you have accidentals (sharps and flats) for your instruments, use these notes to play the song: DDAABBA, GGF#F#EED.

Twinkle Twinkle Little Star (Variations)

W.A. Mozart (arranged by C. Wilson)

Twink - kle Twink - kle lit - tle star,_____ How_ I won - der what_ you are.

Up_ a - bove_ the world so high,_____ like_ a dia - mond in___ the sky,_

Twink - kle twink - kle lit - tle star,_ How_ I won - der what_ you are.

Listening to Music and Revisit Ball Handling

National Standards for Physical Education: 1, Demonstrates competency in motor skills and movement patterns needed to perform a variety of physical activities.

National Standards for Music Education: 4, Composing and arranging music within specified guidelines; 6, Listening to, analyzing, and describing music; 8, Understanding relationships between music, the other arts, and disciplines outside the arts.

Equipment: Balls that bounce for PE, A recording of "Putnam's Camp, Redding, Connecticut" by Charles Ives for music.

Lesson Focus:

- Ball handling in rhythm in PE.
- Listening to polytonality in music.

Related Literature: *What Charlie Heard* by Mordicai Gerstein.

READ THE STORY

Read the story aloud to the class.

PE ACTIVITY

The story deals with composing a song based on sounds that the composer, Charles Ives, heard. The students are going to compose a song using the sounds that sports equipment makes.

Divide the class into small groups. Explain to the students that they will need to be quiet so that all you hear is the equipment. Give each group something that will make a sound. Examples could be basketballs to dribble, soccer balls to kick, jumping rope, and so on. Ask the students what kinds of "instruments" among the equipment become woodwinds, brass, strings, or percussion.*

Have the students come up with a rhythmic pattern using their piece of equipment. Practice the rhythm several times and then share it with the other groups. Next, have the class put the sounds' rhythms together to make a song. Do the song several times and tell the students that there are a lot of ways to make sounds and develop them into songs. If the groups would enjoy singing sounds or words with their rhythmic pattern, this could also be incorporated into their song. Limiting their choices to a particular category, such as animal words or sports words, could help spark their lyrical imaginations.

MUSIC ACTIVITY

Have the students listen to "Putnam's Camp, Redding, Connecticut" by Charles Ives. Explain to them that they will hear a lot of different sounds. Ives loved working with many different sounds, all at the same time. He was original and imaginative. He enjoyed composing music in two different keys at the same time throughout the same composition. Sing "Happy Birthday" with the students in two different keys at the same time to demonstrate polytonality. (Another adult can assist. Have them sing "Happy Birthday" in D major while you sing it in G major.) Do not worry about explaining polytonality in detail at this age. You probably have some unintentional examples of polytonality in your classroom already. Have the students make a picture with crayons to represent the sounds they hear in "Putnam's Camp, Redding, Connecticut."**

Conclude the lesson by having your students tell you which instruments they might like to use to represent different nonmusical sounds.

If you are a classroom teacher with limited space, use classroom equipment (e.g., pencils, rulers, and other things that make distinctive sounds) to compose your song. The listening and art sections of this lesson may proceed as described.

If you have paraprofessionals or other adults assisting in your classroom, they will be of great help in supervising groups and helping them to get started. They can also assist with the art and listening sections.

NOTES

*The percussion family of instruments must be struck with an object or the hand to produce a sound.
**A recording of "Putnam's Camp, Redding, Connecticut" may be downloaded from iTunes. You may find it listed as *Three Places in New England 2: Putnam's Camp.*

Lesson 40

Joseph Haydn and the Farewell Symphony and Revisit Body Shapes

National Standards for Physical Education: 2, Demonstrates understanding of movement concepts, principles, strategies, and tactics as they apply to the learning and performance of physical activities; 6, Values physical activity for health, enjoyment, challenge, self-expression, and social interaction.

National Standards for Music Education: 6, Listening to, analyzing, and describing music; 8, Understanding the relationships between music, the other arts, and disciplines outside the arts.

Equipment: Paper and crayons for music and PE (scarves are optional).

Lesson Focus:

- Creative movement with shapes to music.
- The movements of a symphony.

Related Literature: *The Farewell Symphony* by Anna Harwell Celenza.

READ THE STORY

Read the story aloud to the class.

PE AND MUSIC ACTIVITY

Listen to the music of *The Farewell Symphony*. Have the students give some verbal descriptions of the emotions the music makes them feel. Tell them that they are going to make a creative dance or movement sequence using the four main body shapes of narrow, wide, twisted, and round. Practice the shapes.

Play the music again and lead the group with some shapes as the music continues. At times during the song, allow the students to do their own shapes. Tell them to make their shape match the emotion of the music. If scarves enhance creative movement, give the students scarves to dance with.

Listening to the story and moving to the music will most likely take a full period. Review the song and work on the music activity the following class period.

If you are a classroom teacher with limited space, make sure the students have a self-space for creative movement. The listening and art sections of the lesson may be done at the tables or on the floor.

If you have paraprofessionals or other adults assisting in your classroom, have them dance with the students and give suggestions for creative movement. When the students are making pictorial representations of the movements of the symphony, have helpers monitor students, give encouragement, and ask the students questions about their art.

NOTE

Some students are uncomfortable with dancing. If this is an issue in your classroom, use the term *creative movement*.

Lesson 41

Joseph Haydn and the Farewell Symphony and Revisit Body Shapes

---

National Standards for Physical Education: 2, Demonstrates understanding of movement concepts, principles, strategies, and tactics as they apply to the learning and performance of physical activities; 6, Values physical activity for health, enjoyment, challenge, self-expression, and social interaction.

National Standards for Music Education: 6, Listening to, analyzing, and describing music; 8, Understanding the relationships between music, the other arts, and disciplines outside the arts.

Equipment: Paper and crayons for music and PE (scarves are optional).

Lesson Focus:

* Creative movement with shapes to music.
* The movements of a symphony.

Related Literature: *The Farewell Symphony* by Anna Harwell Celenza.

READ THE STORY

Read the story aloud to the class.

PE AND MUSIC ACTIVITY:

Discuss the story again, showing the students the pictures from the story *The Farewell Symphony* to refresh their memories. Have the students listen to and move to brief sections of *The Farewell Symphony*. (Scarves are optional). Tell them there are usually four movements, or sections, to a symphony. The movements are usually named by the tempo or speed of the movement. In the *Farewell Symphony,* the movements are as follows:

I: *Allegro assai* (rather fast)
II: *Adagio* (a little bit slow)
III: *Minuet Allegretto* (A graceful, up-tempo waltz)
IV: Finale: *Presto; Adagio* (the final movement, fast at first, then slowing down to not so fast).

Talk about how each movement makes the students feel.

Next, give each student a piece of paper that is divided into four rectangles, with one of each of the movements listed at the top of each rectangle. Show the students which movement is playing by showing them the label on their paper, and have them color a picture of how each movement makes them feel. Have the students move to the music one more time.

Conclude the lesson by discussing the movements in a symphony. Let the students take their artwork home.

If you are a classroom teacher with limited space, make sure that the students have a self-space for creative movement. The listening and art sections of the lesson may be done at the tables or on the floor.

228

If you have paraprofessionals or other adults assisting in your classroom, have them dance with the students and give suggestions for creative movement. When the students are making pictorial representations of the movements of the symphony, have helpers monitor students, give encouragement, and ask the students questions about their art.

NOTE

Some students are uncomfortable with dancing. If this is an issue in your classroom, use the term *creative movement*.

Lesson 42

Johann S. Bach's Musical Themes and Variations and Revisit Traveling

⟨⟨⟨⟨⟨⟨⟩⟩⟩⟩⟩

National Standards for Physical Education: 2, Demonstrates understanding of movement concepts, principles, strategies, and tactics as they apply to the learning and performance of physical activities.

National Standards for Music Education: 6, Listening to, analyzing, and describing music; 9, Understanding music in relation to history and culture.

Equipment: Scarves.

Lesson Focus:

• Moving in varying ways in PE and music.

Related Literature: *Bach's Goldberg Variations* by Anna Harwell Celenza.

READ THE STORY

Read the story aloud to the class.

PE AND MUSIC ACTIVITY

Help the students define the word *variation*. Use the definition of doing one thing in many different ways. Ask them about variations in walking, running, pizza, popsicles, and cookies.

Have the students spread out in general space. Tell them they are going to use the locomotor movement of walking, but they are going to invent different variations of walking. Give one example such as walking on tiptoes.

Let the students come up with different variations of walking while playing *Bach's Goldberg Variations*. Practice all of the suggestions the students give. Each time the students come up with a new way to walk, play a new variation.

In closing, see if the students can explain why *Bach's Goldberg Variations* are referred to as variations.

If you are a classroom teacher with limited space, remind your students to move carefully in your room when practicing their walking variations. Musical variations with scarves can proceed as described.

If you have paraprofessionals or other adults assisting in your classroom, have them help students think of various ways to walk and various ways to move with their scarves to the music.

Twinkle Twinkle Little Star (Variations)

W.A. Mozart (arranged by C. Wilson)

Twink - le Twink - le lit - tle star, how I won - der what you are.

Up a - bove the world so high, like a dia - mond in the sky,

Twink - le twink - le lit - tle star, how I won - der what you are.

Twink - le Twink - le lit - tle star,

How I won - der what you are.

Up a - bove the word so high,

Like a dia - mond in the sky,

Twink - le twink - le lit - tle star,

How I won - der what you are.

Twink - kle Twink - kle lit - tle star,_____ How__ I won - der what__ you are.

Up__ a- bove__ the world so high,_____ like__ a dia - mond in__ the sky,__

Twink - kle twink - kle lit - tle star,__ How__ I won - der what__ you are.

A Segment of Bach's Goldberg Variations, #1

J.S. Bach (simplified and arranged by C. Wilson)

This is a segment for the students to sing on *la* so that the students learn to recognize the beginning of *Bach's Goldberg Variations*. It is simplified.

Lesson 43

Johann S. Bach's Musical Themes and Variations and Revisit Traveling

⁓❧⁓

National Standards for Physical Education: 2, Demonstrates understanding of movement concepts, principles, strategies, and tactics as they apply to the learning and performance of physical activities.

National Standards for Music Education: 6, Listening to, analyzing, and describing music; 9, Understanding music in relation to history and culture.

Equipment: Scarves.

Lesson Focus:

• Moving in varying ways in PE and music.

Related Literature: *Bach's Goldberg Variations* by Anna Harwell Celenza.

READ THE STORY

Read the story aloud to the class.

PE AND MUSIC ACTIVITY

Review the story of *Bach's Goldberg Variations* with the students. Show the pictures of the story and refresh their memories. Explain musical variations to the students. You can do this by singing a song (e.g., "Twinkle, Twinkle, Little Star"). First sing it the way you always would. Sing it again in a different meter, such as three-quarter time. Sing it again with a vocal improvisation. Then explain that Bach wrote his variations based on a musical theme or thought. Have the students listen to segments of *Bach's Goldberg Variations*. Have them tell you what is different about each variation. Next, give the students each a scarf, and have them move the scarf to the tempo of the variation they hear.

If time permits, have the students draw you a picture of "variations." Conclude the lesson by discussing the variations the students heard.

If you are a classroom teacher with limited space, remind your students to move carefully in your room when practicing their walking variations. Musical variations with scarves can proceed as described.

If you have paraprofessionals or other adults assisting in your classroom, have them help students think of various ways to walk and various ways to move with their scarves to the music.

Lesson 44

Composers and Rhythms

National Standards for Physical Education: 5, Exhibits responsible personal and social behavior that respects self and others in physical activity settings.

National Standards for Music Education: 6, Listening to, analyzing, and describing music; 9, Understanding music in relation to history and culture.

Equipment: Lummi sticks and scarves or long strips of gift ribbon for PE and music, Figure 4.45.

Lesson Focus:

• Tapping out rhythms and understanding the conductor's role in the orchestra in PE and music.

Related Literature: *Beethoven's Heroic Symphony* by Anna Harwell Celenza.

READ THE STORY

Read the story aloud to the class.

PE AND MUSIC ACTIVITY

After reading the book, spend some time listening to a small section of each of the movements of Beethoven's music. The books by Anna Harwell Celenza come with CDs. If you are missing the CDs, this music may be downloaded from iTunes. Talk to the students about the emotions the music evokes when they hear it.

Before giving the students Lummi sticks, review safety and respect rules. They should either put the sticks down when not in use or place them on their shoulders while holding on to the lower portion of the sticks.

Play Follow the Leader with Lummi sticks. Have the students begin to tap out the rhythm you have shown them with the Lummi sticks. After doing this for several minutes, have the students stand. Show them a three-beat pattern that can be used to conduct movement I of *The Heroic Symphony*. They may use the Lummi sticks, or hands, to conduct. Do this in a way that you are most comfortable. Because the students are young, have them use both hands. Do not worry about perfection. Exposure to conducting is the goal. Practice the pattern slowly at first, showing the students how to conduct the three-quarter meter pattern using the words *down, out, up*. Slowly accelerate the pattern until it reaches the correct tempo. When you have done this for several minutes, have them sit down and tap out another Lummi stick pattern. Alternate Lummi stick patterns with conducting. Show the students some conducting patterns that fit the music of *The Heroic Symphony*. Explain how a conductor conducts the orchestra. Let the students pretend to conduct.

If you are a classroom teacher with limited space, the PE and music activities may proceed as described. It may be easier to have the students sit at their tables or desks, rather than on the floor. If you do not have Lummi sticks, make them from rolled-up newspaper. These paper sticks will be quieter.

If you have paraprofessionals or other adults assisting in your classroom, have them circulate around and help where needed as well as supervise.

NOTE

The plans of Lessons 44 and 45 take two days to accomplish because of the length of the story. You may either read the entire story one day and do some of the movement activity or read half of the story one day and the other half of the story the following day followed by movement activity.

Lesson 45

Composers and Rhythms

—⁓⊸⊸⊸⟋⟍⊶⊶⊶—

National Standards for Physical Education: 5, Exhibits responsible personal and social behavior that respects self and others in physical activity settings.
National Standards for Music Education: 6, Listening to, analyzing, and describing music; 9, Understanding music in relation to history and culture.
Equipment: Lummi sticks and scarves or long strips of gift ribbon for PE and music, Figure 4.45.
Lesson Focus:

• Tapping out rhythms and understanding the conductor's role in the orchestra in PE and music.

Related Literature: *The Heroic Symphony* by Anna Harwell Celenza.

READ THE STORY

Read the story aloud to the class.

PE AND MUSIC ACTIVITY

Review the story of *The Heroic Symphony*. Show the students the pictures of the story to refresh their memories.

Play movement I of *The Heroic Symphony*. Have the students alternate playing Follow the Leader with the Lummi sticks and conducting the three-quarter pattern. When you feel it is time to change movements, play movement II for the students. This movement is much slower. Have the students use the scarves or long pieces of gift ribbon to move creatively in a self-space to this slow, sad section. When you feel it is time for a change, play movement III. Alternate having the students tap a Lummi stick pattern with conducting a two-beat pattern. Again, have the students conduct with both hands. Teach them the pattern by using the words *out* and *up*. When it is time for a change, play movement IV. Alternate having the students play a Lummi stick pattern with conducting a four-beat pattern. Teach the pattern using the words *down*, *in*, *out*, and *up*. Again, slow the pattern down for teaching purposes. Accelerate when appropriate. If your students crave variety, alternate the conducting pattern with Lummi stick patterns and creative movement with the scarves or ribbons.

If you are a classroom teacher with limited space, the PE and music activities may proceed as described. It may be easier to have the students sit at their tables or desks, rather than on the floor. If you do not have Lummi sticks, make them from rolled-up newspaper. These paper sticks will be quieter.

If you have paraprofessionals or other adults assisting in your classroom, have them circulate around and help where needed as well as supervise.

236

NOTE

The plans of Lessons 44 and 45 take two days to accomplish because of the length of the story. You may either read the entire story one day and do some of the movement activity or read half of the story one day and the other half of the story the following day followed by movement activity.

CONDUCTING PATTERNS
Unit 4 Lessons 44 and 45

2/4 METER

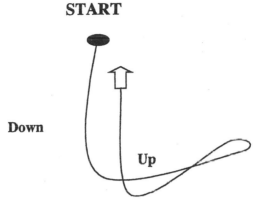

3/4 METER

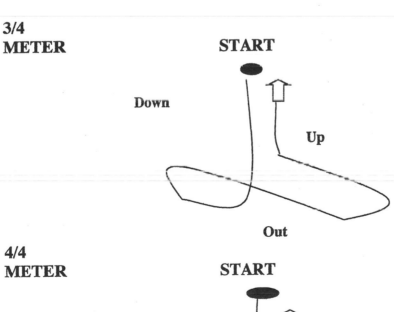

4/4 METER

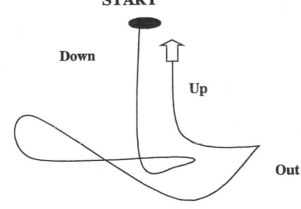

Lesson 46

Rock and Roll and Dance

National Standards for Physical Education: 4, Achieves and maintains a health-enhancing level of physical fitness.
National Standards for Music Education: 6, Listening to, analyzing, and describing music.
Equipment: Musical selections.*
Lesson Focus:

• Rock and roll, keeping a steady beat, and moving to music in PE and music.

Related Literature: *Bats Around the Clock* by Kathi Appelt.

READ THE STORY

Read the story aloud to the class.

PE AND MUSIC ACTIVITY

The students are going to dance to rock and roll. Here is a list of songs and movements that are the same as in Unit 4 Lesson 47.

Use the following movement pattern:

"Surfin' USA" (Beach Boys)
Sidestep while doing swimming freestyle arms sixteen counts
Sidestep while doing swimming backstroke arms sixteen counts
Repeat

"The Twist" (Chubby Checker)
Twist to the right
Twist to the left

"Rock Around the Clock" (Bill Haley)
Do the jitterbug hand motions
Pat legs twice
Clap twice
Both palms down, right hand over left, fingers straight,
(Keep beat with right hand on top for two beats)
Both palms down, left hand over right, fingers straight,

(Keep beat with the left hand over for two beats)
Right fist over left, two beats
Left fist over right, two beats
Right thumb over right shoulder, two beats
Left thumb over left shoulder, two beats
Repeat

"Lollipop" (The Chordettes)
Sidestep, swing arms overhead right then left, sixteen counts
Sidestep, swing arms under shoulders right then left, sixteen counts
Bend knees up and down, swing arms back and forth, sixteen counts

"Bones" (Jim Valley, Rainbow Planet)
Use suggested steps on the recording

"Eye of the Tiger" (Survivor)
Allow students to make up their own movements in self-space

"The River of Dreams" (Billy Joel)
Walk in place to the beat, creating movements with the arms

"Crocodile Rock" (Elton John)
Twist during the verses,
Sidestep while making crocodile arms during the refrain

If you are a classroom teacher with limited space, have the students do the movements in a self-space.

If you have paraprofessionals or other adults assisting in your classroom, have them help you choreograph songs and supervise students when they are moving.

NOTE

*Musical selections can be downloaded from iTunes.

Lesson 47

Rock and Roll and Dance

⊸∿⊶

National Standards for Physical Education: 4, Achieves and maintains a health-enhancing level of physical fitness.
National Standards for Music Education: 6, Listening to, analyzing, and describing music.
Equipment: Musical selections.*
Lesson Focus:

• Rock and roll, keeping a steady beat, and moving to music in PE and music.

Related Literature: *Pigs Rock* by Melanie Jones and Bob Staake.

READ THE STORY

Read the story aloud to the class.

PE AND MUSIC ACTIVITY

The students are going to dance to rock and roll again. Here is a list of songs and movements that are the same as in Unit 4 Lesson 46.
    Use the following movement pattern:

"Surfin' USA" (Beach Boys)
Sidestep while doing swimming freestyle arms sixteen counts
Sidestep while doing swimming backstroke arms sixteen counts
Repeat

"The Twist" (Chubby Checkers)
Twist to the right
Twist to the left

"Rock Around the Clock" (Bill Haley)
Do the jitterbug hand motions
Pat legs twice
Clap twice
Both palms down, right hand over left, fingers straight,
(Keep beat with right hand on top for two beats)
Both palms down, left hand over right, fingers straight,
(Keep beat with the left hand over for two beats)
Right fist over left, two beats

Left fist over right, two beats
Right thumb over right shoulder, two beats
Left thumb over left shoulder, two beats
Repeat

"Lollipop" (The Chordettes)
Sidestep, swing arms overhead right then left, sixteen counts
Sidestep, swing arms under shoulders right then left, sixteen counts
Bend knees up and down, swing arms back and forth, sixteen counts

"Bones" (Jim Valley, Rainbow Planet)
Use suggested steps on the recording

"Eye of the Tiger" (Survivor)
Allow students to make up their own movements in self-space

"The River of Dreams" (Billy Joel)
Walk in place to the beat, creating movements with the arms

"Crocodile Rock" (Elton John)
Twist during the verses,
Sidestep while making crocodile arms during the refrain

If you are a classroom teacher with limited space, have the students do the movements in a self-space.

If you have paraprofessionals or other adults assisting in your classroom, have them help you choreograph songs and supervise students when they are moving.

NOTE

*Musical selections can be downloaded from iTunes.

Lesson 48

Opera and Creative Movement

National Standards for Physical Education: 5, Exhibits responsible personal and social behavior that respects self and others in physical activity settings.
National Standards for Music Education: 1, Singing, alone and with others, a varied repertoire of music.
Equipment: Construction paper, small paper bags, crayons, and cue cards for the opera.
Lesson Focus:

- Creative movement in PE.
- Learning about opera in music.

Related Literature: *The Three Little Pigs* by James Marshall.

READ THE STORY

Read the story aloud to the class.

PE AND MUSIC ACTIVITY

Opera is fun for young children to explore. An opera is a story that is entirely sung. The "songs" in an opera are called *arias*, and the sung parts in between the songs are called *recitative*. Opera is usually colorful and dramatic. Our next four lessons will focus on creating an opera.

The children can be creative when creating an opera if they use a story they are familiar with. The children will sing the story of *The Three Little Pigs* as an opera. Make sure that all of the children know the story of *The Three Little Pigs* well. You can use the cue cards during rehearsals and performances to make sure that they understand the progression of the story.

Begin by having the students make paper bag puppets from the patterns provided and small paper bags. Precut the patterns to save time. You will want to have five different groups. Split the class equally and have three different groups of pigs (i.e., stick pigs, straw pigs, and brick pigs), one group of wolves and one group of chorus members (boys and girls). Let the students glue on the ears and tails or hair and then decorate the puppet.

Make sure that all of your students have been assigned a part in the story of *The Three Little Pigs*. Let them know that when their character sings, they will stand up and use their voice and puppet to sing the story.

Practice your opera many times over, so that the students are comfortable with their parts. Use large cue cards to make sure that all students know when to perform. Have the students make puppets and become familiar with the story. Practice singing the opera and when to stand and when to sit during Unit 4 Lessons 49 to 51. Feel free to have each group invent a "signature move." When the opera is ready, perform for your principal and other teachers, or a class of students.

Conclude the lessons by asking the students what they learned about opera. Opera is a story that is completely sung. The songs in an opera are called *arias*. The sung lines in between the songs are called *recitative*. Opera is usually colorful and dramatic, which is why we use the term *soap opera* to describe daytime television drama today.

If you are a classroom teacher with limited space, this lesson may proceed as described. Arrange your students so that the same characters are sitting next to one another.

If you have paraprofessionals or other adults assisting in your classroom, they can help with cue cards and directing students as to when to stand and sit.

A Three Piggy Opera in One Act (The Three Little Pigs)

C. Wilson

Lesson 49

Opera and Creative Movement

—◦◦◦—

National Standards for Physical Education: 5, Exhibits responsible personal and social behavior that respects self and others in physical activity settings.
National Standards for Music Education: 1, Singing, alone and with others, a varied repertoire of music.
Equipment: Construction paper, small paper bags, crayons, and cue cards for the opera.
Lesson Focus:

- Creative movement in PE.
- Learning about opera in music.

Related Literature: *Bantam of the Opera* by Mary Jane Auch.

READ THE STORY

Read the story aloud to the class.

PE AND MUSIC ACTIVITY

This lesson is a continuation of Unit 4 Lesson 48.

Make sure all of your students have been assigned a part in the story of *The Three Little Pigs*. Let them know that when their character sings, they will stand up and use their voice and puppet to sing the story.

Practice your opera many times over, so the students are comfortable with their parts. Use large cue cards to make sure all students know when to perform. Have the students make puppets and become familiar with the story. Practice singing the opera and when to stand and when to sit. Feel free to have each group invent a "signature move." When the opera is ready, perform for your principal, and other teachers, or a class of students.

Conclude the lessons by asking the students what they learned about opera. Opera is a story that is completely sung. The songs in an opera are called *arias*. The sung lines in between the songs are called *recitative*. Opera is usually colorful and dramatic, which is why we use the term *soap opera* to describe daytime television drama today.

If you are a classroom teacher with limited space, this lesson may proceed as described. Arrange your students so that the same characters are sitting next to one another.

If you have paraprofessionals or other adults assisting in your classroom, they can help with cue cards and directing students as to when to stand and sit.

Lesson 50

Opera and Creative Movement

—⁓⁓—

National Standards for Physical Education: 5, Exhibits responsible personal and social behavior that respects self and others in physical activity settings.
National Standards for Music Education: 1, Singing, alone and with others, a varied repertoire of music.
Equipment: Construction paper, small paper bags, crayons, and cue cards for the opera.
Lesson Focus:

• Creative movement in PE.
• Learning about opera in music.

Related Literature: *Opera Cat* by Tess Weaver.

READ THE STORY

Read the story aloud to the class.

PE AND MUSIC ACTIVITY

This lesson is a continuation of Unit 4 Lessons 48 and 49.

Make sure all of your students have been assigned a part in the story of *The Three Little Pigs*. Let them know that when their character sings, they will stand up and use their voice and puppet to sing the story.

Practice your opera many times over, so the students are comfortable with their parts. Use large cue cards to make sure all students know when to perform. Have the students make puppets and become familiar with the story. Practice singing the opera and when to stand and when to sit. Feel free to have each group invent a "signature move." When the opera is ready, perform for your principal and other teachers, or a class of students.

Conclude the lessons by asking the students what they learned about opera. Opera is a story that is completely sung. The songs in an opera are called *arias*. The sung lines in between the songs are called *recitative*. Opera is usually colorful and dramatic, which is why we use the term *soap opera* to describe daytime television drama today.

If you are a classroom teacher with limited space, this lesson may proceed as described. Arrange your students so that the same characters are sitting next to one another.

If you have paraprofessionals or other adults assisting in your classroom, they can help with cue cards and directing students as to when to stand and sit.

Lesson 51

Opera and Creative Movement

National Standards for Physical Education: 5, Exhibits responsible personal and social behavior that respects self and others in physical activity settings.

National Standards for Music Education: 1, Singing, alone and with others, a varied repertoire of music.

Equipment: Construction paper, small paper bags, crayons, and cue cards for the opera, Figures 4.51.1, 4.51.2, and 4.51.3.

Lesson Focus:

- Creative movement in PE.
- Learning about opera in music.

Related Literature: *The Dog Who Sang at the Opera* by Marshall Izen and Jim West.

READ THE STORY

Read the story aloud to the class.

PE AND MUSIC ACTIVITY

This lesson is a continuation of Unit 4 Lessons 48, 49, and 50.

Make sure all of your students have been assigned a part in the story of *The Three Little Pigs*. Let them know that when their character sings, they will stand up and use their voice and puppet to sing the story.

Practice your opera many times over, so the students are comfortable with their parts. Use large cue cards to make sure all students know when to perform. Have the students make puppets and become familiar with the story. Practice singing the opera and when to stand and when to sit. Feel free to have each group invent a "signature move." When the opera is ready, perform for your principal and other teachers, or a class of students.

Conclude the lessons by asking the students what they learned about opera. Opera is a story that is completely sung. The songs in an opera are called *arias*. The sung lines in between the songs are called *recitative*. Opera is usually colorful and dramatic, which is why we use the term *soap opera* to describe daytime television drama today.

If you are a classroom teacher with limited space, this lesson may proceed as described. Arrange your students so that the same characters are sitting next to one another.

If you have paraprofessionals or other adults assisting in your classroom, they can help with cue cards and directing students as to when to stand and sit.

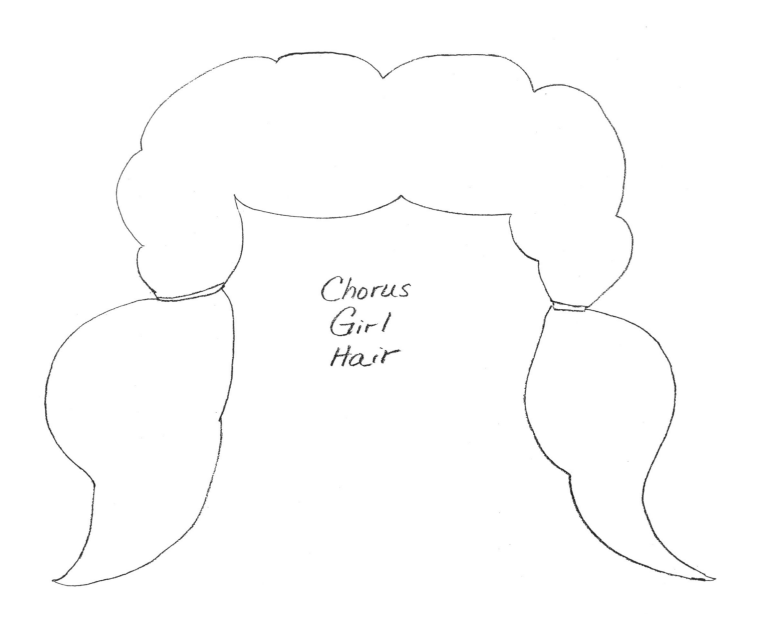

Chorus
Girl
Hair

Pig

Chorus
Boy
Hair

Wolf

Lesson 52

Jazz and Revisit Traveling

—⌇⌇⌇—

National Standards for Physical Education: 1, Demonstrates competency in motor skills and movement patterns needed to perform a variety of physical activities.

National Standards for Music Education: 1, Singing, alone and with others, a varied repertoire of music; 6, Listening to, analyzing, and describing music.

Equipment: Recordings of jazz music for PE. Download from iTunes "The Feeling of Jazz" by Duke Ellington and John Coltrane; "Before I Let Go" by Frankie Beverly and Maze Smooth Jazz; "Squatty Roo" by The Clayton Hamilton Jazz Orchestra; "Dr. Jazz" by Songs of New Orleans; and "On and On" by Smooth Jazz All-Stars; a recording of "Sir Duke" by Stevie Wonder for music.

Lesson Focus:

- Traveling in different ways to jazz music in PE.
- Appreciating and moving to jazz in music.

Related Literature: *Lookin' for Bird in the Big City* by Robert Burleigh.

READ THE STORY

Read the story aloud to the class.

PE ACTIVITY

The students are going to revisit different ways to travel. Begin with a review. Ask the students how many ways they remember to travel on foot. Ask the students about their favorite way of traveling.

Have the students travel to different jazz pieces. Go through the main traveling skills such as skipping, galloping, leaping, hopping, running, jogging, walking, and so on. Give the students plenty of practice time.

MUSIC ACTIVITY

Play the song "Sir Duke" for the students. Tell the students that the artists named in the song are famous jazz musicians (Basie, jazz pianist, organist, composer, band leader; Duke Ellington, pianist, composer, and band leader; Miller, trombonist, Big Band leader; Satchmo (Louis Armstrong), jazz trumpeter, and Ella, jazz vocalist). Explain to the students that these musicians helped jazz to develop into the popular musical genre that it is today. Jazz developed from ragtime and blues music, which was popular in the United States in the 1920s. New Orleans was a place where jazz music developed. Some of the characteristics of jazz include syncopation (i.e., playing or singing off of the beat), planing chords (i.e., playing chords or extended chords in parallel motion), and chords that use seventh, ninth, and eleventh degrees of chords in varied augmented and diminished forms for extension. The children do not need to understand this, but if you play a few jazzy sounding chords for them, they will get the idea. For more information about jazz music, go to www .wikipedia.org.

Listen to "Sir Duke" again. Have the students identify some of the instruments they hear performing. Teach the students to sing the refrain. Have the students sidestep in a self-space as they sing "Sir Duke." They may also clap or dance.

Conclude the lesson by playing some jazz music for the students and asking them how it makes them feel.

If you are a classroom teacher with limited space, make sure you have plenty of room for the PE traveling review. The music lesson may proceed as described.

If you have paraprofessionals or other adults assisting in your classroom, have them supervise the traveling activities and sing the refrain of "Sir Duke" with the students. The helpers can also assist you in inventing jazz-style choreography.

NOTE

You can download lyrics for "Sir Duke" at www.lyricsdomain.com.

Lesson 53

Jazz and Revisit Catching

—⁓⁓—

National Standards for Physical Education: 1, Demonstrates competency in motor skills and movement patterns needed to perform a variety of physical activities.

National Standards for Music Education: 6, Listening to, analyzing, and describing music; 9, Understanding music in relation to history and culture.

Equipment: Small balls to catch for PE, jazz recordings* and paper and crayons for music.

Lesson Focus:

- Quick catches in PE.
- Jazz music in music.

Related Literature: *Charlie Parker Played Be Bop* by Chris Raschka.

READ THE STORY

Read the story aloud to the class.

PE ACTIVITY

Divide your students into small groups of five or six students. Have them get in circles and spread out. This game is like Hot Potato. Use fleece balls or any small ball to play. Fleece balls are preferred. Give each group of students a ball.

Turn on the jazz music, and the students begin tossing the ball to someone in the circle. They can toss to anyone. When the music stops, the student holding the ball jogs around the circle while the other students pretend to play the saxophone. When the music begins, the students start the game again. Play several times.

If students are having a difficult time throwing the ball to anyone, simply have them toss it in order around the circle.

MUSIC ACTIVITY

After you have read the book to the students, let them look at the pictures once more. Play "Sir Duke" and have the students sing and move to the song again. Next, play the recordings of jazz music that are on the equipment list from Unit 4 Lesson 52. Pass out a piece of paper and crayons for every child. Tell the children to draw a picture about the music they are listening to or a picture of the musicians who are playing. You will get an assortment of pictures. Some will be very concrete, and others will be abstract. Tell the children that many jazz musicians improvise during their songs. Explain that improvising is making up part of the song as you are playing it.

Conclude the lesson by having the students tell you how jazz music makes them feel. Let them take their pictures home.

If you are a classroom teacher with limited space, make sure you have plenty of space to play Hot Potato Jazz. The music lesson may proceed as described.

If you have paraprofessionals or other adults assisting in your classroom, have them supervise Hot Potato Jazz. During the jazz picture coloring, have the helpers walk around and ask students about their artwork.

NOTE

*Refer to the list from Unit 4 Lesson 52.

Lesson 54

Jazz and Fitness

—⟪⟫—

National Standards for Physical Education: 4, Achieves and maintains a health-enhancing level of physical fitness.

National Standards for Music Education: 6, Listening to, analyzing, and describing music; 1, Singing, alone and with others, a varied repertoire of music.

Equipment: Poly spots with letters, poker chips, and index cards with jazz words for PE, A recording of "What A Wonderful World" sung by Louis Armstrong for music.*

Lesson Focus:

- Maintaining movement for a set period of time in PE.
- Singing and movement in music.

Related Literature: *Rent Party Jazz* by William Miller.

READ THE STORY

Read the story aloud to the class.

PE ACTIVITY

This activity is to keep the students moving. When they enter the gym have them go to a self-space. Lay out poly spots on the floor spread out with the letters up. If you do not have poly spots with letters on them, write the alphabet on index cards and tape them to the spots.

Give each student a handful of poker chips. Tell the student that they are going to be spelling words that are related to jazz music (i.e., trumpet, sax, piano, jazz, drum, rent, and so on). Give every child an index card and tell the students to start on the first letter of their word. For instance, if the word were *jazz*, they would jog to the poly spot with the letter *J* and place a chip on it. They would then jog to the letter *A* and place a chip on it. Have them continue until the word is spelled. If time allows, they could do several words.

Make sure they are not covering up the letter with the chips when they place them on the spot. You could also change the locomotor movement if they are getting tired of jogging. If you want to play background music during the game, use the music list from Unit 4 Lessons 52 and 53.

MUSIC ACTIVITY

Discuss the story *Rent Party Jazz*. Talk about how music helps people to endure hardships and makes people feel better. Many people use music to help them work. In days before the radio existed, sailors and cowboys sang songs while they worked. Music makes the world a better place.

Teach the students the song "What a Wonderful World" by George Davis Weiss and Bob Theile. Play the recording of the song for them with Louis Armstrong singing. Ask them to tell you about Armstrong's voice. Was it smooth, bouncy, scratchy, young or old sounding, high or low? You will get a variety of answers.

Give every student a colored scarf. Have the students find a self-space and move their scarf to the music. Let them do this activity several times.

Conclude the lesson by having the students tell you what they know about jazz.

If you are a classroom teacher with limited space, the students may do both of these activities in a regular classroom. Remind the students how to move safely in your classroom.

If you have paraprofessionals or other adults assisting in your classroom, have them help students spell their jazz words. The can also think of creative movement during "What a Wonderful World." Have them help you pass out and collect scarves.

NOTE

*This song can be downloaded from iTunes.

Lesson 55

Country and Folk Music and Rhythms

—⁓⁓—

National Standards for Physical Education: 3, Participates regularly in physical activity.
National Standards for Music Education: 1, Singing, alone and with others, a varied repertoire of music; 6, Listening to, analyzing, and describing music.
Equipment: Recordings of "The Farmer in the Dell" from Wee Sing, "Hokey Pokey" from iTunes, Ultimate Party Mix, "Hamster Dance" from iTunes, More Kids Fun.
Lesson Focus:

• Country and folk music and dancing.

Related Literature: *The Old Banjo* by Dennis Haseley.

READ THE STORY

Read the story aloud to the class.

PE AND MUSIC ACTIVITY

Children usually enjoy country and folk music. Teach the students the song and game "The Farmer in the Dell." Have the students form several circles to play the games so that the students get more turns to be a character. Next, teach the students the song and the dance of the "Hokey Pokey." (This can be downloaded from iTunes.) The children do this dance by forming a circle and following the directions on the recording. Finally, teach the students "The Hamster Dance." The following movements are for the song "The Hamster Dance."

Form a circle and hold hands.
Step to the side going to the right eight counts.
Step to the side going to the left eight counts.
Boys walk to the center for four counts and out from the center four counts.
Girls walk to the center for four counts and out from the center four counts.
Repeat.

This dance can be used for many country or folk songs. Conclude the lesson by having the students do their favorite dance.

If you are a classroom teacher with limited space, make sure you have plenty of room to make circles and dance safely.

If you have paraprofessionals or other adults assisting in your classroom, use them to supervise the circles and help get students in the center for "The Farmer in the Dell."

Lesson 56

Country Music and Rhythms

National Standards for Physical Education: 6, Values physical activity for health, enjoyment, challenge, self-expression, and or social interaction.

National Standards for Music Education: 1, Singing, alone and with others, a varied repertoire of music.

Equipment: Recordings of the following songs: "The Farmer and the Dell" from Wee Sing, "Hokey Pokey" from iTunes, Ultimate Party Mix, "The Hamster Dance" from iTunes, More Kids Fun.

Lesson Focus:

• Country and folk songs and dances in PE and music.

Related Literature: *The Little Red Hen* by Jerry Pinkney.

READ THE STORY

Read the story aloud to the class.

PE AND MUSIC ACTIVITIES

Start the class by reviewing the songs and dances that were taught in the Unit 4 Lesson 55 (e.g., "The Farmer in the Dell," "Hokey Pokey," and "The Hamster Dance").

Teach the students the song "Old MacDonald." After the students are comfortable singing this song, have them suggest movements and sounds for various animals. List three animals on a dry-erase board to give the students visual cues regarding which animal comes next.

Have the students sing "The Farmer in the Dell." Next, have the students play the game in several circles as they did in Unit 4 Lesson 55.

Finally, teach the students the song "Little Boy Blue." Have the students sing the song several times until they are comfortable with it. Have the students form a circle. Pick one child to be in the center as Little Boy Blue. Have the other students sing to him. When the song is over, have him pick another student to be Little Boy Blue or Little Girl Sue (for a girl).

Conclude the lesson by having the students tell you about other country songs and games they know.

If you are a classroom teacher with limited space, find an area with enough space to enjoy the circle dances.

If you have paraprofessionals or other adults assisting in your classroom, have them help the students remember the "Hokey Pokey," "The Farmer in the Dell," "The Hamster Dance," and "Little Boy Blue."

Lesson 57

Folk Music and Rhythms

—⋙∿⋘—

National Standards for Physical Education: 5, Exhibits responsible personal and social behavior that respects self and others in physical activity settings.
National Standards for Music Education: 1, Singing, alone and with others, a varied repertoire of music; 6, Listening to, analyzing, and describing music.
Equipment: None.
Lesson Focus: Folk music in PE and music.

Related Literature: *The Little Red Hen* by Barry Downard.

READ THE STORY

Read the story aloud to the class.

PE AND MUSIC ACTIVITY

Read the same story as the previous lesson. Involve the students in acting out the story as it is read. You may need to do this several times so that all of the students get the chance to be a character. If necessary, have groups of students be hens, ducks, pigs, and cats.

Review the songs and dances that the students did in the last two lessons. Have the students sing and play "The Farmer in the Dell," "Old MacDonald," "The Hamster Dance," and any other folk dances or polkas you may have taught.

Conclude the lesson by asking the students which dances and games they enjoyed the most.

If you are a classroom teacher with limited space, find an area that has enough space to allow the students to dance. The gym or another large room will work. You may also consider moving the desks to make space.

If you have paraprofessionals or other adults assisting in your classroom, have the students divide into more circles to play. Make sure there is an adult supervisor for every circle. The students will get more turns in smaller groups.

Country Music and Rhythms

—ᴍᴍᴨᴨ ᴨ ᴨᴍᴍᴍ—

National Standards for Physical Education: 3, Participates regularly in physical activity.
National Standards for Music Education: 3, Improvising melodies, variations, and accompaniments; 6, Listening to, analyzing, and describing music.
Equipment: Rhythm band instruments.
Lesson Focus:

• Country songs, folk songs, and dance in PE and music.

Related Literature: *Barnyard Boogie* by Jim and Janet Post or *Today Is Monday* by Eric Carle.

READ THE STORY

Read one of the selected stories aloud to the class.

PE AND MUSIC ACTIVITY

Discuss the *Barnyard Boogie* story. Have the students make up movements for each animal as the story is read again. Let them practice the animal movements. Next, show the students the rhythm band instruments. Have the students use different types of instruments to make the animal sounds. Have some of the students make the animal sounds with the instruments, while other students do the animal motions as you read the story. Be sure to list the animals on a dry-erase board with their movements and instrument sounds listed to give the students visual cues for the order of the story.

Conclude the lesson by reviewing the songs and dances from Unit 4 Lessons 55 to 57.

If you are a classroom teacher with limited space, the "Barnyard Boogie" activity can be taught with the students staying in a self-space. If you do not have rhythm band instruments, use homemade percussion instruments. You may also use "kitchen band instruments" (i.e., pots, pans, cookie sheets, plastic ware, wooden spoons, and so on) to invent the animal sounds. Vocal sounds can also be used.

If you have paraprofessionals or other adults assisting in your classroom, have them help supervise students and pass out instruments and other various items as needed. They can also choreograph parts and make lists of animal sounds and movements.

Lesson 59

Country and Folk Music and Rhythms

National Standards for Physical Education: 1, Demonstrates competency in motor skills and movement patterns needed to perform a variety of physical activities.

National Standards for Music Education: 6, Listening to, analyzing, and describing music.

Equipment: "Cotton Eyed Joe" (Star Sound Orchestra),* "Grandma's Featherbed" (John Denver),* "Life Is a Highway" (Rascal Flatts),* "Thank God I'm a Country Boy" (John Denver).*

Lesson Focus:

• Country and folk songs and dances in PE and music.

Related Literature: *Goldilocks* by James Marshall.

READ THE STORY

Read the story aloud to the class.

PE AND MUSIC ACTIVITY

Teach the activity called Meet in the Middle. Line up equal numbers of students on two opposite sides of the gym. Make sure that each student is across from another student. Use the country songs in the equipment list above as you play Meet in the Middle.

Give the students instructions for meeting in the middle. Have both groups of students step to the steady beat of the music to the middle of the gym facing their partner. Have each student give his partner across from him a high five. Have the students walk to the steady beat back to their place on the opposite side of the gym. Have the students walk to the steady beat to the middle of the gym again. This time, have each give his partner a right high five and then a left high five. Once again, walk to the steady beat back to the original place. Walk to the middle of the gym again to the steady beat of the music. Have each student give his partner a right high five, a left high five, and add a high ten. Continue to repeat and add on as the song continues. Watch your students carefully. Observe the students' abilities and decide how many more steps you can add. Repeat the actions if you choose or invent new actions. You might even try adding some square dancing calls (i.e., bow to your partner, bow to your neighbor, do-si-do). When you begin a new song, start the motions from the list over again.

Conclude the lesson by having the students describe the sounds of some of the country and folk music they heard.

If you are a classroom teacher with limited space, make sure you have plenty of room to play Meet in the Middle.

If you have paraprofessionals or other adults assisting in your classroom, have them help supervise Meet in the Middle. They can also partner with a student who does not have a partner.

NOTE

*These songs can be downloaded from iTunes.

Lesson 60

Country and Folk Music and Rhythms

National Standards for Physical Education: 5, Exhibits responsible personal and social behavior that respects self and others in physical activity settings.

National Standards for Music Education: 1, Singing, alone and with others, a varied repertoire of music; 6, Listening to, analyzing, and describing music.

Equipment: Scarves for "mice" in PE and music.

Lesson Focus:

• Playing a game together and enjoying rhythms of country and folk music.

Related Literature: *Hansel and Gretel* by James Marshall.

READ THE STORY

Read the story aloud to the class.

PE AND MUSIC ACTIVITY

Have the students listen to the song "Strings on my Banjo" by Jim Gill. It is on his *Noisy in Boise* CD. As the students listen to the song, have them think of ways they could move to the beat. Have some of the students demonstrate their fancy steps as the music is playing. Make sure each student is in a self-space. Have the students listen to the music again. Have the students do some of their fancy footwork to the music!

Next, teach the students the song "Three Blind Mice." Sing the song several times until the students are comfortable with it. After the students know the song well, have them form a circle. If you have many students, have them form several smaller circles of about twelve students each. Pick three students from each circle to be "blind mice." Have the mice tuck a scarf into their back pocket or down the neck opening of their shirt. Have the mice go and stand facing the wall with their eyes closed so that they cannot see the children in the circle. Pick a child from each circle to be the "cook." Do not let the mice know which student is the cook. Have all of the students start singing the song "Three Blind Mice." As they sing, the mice start walking around the circle. When the teacher claps her hands together (usually on the word *run*), the cook starts chasing the mice and tries to grab the scarf from the back pocket of a "mouse." If a mouse is caught, then that student goes back to his spot in the circle, and the cook becomes the mouse. If the mouse is not caught, he may choose another child who has not had a turn yet to be a mouse. If you find you are running out of time and need to make sure that all students get a turn, pick more than one cook!

Conclude the lesson by having the students tell you what they enjoy about moving and singing with music.

If you are a classroom teacher with limited space, consider going to the gym, playground, or other large space to play the game "Three Blind Mice." This game gets loud.

If you have paraprofessionals or other adults assisting in your classroom, have them help supervise the game "Three Blind Mice," especially if you have more than one circle playing at once. They can also help tuck scarves in appropriate places.

Unit 5

GAMES, SONGS, AND
SEASONS OF OTHER LANDS

Spring and Mexico

—◄◄◄◄╮╲╭╭╭╭—

National Standards for Physical Education: 5, Exhibits responsible personal and social behavior that respects self and others in physical activity settings.
National Standards for Music Education: 1, Singing, alone and with others, a varied repertoire of music.
Equipment: None.
Lesson Focus:

• Culture of Mexico.
• Season of spring.

Related Literature: *Turtle Spring* by Deborah Turney Zagwyn and *Pumpkin Fiesta* by Caryn Yacowitz.

READ THE STORY

Read the stories aloud to the class.

PE ACTIVITY

This is a Mexican game called El Bosque Encantado, which means The Enchanted Forest.

Establish a circle inside of the playing area to be used as the witch's den. One player is chosen to be the witch and all of the other children scatter in the playing area. On the *go* signal, everyone runs to avoid being tagged by the witch. Players can become a "tree" by stopping and raising their hands over their head. They can also become a "rock" by curling into a small ball. When in the tree or rock position, the witch cannot tag them.

When players are tagged, they must go to the witch's den and remain there until the next game. Change the witch often and free those in the den regularly so that everyone stays involved.

MUSIC ACTIVITY

Talk about a farm being a busy place in the springtime. Tell the children about farming in Mexico. Farms are usually smaller, and there are more family farms in Mexico than here in the United States. Discuss the responsibilities of children are on the farm (i.e., feed and care for animals, collect eggs, and clean animal stalls or living areas). Teach the children the Argentinean folk song "Mi Chacra." Have the children make up movements for each of the animals.

Conclude the lesson by talking about farming in Mexico and what things might grow better in a warmer climate. Coffee grows well in Mexico.

If you are a classroom teacher with limited space, make sure you have enough space to play *El Bosque Encantado*. The music lesson may proceed as described.

If you have paraprofessionals or other adults assisting in your classroom, have them help supervise the game. They can also help make up animal movements during "Mi Chacra."

Lesson 2

Spring and Mexico

—⸎—

National Standards for Physical Education: 4, Achieves and maintains a health-enhancing level of physical fitness.
National Standards for Music Education: 1, Singing, alone and with others, a varied repertoire of music.
Equipment: Strips of crepe paper for PE.
Lesson Focus:

- Culture of Mexico.
- Season of spring.

Related Literature: *Erandi's Braids* by Antonio Hernández Madrigal and Tomie de Paulo.

READ THE STORY

Read the story aloud to the class.

PE ACTIVITY

Discuss how children all over the world play many different games. In Mexico, the weather stays warm like spring in the United States, so children can play outdoors year-round. Today's game from Mexico is called Gallo Desplumado, which means, "plucked rooster." Each player will need to attach three strips of crepe paper to each arm so they hang down.

On the *go* signal, the players begin moving through general space keeping their arms away from their sides. Each player will try to remove the strips from the other player's arms. The winner is the one at the end of the game with the most strips left on her arms. Play the game several times.

MUSIC ACTIVITY

Review the song "Mi Chacra." Ask the students what they remember about Mexico and farming in Mexico. Review the animal names and animal sounds. Teach the children the song "El Coqui." Have them sing the song several times until they are comfortable with it. Next, have the children go to a self-space on the floor and pretend to be a sleeping frog. The teacher will sing the beginning of the song. When the teacher sings the phrase *in my dream comes his sweet little song*, the teacher will gently tap several students to wake up and sing the "coqui" part (the refrain). The "tapped" students sing the frog part together. Tell all of the frogs to go to sleep again and start the game again. Give each student a chance to sing the frog line. If you wish, have the students hop in place like the frog as they sing the refrain.

Conclude the lesson by having the students sing their Spanish folk songs.

If you are a classroom teacher with limited space, make sure you have plenty of room for the plucking chickens. The music portion of the lesson may proceed in a self-space.

If you have paraprofessionals or other adults assisting in your classroom, have them help supervise Gallo Desplumado. They can also assist with attaching feathers to students. During "El Coqui," helpers can assist by gently tapping frogs to sing.

Lesson 3

Spring and Mexico

—◅⁓‖∫‖⁓▻—

National Standards for Physical Education: 5, Exhibits responsible personal and social behavior that respects self and others in physical activity settings.

National Standards for Music Education: 1, Singing, alone and with others, a varied repertoire of music; 2, Performing on instruments, alone and with others, a varied repertoire of music.

Equipment: Plastic lids and poly spots for PE, Rhythm band instruments for music.

Lesson Focus:

• Culture of Mexico in PE and music.

Related Literature: *Under the Lemon Moon* by Edith Hope Fine.

READ THE STORY

Read the story aloud.

PE ACTIVITY

Discuss the games from Mexico that the students have played in Unit 5 Lessons 1 and 2. In this lesson, the game the students will play is called Ting, Ting, Ting. This game involves throwing or sliding plastic lids. Yogurt lids or other plastic lids work well for this activity. If lids are not available, use beanbags.

Designate and mark a square on the floor. The size will depend on your students' throwing ability and the space you have. In the middle of the square, place four poly spots in a row. Each player will stand on a corner of the square and either toss or slide a lid, trying to get it to land on a poly spot. The game continues with players taking turns and trying to get the most lids on the spots.

MUSIC ACTIVITY

Teach the children to sing the song "La Raspa" (Mexican Dance). It is commonly known as the "Mexican Hat Dance." Have the students sing the notes on *la* and clap in between each phrase. When the students are comfortable singing the song, have them learn how to do the Mexican Dance to the song. The movement to the song is found in the book *Diez Ditos (Ten Little Fingers and Other Play Rhymes and Action Songs from Latin America)*, selected, arranged, and translated by Jose-Luis Orozco and illustrated by Elisa Kleven. The book also has an accompanying CD, so the students can hear how all of the songs and rhymes sound. "La Raspa" can also be downloaded from iTunes (Reader's Digest Music, "Perfidia," *All-Time Latin Favorites*). Next, pass out rhythm band instruments to each student. Have the students play the instruments to the steady beat of the song.

Conclude the lesson by having the children tell you what they know about Mexico.

"La Raspa" Dance
(Have students choose a partner)
Movement for the verses:
Right foot on the downbeat: heel, toe, heel, (clap, clap)
Left foot on the downbeat: heel, toe, heel, (clap, clap)
Do this sequence four times.

Movement for the refrain:
Link elbows; swing right on the first phrase.
Link elbows; swing left on the second phrase.
Do this sequence two times.

    If you are a classroom teacher with limited space, these activities may be done in your classroom. Be sure to remind students how to move safely in the space you have designated. If you do not have any rhythm band instruments, use homemade percussion instruments or rhythm sticks.

    If you have paraprofessionals or other adults assisting in your classroom, have them help supervise students as they play Ting, Ting, Ting. If you have an odd number of students, have an assistant dance "La Raspa" with a child who needs a partner.

La raspa (Mexican Dance)

Spring and Mexico

—⟨⟨⟨∫⟩⟩⟩—

National Standards for Physical Education: 1, Demonstrates competency in motor skills and movement patterns needed to perform a variety of physical activities.
National Standards for Music Education: 1, Singing, alone and with others, a varied repertoire of music.
Equipment: None.
Lesson Focus:

• Mexican culture, games, and singing in PE and music.

Related Literature: *Mice and Beans* by Pam Muñoz Ryan.

READ THE STORY

Read the story aloud to the class.

PE AND MUSIC ACTIVITIES

This lesson is a review lesson. Sing the songs from Unit 5 Lessons 1, 2, and 3, and do the dances. If time allows, let the students choose which of the three Mexican games they would like to play.

PE ACTIVITY

Ask the children what they know about Mexico. Ask them about things that happen during the springtime. Play El Bosque Encantado from Unit 5 Lesson 1. Play Gallo Desplumado from Unit 5 Lesson 2. Finally, play Ting, Ting, Ting from Unit 5 Lesson 3. Have the children vote on their favorite Mexican game.

MUSIC ACTIVITY

Sing and make animal sounds to the song "Mi Chacra" from Unit 5 Lesson 1. Ask the children what they remember about farming in Mexico. Next, sing the song "El Coqui" from Unit 5 Lesson 2. Have them play the "frog game." Finally, have the children dance to "La Raspa" (Mexican Dance). Have the children vote on their favorite Mexican song or dance.

    If you are a classroom teacher with limited space, make sure you have sufficient room for all games and activities.

    If you have paraprofessionals or other adults assisting in your classroom, have them help supervise games, sing songs, and dance to "La Raspa."

Lesson 5

Summer and Africa

National Standards for Physical Education: 5, Exhibits responsible personal and social behavior that respects self and others in physical activity settings.

National Standards for Music Education: 1, Singing, alone and with others, a varied repertoire of music.

Equipment: A medium-sized rock, an eraser, or a small stuffed animal for music.

Lesson Focus:

• Culture of Africa in PE and music.

Related Literature: *Summer* by Núria Roca from Barrons Publishing.

READ THE STORY

Read the story aloud to the class.

PE ACTIVITY

Hopefully the weather is decent today because this activity requires sunshine. It is a great way to introduce the sunny weather of summer as well as the heat in Africa. The game is called Shadow Tag.

Take the students outside and establish boundaries. The object of this game is for every student to tag or step on as many shadows of other students as they can, trying to avoid getting their own shadow stepped on.

During the first game, have the students count how many shadows they were able to tag. During the second game, have them count how many times their own shadow was tagged. Play the game several times, enjoying the fresh air and sunshine.

MUSIC ACTIVITY

Teach the students the song "Obwisana." The translation of the song is "Ouch, I hurt my finger on a rock." Explain to the students that children all over the world have songs they sing and games they play. Have the students clap the steady beat of the song. Next, have the students get into a circle. Have them pass the "rock" on the steady beat to the student who is to their right as they sing the song. Have them pass the rock with their right hand. If you want to challenge them more, add more rocks or reverse the rock and have them pass it to their left.

Most children will take a lot of practice before they can pass the rock on the beat to another student. Do not be surprised if their passing is not perfect. Give them the experience of enjoying the activity and of learning about a game from another country.

If you are a classroom teacher with limited space, these activities may proceed as described.

If you have paraprofessionals or other adults assisting in your classroom, have them help supervise Shadow Tag. During "Obwisana" they can supervise a circle of students while they play the game. More circles with fewer students give each child more opportunities for turns.

Lesson 6

Summer and Africa

National Standards for Physical Education: 4, Achieves and maintains a health-enhancing level of physical fitness.

National Standards for Music Education: 1, Singing, alone and with others, a varied repertoire of music; 2, Performing on instruments, alone and with others, a varied repertoire of music.

Equipment: Hand drums and maracas for music.

Lesson Focus:

• Learning about Africa in PE and music.

Related Literature: *Pinduli* by Janell Cannon.

READ THE STORY

Read the story aloud to the class.

PE ACTIVITY

This game originated in Nigeria. It is called Lion's Den. You can play this inside or outside.

Establish a large circle in the center of the playing area. One student is the "lion" and sits in the middle of the circle (lion's den). All other students run around the den calling "Lion, lion come out of your den." At any moment the lion runs out and tries to tag as many players as he or she can. All tagged players become lions and enter the lion's den. Each time the lions leave the den, the original lion has to leave first to start the chase. The last player to be caught becomes the new lion.

MUSIC ACTIVITY

Review the song "Obwisana" from Unit 5 Lesson 5. Remind the children about the game they played with the "rock." Have the children clap to the steady beat of the song as they sing it. Next, pass out various kinds of rhythm band instruments to half of the class. Have one half of the class play the steady beat of the song while the other half of the class sings the song. Have the students trade. The players become the singers, and the singers get to play the instruments. If you have time, let the children try various kinds of instruments with the song "Obwisana."

Conclude the lesson by asking the students which instruments were their favorite instruments to play during the song "Obwisana."

If you are a classroom teacher with limited space, go to the gymnasium or outside to play Lion's Den. If you do not have rhythm band instruments, use homemade percussion instruments from previous lessons. Rhythm sticks and "kitchen band" instruments also work well.

If you have paraprofessionals or other adults assisting in your classroom, have them help supervise Lion's Den. They can also help "pass on the beat" and distribute instruments during "Obwisana."

Lesson 7

Summer and Africa

—⟨⟩—

National Standards for Physical Education: 1, Demonstrates competency in motor skills and movement patterns needed to perform a variety of physical activities.

National Standards for Music Education: 1, Singing, alone and with others, a varied repertoire of music; 2, Performing on instruments, alone and with others, a varied repertoire of music.

Equipment: Batting tee, beanbags, and fleece balls for PE, Rhythm band instruments and scarves for music.

Lesson Focus:

• Culture of Africa in PE and music.

Related Literature: *Water Hole Waiting* by Jane and Christopher Kurtz.

READ THE STORY

Read the story aloud to the class.

PE ACTIVITY

The game of Beanbag Smash originated in South Africa. It is played in groups of three students.

Place a beanbag on top of a batting tee. The three players form a triangle around the tee standing at least three feet away. Each group has a soccer ball. The object of the game is to use any part of the body, except hands, to move the ball so that it knocks the beanbag off of the tee. The player knocking off the ball scores a point, and the game begins again.

Play several games. If time allows, change the students in each group so that they get to play with different students.

MUSIC ACTIVITY

Review the song "Obwisana." Have the students clap to the steady beat of the song. Next, pass out scarves, and have the students form a circle. Have them dance to the music with their scarves. Have them walk clockwise in the circle and try different things with their scarves. See if someone comes up with a nice movement pattern to go with the song. Have several students show the class their patterns with their scarf, and then have the rest of the class try the new patterns. Next, have half of the class walk in the circle using the scarves, and the other half play rhythm band instruments to the steady beat of the song. Have the students who waved scarves use rhythm band instruments, and have the students who played instruments wave scarves. If time allows, review the stone passing game.

Conclude the lesson by having the students tell you what they learned about the continent and culture of Africa.

If you are a classroom teacher with limited space, make sure you have sufficient space for Beanbag Smash. If you do not have batting tees, use cones to hold the beanbags. If you have no rhythm band instruments, substitute homemade percussion instruments during "Obwisana."

If you have paraprofessionals or other adults assisting in your classroom, have them help supervise Beanbag Smash. During "Obwisana," they can help distribute scarves and instruments. They can also lead scarf movement and help to keep the steady beat.

Lesson 8

Summer and Africa

—⁓⁓—

National Standards for Physical Education: 1, Demonstrates competency in motor skills and movement patterns needed to perform a variety of physical activities.
National Standards for Music Education: 1, Singing, alone and with others, a varied repertoire of music.
Equipment: Cups or cans and small balls for PE.
Lesson Focus:

• The culture of Africa in PE and music.

Related Literature: *Mufaro's Beautiful Daughters* by John Steptoe.

READ THE STORY

Read the story aloud to the class.

PE ACTIVITY

Double or Nothing is a game that originated in Zimbabwe. Have the students find partners and work in groups of four.

Two players on team A stand on a line and hold a can or cup with both hands. The two opposing players on team B stand on a line five meters away and hold a small ball in their hands. The game begins with two players on team B simultaneously throwing the balls into the air and toward team A. Both players on team A try to catch the balls in their cup or can. If both players are successful, team A gets one point. If one or both players fail to catch the ball, they exchange positions with team B. The first team to score five points wins the game.

MUSIC ACTIVITY

Teach the children the song "Che Che Koolay" from Ghana, a country in Africa. On a world map, show the children where the continent of Africa is located. This song is sung in a solo/chorus form. Sing each phrase of the song, and have the children repeat it after you. When the children are comfortable with the song, have them take turns being the soloist for the class while they sing. Discuss the translation for "Che Che Koolay." This is a song about being thankful.

Conclude the lesson by having the students sing the song one last time and tell you what they are thankful for. People all over the world are thankful for many things.

If you are a classroom teacher with limited space, find sufficient room to play Double or Nothing. If this is not possible, use rolled sock balls for tossing and big paper bags for catching.

If you have paraprofessionals or other adults assisting in your classroom, have them help supervise double or nothing. During "Che Che Koolay," an assistant can help lead singing and making up movements for the song.

Lesson 9

Fall and Australia

—◀══◆══▶—

National Standards for Physical Education: 4, Achieves and maintains a health-enhancing level of physical fitness.
National Standards for Music Education: 1, Singing, alone and with others, a varied repertoire of music.
Equipment: Hula hoops and cones for PE.
Lesson Focus:

• Culture of Australia in PE and music.

Related Literature: *Do Cows Turn Colors in the Fall?* by Viki Woodworth.

READ THE STORY

Read the story aloud to the class.

PE ACTIVITY

This game from Australia is called "Snow White" Tag.

Divide the students into seven teams. Each team is given a name of one of the "Seven Dwarfs" (i.e., Happy, Dopey, Sleepy, Bashful, Doc, Grumpy, and Sneezy). One child is selected to be the "witch" or tagger; another student is Snow White. Hula hoops are on one side of the gym, and they serve as a "dungeon." Snow White stands in a hula hoop near the dungeon. All teams line up behind a home-base line with the witch standing anywhere within the playing area. The witch calls a name of a dwarf, and the dwarfs who are on the team that the witch calls out try to run to the opposite line without being tagged. The only safe area is behind the home-base line. Students who are tagged are sent to the dungeon (hoops). Snow White can at any time sneak into the hoops to free the caught dwarfs by touching them. If Snow White gets tagged, another student replaces her. The game ends when each group of dwarfs has been chosen to run. A new witch is chosen to start a new game.

MUSIC ACTIVITY

Teach the students the song "Kookaburra," a song from Australia. Explain to the students that a kookaburra is a bird that is native to Australia. Explain that when Australians refer to "the bush" or "the outback," they are referring to the country and the wilderness in Australia. Have them sing the song "Kookaburra" with you several times until they are comfortable with the tune. Have the students clap and stomp to the steady beat of the song. Next, divide the class in half, and have the students sing the song as a round. If you have another adult with you who can sing with the students, it is helpful to have him sing with the students on part one while you sing with the students on part two. Have the students sing the song in a round several times. They will enjoy the harmony that singing in a round creates. It will take practice for students of this age to be able to sing in a round. They will get experience and understand rounds.

Conclude the lesson by having the students tell you what they learned about Australia.

If you are a classroom teacher with limited space, go to the gymnasium or outside to play "Snow White" Tag. The music lesson may proceed as described.

If you have paraprofessionals or other adults assisting you in your classroom, have them supervise "Snow White" Tag. It will also be helpful to have assistants help students when attempting round singing.

Kookaburra

Traditional Australian (arranged by C. Wilson)

2). Kookaburra sits in the old gum tree,
    Eating all the gum drops he can see.
    Stop, kookaburra, stop, kookaburra,
    Leave some there for me!

Lesson 10

Fall and Australia

National Standards for Physical Education: 4, Achieves and maintains a health-enhancing level of physical fitness.
National Standards for Music Education: 1, Singing, alone and with others, a varied repertoire of music; 2, Performing on instruments, alone and with others, a varied repertoire of music.
Equipment: Something soft to tag with for PE, Xylophones for music.
Lesson Focus:

• The culture of Australia in PE and music.

Related Literature: *The Old Woman Who Loved to Read* by John Winch.

READ THE STORY

Read the story aloud to the class.

PE ACTIVITY

The Australian game the students will play is called "What Time Is It Mr. Wolf?" This is also played in Italy, where it is referred to as "Lupo Della Ore."

One student is the wolf, and he or she will stand with his or her back turned to the other students. The others call out, "What's the time Mr. Wolf?" and the wolf turns to face the others and shouts out a time. If the wolf says 10 o'clock, the others take ten steps toward the wolf. The others will always take the number of steps the wolf says in hours of time. Each time the wolf will turn his back on the other students when they start taking steps toward him. When the group is close to the wolf, instead of stating a time, he will yell "Dinner Time!" and run after the group who will be trying to get back to the starting line. Anyone caught becomes the next wolf.

Make sure to emphasize safe tagging and for students to watch where they are going to avoid collisions.

MUSIC ACTIVITY

Have the students sing the song "Kookaburra" that they learned in Unit 5 Lesson 9. Have them sing the song in the key of D major. It is a comfortable key for young children when they sing this song. That means you will start on the note A. After you are sure they remember the song, set out your xylophones. They will be playing half notes on D and A. Have them play the D and the A at the same time, D with the left hand and A with the right hand. If you have five xylophones, let five children play together while the other students sing the song "Kookaburra." Next, let some of the other children

285

have a turn playing the instruments, until all children have had a turn playing the xylophones. Tell the students that they played an ostinato on the instruments. An ostinato is a pattern that repeats throughout a song.

Conclude the lesson by asking the children what a musical round is, and what an ostinato is. It will take some time before the students remember these terms. Ask them what they have learned about the country of Australia.

If you are a classroom teacher with limited space, make sure you have a space large enough to play "What Time Is It Mr. Wolf?" If you have a carpet or mats, you may be able to play on these surfaces with the children moving on their hands and knees. Make the area outside of the carpet or mats "out of bounds." Emphasize safety. If you have no xylophones, have the students bring xylophones from home.

If you have paraprofessionals or other adults assisting in your classroom, have them help supervise "What Time Is It Mr. Wolf?" Have assistants also help students playing instruments during the song "Kookaburra."

Lesson 11

Fall and Australia

National Standards for Physical Education: 5, Exhibits responsible personal and social behavior that respects self and
others in physical activity settings.
National Standards for Music Education: 1, Singing, alone and with others, a varied repertoire of music.
Equipment: Beanbags for PE.
Lesson Focus:

• Culture of Australia in PE and music.

Related Literature: *The Pumpkin Runner* by Marsha Diane Arnold.

READ THE STORY

Read the story aloud to the class.

PE ACTIVITY

This activity from Australia is called Partner Beanbag Tag. Have students find a partner. Have one of the students in each
pair get a beanbag. Play music of your choice. When the music is playing, the partners should be close together playing
catch with the beanbag. When the music stops, the student with the beanbag is "it." The child that is it then chases his or
her partner and tries to tag him or her with the beanbag. When the partner is tagged, he or she becomes it and the chase
continues. Once the music begins to play again, the partners resume playing catch.

MUSIC ACTIVITY

Review the song "Kookaburra." Teach the children the song "Waltzing Matilda," a song that is from Australia. This song
has some words that are used only in Australia. Even though people speak English in Australia, they use some different
expressions that people in other English-speaking countries do not use. The song is a story about a *swagman* (hobo)
who camps by a *billabong* (river). He sings as he waits for his *billy* (tea) to boil. "Waltzing Matilda" is an expression for
going for a walk in the outback. The *jumbuck* is a sheep. His *tuckerbag* is a knapsack or backpack. Make sure that the
children understand the story of the song. They will enjoy singing the refrain of this lively tune!

Have the students march in place to the steady beat of the song. Next, have the students play Follow the Leader, walking behind you to the steady beat of the song as they sing. You will go "Waltzing Matilda" through the room.

Conclude the lesson by asking the students to tell you what a swagman, a billabong, billy, a tuckerbag, and a jumbuck
are. When someone goes "Waltzing Matilda," what is he doing (going for a walk in the outback)?

If you are a classroom teacher with limited space, take the students outside or to the gymnasium to play Partner Beanbag Tag. The music lesson may proceed as described.

If you have paraprofessionals or other adults assisting in your classroom, have them help supervise Partner Beanbag Tag. Helpers can also lead a group of students in a game of Follow the Leader as they sing "Waltzing Matilda."

Lesson 12

Fall and Australia

National Standards for Physical Education: 4, Achieves and maintains a health-enhancing level of physical fitness.

National Standards for Music Education: 1, Singing, alone and with others, a varied repertoire of music; 2, Performing on instruments, alone and with others, a varied repertoire of music.

Equipment: Something soft to tag with for PE, Xylophones for music.

Lesson Focus:

• Culture of Australia in PE and music.

Related Literature: *Wombat Stew* by Marsha K. Vaughn and Pamela Lofts.

READ THE STORY

Read the story aloud to the class.

PE ACTIVITY

Stuck-in-the-Mud Tag is a game commonly played in Australia. It is equivalent to freeze tag in the United States.

Give the person or persons who are "it" something soft to tag with. On the *go* signal, the child who is it tries to tag as many people as possible. When someone gets tagged, she must freeze in a straddle position. To get "unstuck," a classmate must crawl through her legs. Play for one minute, change taggers, and release those students who are stuck.

MUSIC ACTIVITY

Have the students review the song "Kookaburra." Have them sing it in a round. Next, have them play the ostinato on the xylophones that they played in Unit 5 Lesson 10 as they sing the song. Review the song "Waltzing Matilda." Have them tell you what the Australian words *swagman*, *billabong*, *billy*, *jumbuck*, *tuckerbag*, and *Waltzing Matilda* mean. Have them play Follow the Leader as they go "Waltzing Matilda" through the classroom.

Conclude the lesson by having the students tell you what they learned about Australian music and culture.

If you are a classroom teacher with limited space, find a larger space to play Stuck-in-the-Mud Tag. The music lesson may proceed as described.

If you have paraprofessionals or other adults assisting in your classroom, have them help supervise the tag game. They can also lead a group of students singing "Kookaburra" in a round.

Lesson 13

Winter and Russia

National Standards for Physical Education: 2, Demonstrates understanding of movement concepts, principles, strategies, and tactics as they apply to the learning and performance of physical activities.

National Standards for Music Education: 1, Singing, alone and with others, a varied repertoire of music.

Equipment: Poker chips or coins for PE, A recording of *Nutcracker Suite* by Pyotr Ilyich Tchaikovsky and scarves for music.

Lesson Focus:

• The culture of Russia in PE and music.

Related Literature: *Winter* by Núria Roca from Barrons Publishing.

READ THE STORY

Read the story aloud to the class.

PE ACTIVITY

This Russian game is called The Ring. The rules have been modified to make it more appealing to young students. Divide the students into groups of six. Have each group play the game in a designated area.

Have one child in each group be the "chief." The chief stands with his or her back turned from the other students. The other students are in a line ten feet from the chief. The students in line begin to pass a ring back and forth (a poker chip or coin also work well). The chief then turns and says, "Ring, ring go out to the porch!" The student who is holding the object tries to run past the chief without getting tagged. If he or she is tagged, he or she joins the chief and helps to tag other students. Use more than one object to pass to make the game move more quickly.

MUSIC ACTIVITY

Teach the students about the composer Pyotr Ilyich Tchaikovsky. Tell them he was born a long time ago in Russia, in the year 1840. He died in 1893, at the age of fifty-three. He started taking piano lessons when he was four years old, and he began to compose music as a young child. When he was ten years old, he started law school and he became a clerk in the Ministry of Justice. He was not a successful law clerk. He did not enjoy the work. He decided to devote his life to music. Tchaikovsky became one of the leading composers of the Romantic period of music. He wrote several beautiful ballets. His most famous work is the *Nutcracker Suite.*

Play the "Overture" of the *Nutcracker Suite* for the students. Ask them if any of them have heard the music before. Briefly tell the children the story of the Nutcracker. Clara is a little girl. There is a big fancy party at her house the night before Christmas. Everyone is dressed up in the finest clothes. Clara gets a beautiful Nutcracker as a Christmas gift from Herr Drosselmeyer, a family friend. Clara's brother accidentally breaks the Nutcracker. Clara is sad. Before she goes to bed, she puts the nutcracker under the Christmas tree. Her father promises to fix the nutcracker doll in the morning. In a dream during the night, Clara goes back to the Christmas tree to see the Nutcracker. He becomes life-sized, and he jumps up to greet Clara. All of the toy soldiers come to life as well. They surge into a battle against an invading army of mice. Just when it looks like the mice will win the battle, Clara removes her shoe and throws it at the Mouse King. He dies, and the Nutcracker is saved. He turns into a handsome prince, and he takes Clara to the Kingdom of Sweets with him. Clara is welcomed and honored with many dances. At the end of the story, Clara leaves the Kingdom of Sweets with beautiful memories of her visit.

Play a small portion of the "Dance of the Sugar Plum Fairy," the "Russian Dance," the "Arabian Dance," the "Chinese Dance," and the "Waltz of the Flowers" for the students. Have the students move to the music while using scarves.

Conclude the lesson by asking the children to tell you what happens in the story of the *Nutcracker Suite.*

If you are a classroom teacher with limited space, go outside or to the gymnasium to play The Ring. The music lesson may proceed as described.

If you have paraprofessionals or other adults assisting in your classroom, have them help supervise groups of students as they play The Ring. Assistants can also help the children move creatively to the *Nutcracker Suite.*

Lesson 14

Winter and Russia

National Standards for Physical Education: 5, Exhibits responsible personal and social behavior that respects self and others in physical activity settings.

National Standards for Music Education: 6, Listening to, analyzing, and describing music; 8, Understanding relationships between music, the other arts, and disciplines outside of the arts.

Equipment: A large ball and a small ball for PE, A recording of the *Nutcracker Suite*, paper, crayons, and scarves for music.

Lesson Focus:

• Culture of Russia in PE and music.

Related Literature: *Symphony of Whales* by Steve Schuch.

READ THE STORY

Read the story aloud to the class.

PE ACTIVITY

This game is called The Doggie and the Kitten. It is from Romania. The children sit in a large circle. The object of the game is for the large ball (the doggie) to catch up with the small ball (the kitten). Place the balls on opposite sides of the circle.

On a *go* signal, the balls are rolled around or across the circle as fast as possible. The player who ends up with both balls in front of him or her is out. Do not eliminate anyone. Have the player jog a lap around the circle and start the game again.

Use a soccer ball for the large ball and a Wiffle ball for the small ball.

MUSIC ACTIVITY

Have the students tell you what they remember about Pyotr Ilyich Tchaikovsky and the story of the *Nutcracker Suite*. Hand the students a scarf, and make sure that they are in a self-space. Play a small part of each of the movements of the *Nutcracker Suite* for the students. Have them move creatively to the music. Next, have the students share some of their choreography with the class.

Give every student a piece of paper and some crayons. Have the students color a picture of one of the scenes of the *Nutcracker*. Discuss how music is used to inspire dancing, creating pictures, and creating other forms of art.

Conclude the lesson by having the students tell you what they have learned about the country of Russia so far.

If you are a classroom teacher with limited space, all of these activities can take place in a space large enough for "circle time."

If you have paraprofessionals or other adults assisting in your classroom, divide the class in half and have two separate circles of students playing The Doggie and the Kitten. Have the helpers supervise one of the circles. During the music portion of the lesson, have the assistants give the students ideas for creative movement. They can also ask students questions about the pictures they are creating.

Lesson 15

Winter and Russia

—⟨ull⟩⟨lilt⟩—

National Standards for Physical Education: 2, Demonstrates understanding of movement concepts, principles, strategies, and tactics as they apply to the learning and performance of physical activities.
National Standards for Music Education: 1, Singing, alone and with others, a varied repertoire of music.
Equipment: A scarf to identify the giant for PE, A recording of the *Nutcracker Suite* by Pyotr Ilyich Tchaikovsky for music.
Lesson Focus:

• Culture of Russia in PE and music.

Related Literature: *Latkes, Latkes, Good to Eat* by Naomi Howland.

READ THE STORY

Read the story aloud to the class.

PE ACTIVITY

This game from Russia is called "Mother May I?" Have the students form a circle. Choose a "giant." Have the giant tuck a scarf down the back of his or her shirt. The teacher or "mother" stands in the center of the circle. The students ask, "Mother, may we go out to play?" Mother answers, "Yes, but don't go near the giant's cave." The giant is standing in another area in the gym.

The children run about the gym until Mother says, "Hurry home or the giant may catch you!" The children then run back to the home circle, trying not to get caught by the giant. If the giant tags them, they become the next giant.

Play several times so that several children get to be the giant.

MUSIC ACTIVITY

Teach the children the "Russian Slumber Song." Sing the song several times until the children are familiar with the melody. Play or sing some songs in major keys and some songs in minor keys for the children. Some suggestions are "All the Pretty Little Horses" (Unit 4 Lesson 4, minor) and "Michael Row the Boat Ashore" (Unit 4 Lesson 20, minor). Ask the children to describe the difference in the sound of a song in a major key and a minor key. (Most will tell you that major keys sound "happy" and minor keys sound "sad.") The students may not hear the difference in major and minor keys yet. Introduce the terms, keeping in mind that education is a layering process. Ask the children if the "Russian Slumber Song" is in a major or a minor key. Sing the song again.

If you have extra time left, have the students listen to some of the themes of the *Nutcracker Suite* again. Have them move dramatically to the music as they recall the details of the story.

Conclude the lesson by having the children sing the "Russian Slumber Song."

If you are a classroom teacher with limited space, make sure you have plenty of space for "Mother May I?" If weather permits take the students outside to play. The music lesson may take place as described.

If you have paraprofessionals or other adults assisting in your classroom, have them help supervise "Mother May I?" During the music lesson, have them help lead singing and movement.

Russian Slumber Song

Traditional Russian (arranged by C. Wilson)

Lesson 16

Winter and Russia

───◈───

National Standards for Physical Education: 5, Exhibits responsible personal and social behavior that respects self and others.

National Standards for Music Education: 1, Singing, alone and with others, a varied repertoire of music; 2, Performing on instruments, alone and with others, a varied repertoire of music.

Equipment: Hula hoops for PE, Bass xylophones, alto xylophones, alto glockenspiels, and finger cymbals for music.

Lesson Focus:

• Culture of Russia in PE and music.

Related Literature: *The Elf's Hat* by Brigitte Weninger.

───────────

READ THE STORY

Read the story aloud to the class.

PE ACTIVITY

This game is called Little Birds. You will need enough hula hoops spread out on the gym floor so that there is one for every two students. Pretend the hula hoops are bird nests. One student is left out of a nest in the middle of the gym.

When you say *Every little bird needs to find a new nest*, all of the students run to get to a different hoop. There should be a new bird left in the middle each time. Have the teacher or other adult do the signal.

Remind the students that there can be no more than two students in each hula hoop. Encourage safe movement.

MUSIC ACTIVITY

Review the "Russian Slumber Song" with the students. On the bass xylophones, have the students play a whole note bordun on the notes F and C at the same time. Use the words *hold that ba-by* to show them how long to hold the whole note. Have them use their left hand on the F and their right hand on the C. Have some students play the bordun as the other students sing. Next, have the alto xylophones play the bordun with the students who are on the bass xylophones. Add the finger cymbals on beat one of every other measure. Tell the cymbal players that they play only on the word *hold*. Add the alto glockenspiel on beats three and four in the notated measures. Make sure you have the students practice the rhythm of their parts by clapping their hands when they are supposed to play while you sing the song. Tell the glockenspiel players that they play on the word *ba-by*. It will take the children time to make the piece go smoothly. They will enjoy the experience of playing.

Conclude the lesson by having the students sing the "Russian Slumber Song" as they help you put your equipment away.

If you are a classroom teacher with limited space, use the gymnasium or a multipurpose room to play Little Birds. If you have no classroom instruments, use different types of homemade instruments from previous lessons to play the xylophone, glockenspiel, and cymbal parts of the "Russian Slumber Song."

If you have paraprofessionals or other adults assisting in your classroom, have them help supervise Little Birds. During the "Russian Slumber Song," have them assist children playing instruments.

HOLIDAYS AND SPECIAL TIMES

Lesson 1

First Day of School

National Standards for Physical Education: 3, Participates regularly in physical activity.
National Standards for Music Education: 1, Singing, alone and with others, a varied repertoire of music.
Equipment: None.
Lesson Focus:

- What is PE?
- Welcome to music class.

Related Literature: *I Am Too Absolutely Small for School* by Lauren Child.

READ THE STORY

Read the story aloud to the class.

PE ACTIVITY

The first day of school can be scary for young children. Begin by explaining that PE stands for physical education. Explain some of the activities that they will be doing and how important it will be they wear tennis shoes every time they participate in PE activities to keep them safe.

Take a walk around the gym. Show the students some of the equipment that they will be using. Jump ropes, basketballs, soccer balls, and other pieces of equipment will help the students to be excited to come to class.

To conclude, let the students know what days they are coming to the gym and review what they need to wear. If time allows, have them share with you their favorite ways to be active.

MUSIC ACTIVITY

Welcome the children to the music classroom. Show the children some of the instruments they will be using during music. Teach the children the song "The More We Get Together." Have them tell you some of their favorite songs.

Make sure that the children understand the rules for your classroom. Specific rules are easier for young children to understand. Here are examples of specific rules:

1. Respect everyone around you.
2. No gum, candy, or toys.

3. Sit tall.
4. Sing using your best voice.
5. Raise your hand for permission to speak.

Tell the students how they are rewarded when they do well in the class. For example, when they sing or play a song well, draw a star on the board. When the class has earned one hundred stars (this will take time) they have a special music day.

Tell them the consequences for making poor choices. For example, if a student is making a poor choice, he may have to sit in "time out." If the class is making poor choices, you might have to take away some of their stars. The rules will help all of the children to be safe and comfortable.

Have the children tell you about some of their favorite songs and musical experiences.

Conclude the lesson by singing "The More We Get Together" again. Tell the students that you cannot wait to see them again!

If you are a classroom teacher with limited space, the lessons may proceed as described. Show the students some of your PE equipment and musical instruments (i.e., jump ropes, balls, and rhythm band instruments).

If you have paraprofessionals or other adults assisting in your classroom, have them sit near children who are having difficulty adjusting to being at school.

Lesson 2

Halloween

National Standards for Physical Education: 1, Demonstrates competency in motor skills and movement patterns needed to perform a variety of physical activities.

National Standards for Music Education: 1, Singing, alone and with others, a varied repertoire of music.

Equipment: Halloween paper plates and beanbags for PE, Rhythm band instruments to represent five little pumpkins for music.

Lesson Focus:

- Tossing underhand in PE.
- Creating sounds to accompany a poem for music.

Related Literature: *Hoodwinked* by Arthur Howard.

READ THE STORY

Read the story aloud to the class.

PE ACTIVITY

Spread the paper plates around the gym and establish boundaries that the students must not cross when tossing beanbags at the plates. Give each student three beanbags.

If you have not taught an underhand throw, you will need to demonstrate this skill. Teach the cue of stepping with the opposite foot from the throwing hand. Allow the students to toss their beanbags at any of the plates as long as they stay behind the boundaries. If their beanbag lands on a plate they get a point. Ask them to see if they can get ten points.

The plates may move around a little bit during the activity but not enough to cause a problem. Do not get concerned about assessing opposition (i.e., stepping with the opposite foot from the throwing hand). This is a time for a fun activity; the underhand throw will be taught at greater depth in Unit 4.

MUSIC ACTIVITY

Teach the children the rhyme "Five Little Pumpkins." There are many varieties of this rhyme. This is an example of one:

Five little pumpkins sitting on a gate
The first one said, "It's getting late!"
The second one said, "There is frost in the air!"
The third one said, "We don't care!"
The fourth one said, "Let's run and run and run!"
The fifth one said, "I'm ready for some fun!"

So whooooo went the wind,
And out went the lights,
And the five little pumpkins
Rolled out of sight.

Have the children choose a percussion instrument to represent each little pumpkin (e.g., maracas, triangle, finger cymbals, wood block, vibra slap, or other rhythm band instruments). As the poem is spoken, have several children play the chosen instrument to represent each pumpkin as that little pumpkin speaks. Have all of the children speak the poem as they play along. After the children say *and the five little pumpkins rolled out of sight*, have them all play their instruments until you show them the stop signal. (A simple cutoff cue will work nicely.). Continue speaking and playing the poem until all of the children have had a chance to play an instrument.

Conclude the lesson by asking the children why they chose certain instruments to represent the "Five Little Pumpkins." Have them dramatically speak the poem with no instruments before they leave the room.

If you are a classroom teacher with limited space, both of these activities may be done in the classroom. If you do not have rhythm band instruments, use "body percussion" to make sounds to represent the pumpkins (i.e., clapping hands, snapping fingers, drumming feet, patting legs, rubbing hands together, and so on).

If you have paraprofessionals or other adults assisting in your classroom, have them help supervise the pumpkin beanbag toss game. During music, helpers can distribute and collect instruments. They can also help lead the rhythmic chanting of "Five Little Pumpkins."

Five Little Pumpkins
Traditional (arranged by C. Wilson)

Lesson 3

Patriotic Days

—◄◄◄◄◄‖‖‖►►►—

National Standards for Physical Education: 4, Achieves and maintains a health-enhancing level of physical fitness.
National Standards for Music Education: 1, Singing alone and with others, a varied repertoire of music.
Equipment: Something soft to tag with in PE.
Lesson Focus:

• Tag in PE.
• Singing for music.

Related Literature: *By the Dawn's Early Light* by Steven Kroll.

READ THE STORY

Read the story aloud to the class.

PE ACTIVITY

This activity is called Red, White, and Blue Tag. Tell the students that these three colors are considered patriotic. If you have a flag in your room, show them the flag.

Choose three students to be "it." Give each tagger a different color of wristband or vest so that you have a red, white, and a blue tagger. Establish three areas in the gym for students to go to when they have been tagged. You will need a red area, a white area, and a blue area. If a red tagger tags a student, he would go to the red area. If a student is tagged by a blue tagger, he would go to the blue area. If a student is tagged by a white tagger, students go to the white area. Once the students are in the color area, they must think of something that color before they can get out. This works best if there is an adult in each of the three areas to listen to the students as they name items that are the color they are tagged, but if that is not possible, they will have to run to you and tell you an item that is the color of their "tagged area."

Change taggers often. Conclude by having the students think of holidays that would be patriotic (e.g., Fourth of July, Flag Day, Veterans Day, and so on).

MUSIC ACTIVITY

Tell the children that many beautiful patriotic songs have been composed to express a love for the country where we live. Ask them if they know any patriotic songs. Play and sing "The Star-Spangled Banner" for the students. Explain that it is our national anthem. Ask the children if they have ever heard "The Star-Spangled Banner," and where they heard it (e.g., movie theater, before sporting events, on television, or other various places). Play it several more times until they recognize it. You may briefly try to teach the children "The Star-Spangled Banner." The words and the notes will be a little bit difficult for them at this age, but if you keep working on the song, it will happen. Keep the work brief. If you notice that the children are not ready to sing this song, teach another patriotic song. "My Country, 'Tis of Thee," also known as "America," and "You're a Grand Old Flag" will be easier for young children to sing. Teach them these songs after you have introduced "The Star-Spangled Banner." Have the children march on the beat to the song "You're a Grand Old Flag." They will enjoy this!

Conclude the lesson by having the children tell you which patriotic songs they studied today.

If you are a classroom teacher with limited space, go outside or to the gymnasium to play Red, White, and Blue Tag. The music lesson may proceed as described.

If you have paraprofessionals or other adults assisting in your classroom, have them stand in a color area during Red, White, and Blue Tag to listen to students as they identify an item that is the color of their tagger. During music have assistants lead students in a patriotic parade as they sing "You're a Grand Old Flag."

Thanksgiving

—⁓⁓—

National Standards for Physical Education: 5, Exhibits responsible personal and social behavior that respects self and others in physical activity settings.

National Standards for Music Education: 1, Singing, alone and with others, a varied repertoire of music; 2, Performing on instruments, alone and with others, a varied repertoire of music.

Equipment: Construction paper turkey feathers for PE, Sleigh bells for music.

Lesson Focus:

- Tag in PE.
- Singing for music.

Related Literature: *'Twas the Night Before Thanksgiving* by Dav Pilkey.

READ THE STORY

Read the story aloud to the class.

PE ACTIVITY

This game is called Thankful Turkey Tag. Choose two to four students to be "it." Give each tagger a construction paper feather to tag with. Emphasize safety when tagging. Taggers should touch shoulders or backs and not push or grab. When students get tagged, they will go to the teacher and tell him or her something they are thankful for. Some students may need suggestions at first.

Play several times so that most of the children get the chance to be it.

MUSIC ACTIVITY

Talk to the children about Thanksgiving. Teach the children the traditional Thanksgiving songs "Jingle Bells" and "Over the River." Most of the children will think that "Jingle Bells" is a Christmas song, but it was really written for Thanksgiving. A minister named James Pierpoint wrote it for his congregation many years ago when they were coming to church through the snow in their horse-drawn sleighs. The snow was falling, it was Thanksgiving, and his congregation was happy to see the new-fallen snow.

Next, pass out the sleigh bells. As the students sing the Thanksgiving songs, have some children play the bells. Have the children who are not playing the bells "ride" their horses to the beat of the music. Continue singing the Thanksgiving songs and giving the children a chance to play the sleigh bells.

Conclude the lesson by asking the children what they have to be thankful for, and be sure to tell them to have a happy Thanksgiving.

If you are a classroom teacher with limited space, find a large area to play Thankful Turkey Tag. If you do not have sleigh bells for the Thanksgiving songs, use a glass jar with coins in it and shake the jar.

If you have paraprofessionals or other adults assisting in your classroom, have them listen to students as they tell the helpers what they are thankful for. Have assistants lead singing and help with instrument distribution and collection while singing the Thanksgiving songs.

Lesson 5

Hanukah

National Standards for Physical Education: 5, Exhibits responsible personal and social behavior that respects self and others in physical activity settings.

National Standards for Music Education: 1, Singing, alone and with others, a varied repertoire of music.

Equipment: Enough empty two-liter pop bottles for every six students and ten pennies per student for PE.

Lesson Focus:

- The dreydl game in PE.
- The tradition of Hanukah for music.

Related Literature: *Papa's Latkes* by Michelle Edwards.

READ THE STORY

Read the story aloud to the class.

PE ACTIVITY

Put the students in groups of six each. Give each group a two-liter bottle and a set of cards. The cards can be made out of any kind of paper. Each group will need four cards with one of these words on each card:

- Nun—The player gets nothing from the bowl.
- Gimel—The player takes five pennies from the bowl.
- Heh—The player takes two pennies from the bowl.
- Shin—The player puts one penny in the bowl.

Laminate these cards so they can be used again. Set the cards in a small square with the empty bottle in the middle. Place a bowl for the pennies in the middle of the square. The small group of students sits around the square, each with their ten pennies in front of them. Each student puts five pennies in the bowl in the center and keeps five pennies for himself. Begin by having one player spin the bottle. He must do with his pennies as the card that the bottle top lands nearest suggests. It would then be the next person's turn to spin. Continue taking turns spinning and moving pennies in and out of the square. The game ends when someone runs out of pennies or time runs out. If time runs out, the students each count their pennies.

MUSIC ACTIVITY

Tell the children that Hanukah is a religious celebration of Jewish people that takes place during December. Explain that people exchange gifts, enjoy special foods, and enjoy time with their families and friends. The festival lasts for eight days. During the evening of each of the eight days, a candle is lit on a special candleholder called a *menorah*. Hanukah is also known as the Festival of Lights. Teach the children the songs "Hanukah Is Here" and "My Dreydl." Have the students pat their legs to the beat as they sing "Hanukah Is Here." Tell them that they will have a chance to play the dreidel game during PE.*

Conclude the lesson by having the students sing the songs one more time and by asking them what they know about the Festival of Lights.

If you are a classroom teacher with limited space, both the PE and the music activities may proceed as described.

If you have paraprofessionals or other adults assisting in your classroom, have them help supervise the dreidel game. They can help lead singing during "Hanukah is Here" and "My Dreydl."

NOTES

*Here is suggested choreography for "Hanukah is Here":

Have students form a circle. Stand still during the introduction.
A. Grapevine eight counts left
   Grapevine eight counts right
B. Step forward for three counts and clap on beat four
   Step backward for three counts and clap on beat four
   Repeat B section
   Repeat A section

Lesson 6

Christmas

National Standards for Physical Education: 1, Demonstrates competency in motor skills and movement patterns needed to perform a variety of physical activities.

National Standards for Music Education: 1, Singing, alone and with others, a varied repertoire of music; 2, Performing on instruments, alone and with others, a varied repertoire of music.

Equipment: Fleece balls for PE, Xylophones, a hand drum, and finger cymbals for music.

Lesson Focus:

- Catching in PE.
- Singing and keeping a steady beat for music.

Related Literature: *The Christmas Hat* by A. J. Wood.

READ THE STORY

Read the story aloud to the class.

PE ACTIVITY

In this lesson, the students are going to play catch with fleece balls. This activity is called Snowball Catch. Have the students find a partner and play rock, paper, scissors to determine which one goes to get the snowball. Suggest that they stand no farther than five feet from one another when playing catch.

Play holiday music while they play catch and when the song goes off, they should find a new partner. Continue this until the students have had a chance to play with several other students.

MUSIC ACTIVITY

Ask the students what they know about the celebration of Christmas. Tell the children that during Christmas, people exchange gifts, enjoy special foods, and enjoy time with family and friends. Teach the children the song "Christmas Is Coming." Have the children pat the half note on their legs as they sing the song. This will be the rhythm of the xylophone part. Sing the song several times until the children are comfortable singing it. Next, have the children pat on beat one of every other measure. This is going to be the hand drum part. Have the children sing the song again, and have them clap after the words *coming*, *fat*, *hat*, and *hat*. This is going to be the finger cymbal part.

Next, choose some children to play the xylophones. Have them practice their part while the other students sing the song. Next, practice with the students who play the hand drums, and finally practice with the students who play the finger cymbals. Have the students sing the song while they play the instruments. Continue singing the song and choosing other children to play the instruments until all of the children have had a chance to play an instrument. Many of the students will not be able to play their part at the correct time without you right beside them. Do not worry about perfection yet. Give them a chance to play in the ensemble. You will be amazed at their improvement with time and exposure to many kinds of musical experiences.

Conclude the lesson by having the children sing "We Wish You a Merry Christmas" as they help to straighten up the instruments.

If you are a classroom teacher with limited space, the students may play Snowball Catch in the classroom. Use wads of white paper instead of fleece balls. If you have no xylophones, hand drums, or finger cymbals, use kitchen band instruments (i.e., pots, pans, and spoons) for the instrumental parts.

If you have paraprofessionals or other adults assisting in your classroom, have them supervise students playing catch. They can also help students with instruments.

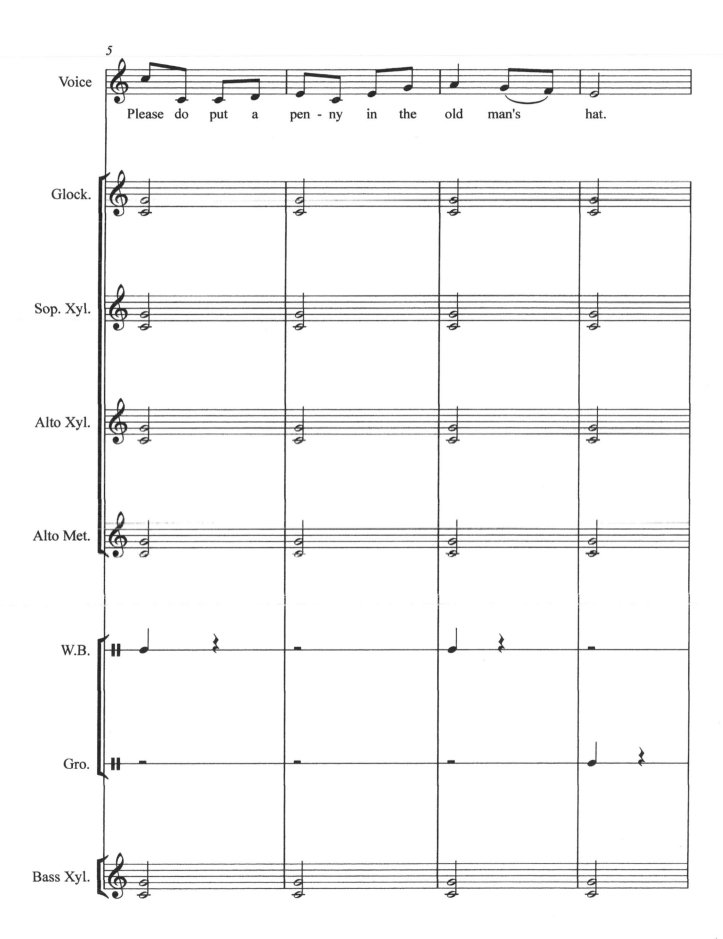

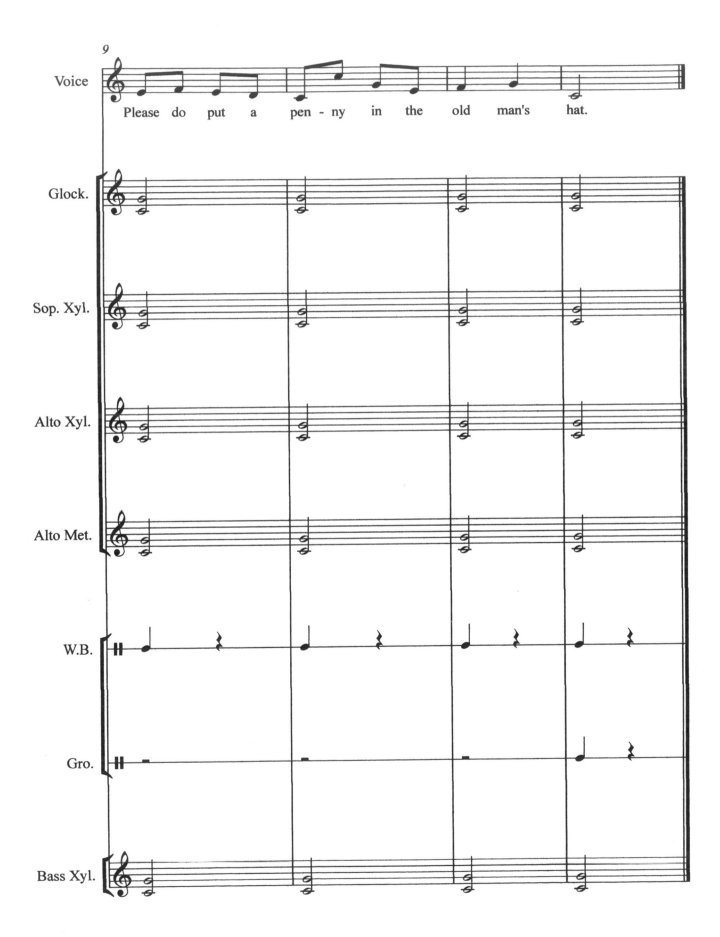

Lesson 7

Kwanzaa

National Standards for Physical Education: 1, Demonstrates competency in motor skills and movement patterns needed to perform a variety of physical activities.

National Standards for Music Education: 1, Singing alone and with others, a varied repertoire of music.

Equipment: Seven large cones with a different color of construction paper on the front of each and beanbags for PE.

Lesson Focus:

- Throwing in PE.
- The celebration of Kwanzaa for music.

Related Literature: *Seven Candles for Kwanzaa* by Andrea Davis Pinkney.

READ THE STORY

Read the story aloud to the class.

PE ACTIVITY

This activity is the Kwanzaa Candle Toss. After reading the story about the Kwanzaa candles, the students should have a good understanding about what they stand for. Line up the seven cones across the middle of the gym and put a different color of construction paper on each one. Explain to the students that these are the candles and that they are going to toss the beanbags at the candles to light them. Choose yellow and orange beanbags to symbolize the fire.

Stand the students five to seven feet away from the cones. Have them try to throw their beanbag and hit the cone. They could use an underhand or an overhand throw. Tell them that all seven candles need to be lit, so they should not just throw at the same cone.

If you have a lot of students at one time, do this activity in pairs. One partner would throw while the other one retrieves.

MUSIC ACTIVITY

Discuss the holiday of Kwanzaa. Ask the students what they remember about Kwanzaa from the book. The seven days of Kwanzaa begin on December 26. This holiday celebrates the struggles and accomplishments of African Americans. Each of the seven days has a special principle and symbol:

Dec. 26–(Day 1)
   Principle: Unity
   Symbol: Straw basket of fruit

Dec. 27–(Day 2)
   Principle: Self-determination
   Symbol: Straw mat

Dec. 28–(Day 3)
   Principle: Working together
   Symbol: Wooden candleholder

Dec. 29–(Day 4)
   Principle: Sharing profit
   Symbol: Ears of corn

Dec. 30–(Day 5)
   Principle: Purpose
   Symbol: Handmade gift or book

Dec. 31–(Day 6)
   Principle: Creativity
   Symbol: Unity cup

Jan. 1–(Day 7)
   Principle: Faith
   Symbol: Seven candles

Teach the students the song "O Kwanzaa." Have the children sing the song until they are comfortable with it. Next, have them sidestep and clap to the beat as they sing. They will enjoy moving to the beat.

Conclude the lesson by asking the children to tell you about Kwanzaa.

If you are a regular classroom teacher with limited space, these activities may be done in a regular classroom. During the Kwanzaa Candle Toss, make adaptations for a smaller area (i.e., throw sock balls at Styrofoam cups placed upside down with different colors on them).

If you have paraprofessionals or other adults assisting in your classroom, have them help supervise the tossing game. During the song "O Kwanzaa," assistants can help lead singing and create movement.

Lesson 8

Ramadan and Eid-ul-fitr

—◁◀▥◍▥▶▷—

National Standards for Physical Education: 5, Exhibits responsible personal and social behavior that respects self and others in a physical activity setting.
National Standards for Music Education: 9, Understanding music in relation to history and culture.
Equipment: Milk cartons with the top half cut off and poker chips for PE.
Lesson Focus:

• Eid-ul-fitr signifies the end of Ramadan. There is feasting and a grand celebration. Ramadan is the most significant holiday of the Muslim countries.
• Traditional music and dance from the Middle East countries.

Related Literature: *Celebrating Ramadan* by Diane Hoyt-Goldsmith.

READ THE STORY

Read the story aloud to the class.

PE ACTIVITY

Children in the Middle East play traditional games during Ramadan. The children are going to learn how to play a traditional Lebanese game, Pebble Toss. Begin by dividing the students into small teams. Each team has a milk carton and two poker chips per student. The object of the game is to toss the chips from a designated line into the milk carton. Each child must wait for her turn and can only toss one chip per turn. The team that gets all of its chips into the milk carton first wins.

MUSIC ACTIVITY

Teach the students that Ramadan is a special month of the year when Muslims fast during daylight hours. They sing special songs and they pray. Ramadan is considered a holy time. Eid-ul-fitr is a holy night that signifies the end of Ramadan. People eat special foods, sing special songs, and play games.

Teach the students the traditional song "Sleep." This song is from Syria, another country in the Middle East. Music for "Sleep" can be found at www.mamalisa.com. An MP3, a translation, and a transliteration are also available. The song begins by naming a child. Change the child's name to the name of one of the children in your class each time you sing the song. Have the children listen to the MP3 so they can hear the soothing rhythms and Oriental flavor of music from the Middle East.

Conclude the lesson by asking the students what they learned about Ramadan and the Middle East.

If you are a classroom teacher with limited space, these lessons may proceed as described.

If you have paraprofessionals or other adults assisting in your classroom, have them help you monitor the Pebble Toss. During the music lesson, they can sit with a small circle of students and sing the name of a different child each time the song is sung. This will ensure that all students have a chance to hear the lullaby sung with their name included.

Lesson 9

Martin Luther King Jr. Day or Black History Month

National Standards for Physical Education: 2, Demonstrates understanding of movement concepts, principles, strategies, and tactics as they apply to the learning and performance of physical activities.
National Standards for Music Education: 1, Singing, alone and with others, a varied repertoire of music.
Equipment: Lummi sticks for PE.
Lesson Focus:

- Traditional African children's games in PE.
- Singing and learning about Martin Luther King Jr. for music.

Related Literature: *A Picture Book of Martin Luther King Jr.* by David Adler or *Let Them Play* by Margot Theis Raven.

READ THE STORY

Read the story aloud to the class.

PE ACTIVITY

In this lesson, you will teach the students a traditional African children's game. It is called Sae Sae Brae Wah a Deisha, pronounced *sa, sa, bray, wah ah deesha.*

Each student will need a Lummi stick and will sit in a large circle close to the person next to him. Memorize the words to the game. Help the students to say it in a cadence. As they speak the cadence they will pass their Lummi stick one person to the right. Continue practicing the words and the pass, gradually getting faster.

Explain to the students that this activity was used to teach coordination and teamwork. These are skills that young African children needed when working in the fields or simply to relieve boredom.

MUSIC ACTIVITY

Ask the students what they remember about Martin Luther King Jr. from the book. Tell the students that African Americans and others in the United States did not always have the rights and freedoms they have today. Martin Luther King Jr. and other civil rights leaders struggled to win rights and freedoms for all human beings. Teach the students the song "Martin Luther King." Teach the children the sign language that goes with the song. Sing the song while signing it.

Conclude the lesson by having the students sing one more time about Martin Luther King Jr.

If you are a classroom teacher with limited space, both of these lessons may proceed as described.

If you have paraprofessionals or other adults assisting in your classroom, divide your students so that you have an assistant for each circle while playing the game. During the song "Martin Luther King," have the assistants help students with the sign language.

Lesson 10

Groundhog Day

—◁◁◁ ∫ ▷▷▷—

National Standards for Physical Education: 4, Achieves and maintains a health-enhancing level of physical fitness.
National Standards for Music Education: 1, Singing, alone and with others, a varied repertoire of music; 2, Performing on instruments, alone and with others, a varied repertoire of music.
Equipment: Hula hoops and something soft to tag with for PE, Resonator bells and finger cymbals or a triangle for music.
Lesson Focus:

- Chasing, fleeing, and dodging in PE.
- Singing and playing instruments to a steady beat in music.

Related Literature: *Go to Sleep, Groundhog!* by Judy Cox.

READ THE STORY

Read the story aloud to the class.

PE ACTIVITY

After the students have heard the story, they will understand why the groundhog comes out of hibernation on Groundhog Day. This game is Groundhog Tag. Choose at least two students to be "it" and give them something soft to tag with.

Have the rest of the students stand in hula hoops spread out on the gym floor. Put two or three students per hoop. On the command, *Groundhogs, come out and play*, the students leave the hoops and run through the gym. If they are tagged, they become it and they help tag students. Go for a minute and start back in the hoops again. Change the beginning taggers each time.

MUSIC ACTIVITY

Briefly discuss Groundhog Day with the students. Teach the children the song "Time to Wake Up." Sing the song until the children are comfortable with it. Next, show the children the resonator bells. Have the students play the notes D, D, D, and E as they sing the phrase *time to wake up*. Give each student a D and an E. If you have many students and only a few resonator bells, have some students play the instruments while other students sing the song. Change instrument players frequently so that all students get a chance to play. You can also add another instrument on the final words *wake up* (e.g., finger cymbals or a triangle). Several children could also play hand drums or claves on the phrase *time to wake up*.

Conclude the lesson by telling the children to have a happy Groundhog Day.

If you are a classroom teacher with limited space, find a larger space for Groundhog Tag. The gymnasium or a multipurpose room or large area will work well. If you do not have xylophones or rhythm band instruments, have your students bring toy xylophones from home. Make sure they can all find a D and an E. If you do not have rhythm band instruments, use your homemade percussion instruments from previous lessons.

If you have paraprofessionals or other adults assisting in your classroom, have them help supervise the tag game. During the song "Time to Wake Up," assistants can help students play instrumental parts. They can also help distribute and collect instruments.

Lesson 11

Valentine's Day

—⚙️𝄞⚙️—

National Standards for Physical Education: 5, Exhibits responsible personal and social behavior that respects self and others in physical activity settings.

National Standards for Music Education: 1, Singing, alone and with others, a varied repertoire of music.

Equipment: Dome markers or poly spots for PE.

Lesson Focus:

- Memory challenge and teamwork in PE.
- Singing in music.

Related Literature: *Heart to Heart* by George Shannon.

READ THE STORY

Read the story aloud to the class.

PE ACTIVITY

This activity is similar to Go Fish. Spread the dome markers or poly spots out on the gym floor. Place paper hearts under half of them. Divide the class into small teams and give them a starting spot. On the signal *go*, the first student in line for each team runs out and looks under one marker. If there is a heart, the student brings it back to the team. If the marker turns up empty, it is simply replaced and the student returns to his team. As the students return, they tag the next team member who then goes out in search of a heart. Each player may only check under one marker per turn.

Conclude the lesson by counting how many hearts the students found.

MUSIC ACTIVITY

Discuss Valentine's Day traditions. People exchange cards, small gifts, and candies. Teach the students the song "Skidamarink." Teach them the actions that go with the song. Sing the song several times until the students can remember it.

Conclude the lesson by telling the students to go home and sing "Skidamarink" to someone they love!

If you are a regular classroom teacher with limited space, the students can still "go fishing" for hearts. Hide the hearts around your classroom and have the students walk through the room to find them. The music lesson may proceed as described.

If you have paraprofessionals or other adults assisting in your classroom, have them help you hide hearts for Go Fish. They can also supervise students during the relay game. Have helpers lead choreography and singing during "Skidamarink."

Lesson 12

St. Patrick's Day

—⟨⟨⟨⟨∫⟩⟩⟩⟩—

National Standards for Physical Education: 3, Participates regularly in physical activity.
National Standards for Music Education: 1, Singing, alone and with others, a varied repertoire of music.
Equipment: Scarves for PE and music.
Lesson Focus:

- St. Patrick's greetings and tag in PE.
- Singing Irish songs in music.

Related Literature: *The Leprechaun's Gold* by Pamela Duncan Edwards.

READ THE STORY

Read the story aloud to the class.

PE ACTIVITY

Teach the students to play a tag game, Pot of Gold. Choose two students to be taggers. The rest of the students will be leprechauns. The taggers will carry a bright-colored scarf.

Give the students the signal to start. The students use a designated locomotor skill to move about the gym (e.g., skipping, jogging, walking, and so on). If a leprechaun is tagged, she turns into a pot of gold. She must scrunch down into a low, curled-up shape. To get back into the game, a classmate comes by and touches her head, greeting her with "Happy St. Patrick's Day!"

Continue playing the game, changing the taggers every few minutes.

MUSIC ACTIVITY

Tell the children that many people came to the United States from the country of Ireland long ago. People who came from Ireland brought many traditions, customs, and songs with them. Play or sing the song "Mrs. Murphy's Chowder" for the students. See if they notice anything funny about the song. Read the ingredient list of the chowder to the students. Explain what some of the ingredients are. Ask the children if they would like to eat Mrs. Murphy's chowder. Play or sing the song several more times for the children. Have them sing along.

Next, have the students review the song "Follow the Rainbow" from Unit 2 Lesson 24. Give the students colored scarves, and have them wave their color of scarf when their color is mentioned in the song.

Conclude the lesson by wishing the students a happy St. Patrick's Day.

If you are a classroom teacher with limited space, play the tag game outside or in the gym. You could also move some classroom furniture if finding an alternate space is not possible. The music lesson can proceed as described.

If you have paraprofessionals or other adults assisting in your classroom, have them make sure that the students keep their fun under control and stay inside the general space boundaries. During the music portion of the lesson, have them assist students singing. They can also help students to wave their scarves at the right time.

Lesson 13

Earth Day

National Standards for Physical Education: 5, Exhibits responsible personal and social behavior that respects self and others in physical activity settings.

National Standards for Music Education: 1, Singing, alone and with others, a varied repertoire of music; 2, Performing on instruments, alone and with others, a varied repertoire of music.

Equipment: None for PE, Resonator bells for music.

Lesson Focus:

• Enjoying nature in PE.
• Singing and playing instruments for music.

Related Literature: *Earth Day—Hooray!* by Stuart J. Murphy.

READ THE STORY

Read the story aloud to the class.

PE ACTIVITY

Take the students outside for a walk and enjoy what nature has to offer. Emphasize the health factors of walking and line up the students. Choose a safe route and take the students for a healthy walk. Discuss the different sights, sounds, and smells as you walk. Observe trees, leaves, and other highlights.

MUSIC ACTIVITY

Review the songs "I Love the Mountains" and "Big Beautiful Planet" from Unit 2. Sing the songs until the students remember them well. See if the students remember how to sing "I Love the Mountains" in a round. It will help greatly if you have another adult in the room who sings well. Divide the students into two groups and try a two-part round while you sing "I Love the Mountains." Next, divide the students into four chord groups: I, VI, IV, V. Assign each student a note to play in his or her chord group. The notes for the chords are as follows:

I—F, A, C
VI—D, F, A
IV—B flat, D, F
V—C, E, G

Have the students strike their bells once each time you point to their group. Have the students play the chords as you sing the song "I Love the Mountains." Use the chord symbols (i.e., hold up the number of the chord with your fingers and look at the students in that group) when you are conducting the students to help them with the chord changes. Next, see if they can sing the song and play at the same time.

Conclude the lesson by having the students sing "Big Beautiful Planet" and "I Love the Mountains" while they help you put away the resonator bells.

If you are a classroom teacher with limited space, these lessons may proceed as described. If you have no resonator bells, have the students bring xylophones from home. Make sure that the students know which notes to play.

If you have paraprofessionals or other adults assisting in your classroom, have them walk at the end of the class line while going on the Earth Day walk to make sure that all of the students stay together. During the song "I Love the Mountains," have assistants distribute and collect resonator bells and mallets. They can also help students play at the correct time.

Lesson 14

Easter

National Standards for Physical Education: 4, Achieves and maintains a health-enhancing level of physical fitness.

National Standards for Music Education: 1, Singing, alone and with others, a varied repertoire of music; 2, Performing on instruments, alone and with others, a varied repertoire of music.

Equipment: Plastic eggs and slips of paper with exercises on them for PE, Resonator bells for music.

Lesson Focus:

- Aerobics in PE.
- Singing and playing instruments in music.

Related Literature: *Rechenka's Eggs* by Patricia Polacco.

READ THE STORY

Read the story aloud to the class.

PE ACTIVITY

This is an Eggsercise Hunt. Throughout the gym, hide plastic Easter eggs with exercises written on small pieces of paper in them. Explain to the students before they enter the gym that they will be hunting for eggs.

As they enter the gym and start to collect eggs, have them bring the eggs to a designated spot. When all of the eggs have been found, have the students return to their special spots.

Begin to open the eggs one at a time. Have the students do the exercise that is written on the slip of paper inside of the egg you have just opened. Continue for as long as time allows. You may play background music for the students as they "eggsercise."

MUSIC ACTIVITY

Teach the students the song "Little Peter Rabbit." Have them repeat the song several times until they are comfortable singing it. Teach the students the actions to the song. Next, divide the students into three groups: a I chord group, a IV chord group, and a V chord group. Give each student a resonator bell to play in his or her chord group. "Little Peter Rabbit" is in the key of G, so the chords are as follows:

I—G, B, D
IV—C, E, G
V—D, F sharp, A

Have the students strike their bell once when you signal to them as they sing the song. Use the chord symbols above the music to help you conduct the students. Sing and play the song several times.

Conclude the lesson by having the students sing the song as they help you put away the bells.

If you are a classroom teacher with limited space, modify the exercises in the eggs to movements and stretches that can be done in a self-space. If you have no classroom instruments, have the students pat the steady beat of the song. They can also hop to the steady beat of "Little Peter Rabbit."

If you have paraprofessionals or other adults assisting in your classroom, have them help you make up exercises and put them in the plastic eggs. Next, have them help you hide the eggs. Assistants can help supervise the egg hunt. During "Little Peter Rabbit," have them distribute and collect instruments. They can also help students to play at the correct time. If you have a creative assistant, have her choreograph the song.

Little Peter Rabbit
(to the tune of "Battle Hymn of the Republic")

Unknown (arranged by C. Wilson)

Lesson 15

May Day

—⁓◍⁓—

National Standards for Physical Education: 6, Values physical activity for health, enjoyment, challenge, self-expression, and social interaction.

National Standards for Music Education: 1, Singing, alone and with others, a varied repertoire of music.

Equipment: Maypole for PE (use a five-foot wood dowel with three yards of colored ribbons in several colors attached to the top) and artificial flowers.

Lesson Focus:

• May Day traditions in PE and music.

Related Literature: *Miss Flora McFlimsey's May Day* by Mariana.

READ THE STORY

Read the story aloud to the class.

PE ACTIVITY

Explain to the children the tradition of the Maypole Dance. People in many cultures celebrate the arrival of spring with dancing and festivities. Assign a student to each of the ribbons on the pole and spread out in a circle. Play cheerful music in the background. Have the students skip around the pole, wrapping the bright ribbons as they go. You will probably need to do this several times so that each student gets a chance to hold a ribbon. Have a group of students toss artificial flowers during the Maypole Dance.

Have an adult hold the Maypole. The adult will get wrapped with ribbon, but it just adds fun to the activity.

MUSIC ACTIVITY

Talk with the children about May Day activities. Tell them that in many cultures springtime is a special time for celebrations. People sing songs about spring and love, have special parties, and give each other flowers. Teach the children the song "Las Mananitas." Explain that it is a special song that is sung in Mexico on special occasions, such as birthdays or festival days. Some of your Spanish-speaking students may already know this song. Another appropriate song for springtime celebrations is "I Love the Mountains" (Unit 6 Lesson 13). "Little Green Frog" is also a good song for celebrating spring. The children love singing about frogs! Teach the actions for "Little Green Frog."

Conclude the lesson by having the children sing their spring songs.

If you are a classroom teacher with limited space, find a larger space for the Maypole dance. The music lesson may proceed as described.

If you have paraprofessionals or other adults assisting in your classroom, have them hold the Maypole. They can also help students toss flowers and skip around the pole. During the music "spring sing," have helpers lead the students in singing songs.

Lesson 16

Mother's Day

━━◅◍▻━━

National Standards for Physical Education: 2, Demonstrates understanding of movement concepts, principles, strategies, and tactics as they apply to the learning and performance of physical activities.

National Standards for Music Education: 1, Singing, alone and with others, a varied repertoire of music.

Equipment: None for PE, Scarves for music.

Lesson Focus:

• Following directions in PE.
• Singing for music.

Related Literature: *I Like Noisy, Mom Likes Quiet* by Eileen Spinelli.

READ THE STORY

Read the story aloud to the class.

PE ACTIVITY

This Mother's Day game is called "Mother, May I." If possible, choose an adult at the beginning of the game to be the mother. The students line up on a designated line facing the mother. Have the student at the end of the line ask the mother if he or she may take a certain number of steps and say what kind of steps he or she would like to take. For example, *Mother, may I take six baby steps?* The mother would reply either *yes, you may* or *no, you may not*. If the mother replies *yes*, the student takes the correct number of steps toward the mother. If the mother replies *no*, the student stands still. The next student in line would ask the mother if he or she could also take some steps. Continue until someone reaches the mother. Choose a new mother and begin the game again. If you have a large group, you may want to have more than one game going at the same time.

MUSIC ACTIVITY

Ask the children what they are planning to do for Mother's Day. Have the students review the song "Skidamarink" from Unit 6 Lesson 11. Practice it several times so that they can go home and sing it to their mothers. Review the song "Las Mananitas" from Unit 6 Lesson 14 (May Day). Some of the children will want to sing "Las Mananitas" for their mothers. Pass each student a colorful scarf. Have the students wave the scarf as they sing "Las Mananitas."

Conclude the lesson by discussing with the children how they will make Mother's Day special for their mothers.

If you are a classroom teacher with limited space, make sure you have sufficient space to play the game "Mother, May I." If weather permits, play the game outside. The music lesson may proceed as described.

If you have paraprofessionals or other adults assisting in your classroom, have them supervise a second group of students playing "Mother, May I." They can also be mother. During the music lesson, have assistants help lead the singing. Assistants can also help by distributing and collecting scarves.

Lesson 17

Multicultural Days: China (Asia)

National Standards for Physical Education: 5, Exhibits responsible personal and social behavior that respects self and others in physical activity settings.

National Standards for Music Education: 1, Singing, alone and with others, a varied repertoire of music; 9, Understanding music in relation to history and culture.

Equipment: Paper and crayons or markers for music.

Lesson Focus:

• Games from the country of China.
• Songs from the country of China.

Related Literature: *The Seven Chinese Brothers* by Margaret Mahy or *Grandfather Tang's Story* by Ann Tompert.

READ THE STORY

Read one of the selected stories aloud to the class.

PE ACTIVITY

This game is called Zhao Lingxiu or "Find the Leader." Have the students stand in a circle. Ask one student to turn around and close his or her eyes. Choose one student to be the leader. The leader will designate an action such as clapping or finger snapping. All of the children must copy what the leader is doing. Tell the leader to change actions often. The student who was not looking turns around and tries to figure out who the leader is. If he or she guesses correctly, the leader is now the one to turn around and close his or her eyes. If he or she guesses incorrectly, that student does a "stunt" that you choose. Stunts can include running a lap or doing five jumping jacks. Next, the teacher would need to choose a new player to close his eyes and a new leader.

MUSIC ACTIVITY

Teach the students some facts about the country of China. China has the world's largest population. The official language of China is Mandarin Chinese. Many people in China ride bicycles to get to work. The traditional music of China is constructed using a five-tone pentatonic scale.

Teach the students the song "Fong Swei" (After School). This song can be found in *Wee Sing, Around the World*, page 55. Play the CD so that the students can hear the song in Mandarin and in English. Draw some of the lyrics on a dry-erase board for the students so that they can see what the written Chinese language looks like. Chinese is written using little "pictures" for words. Give the students a chance to make some of the simpler characters on a piece of paper with crayons or markers. Let them take their work home.

Conclude the lesson by asking the students what they learned about China.

If you are a classroom teacher with limited space, this lesson may proceed as described.

If you have paraprofessionals or other adults assisting in your classroom, have them supervise a second group of students playing Follow the Leader. This will give more students an opportunity to be the leader. During "Fong Swei" have assistants help lead student singing and assist students making Chinese characters.

Lesson 18

Multicultural Days: Caribbean

—◦◦◦◦∫◦◦◦◦—

National Standards for Physical Education: 5, Exhibits responsible personal and social behavior that respects self and others in physical activity settings.

National Standards for Music Education: 1, Singing, alone and with others, a varied repertoire of music; 2, Performing on instruments, alone and with others, a varied repertoire of music; 9, Understanding music in relation to history and culture.

Lesson Focus:

- Games from the Caribbean.
- Songs from the Caribbean.

Related Literature: *Isla* by Arthur Dorros.

READ THE STORY

Read the story aloud to the class.

PE ACTIVITY

This game is called Cuba and Spain. It is a traditional Caribbean game. The class is divided into two teams. One team is Cuba, and the other Spain. A player from Spain is chosen to go to Cuba. The team called Cuba is standing in a line facing Spain. Players from Cuba hold out their hands, palms up. The player from Spain claps the palm of a Cuban player, signaling the Cuban player to chase the Spanish player. If the Cuban player catches the Spanish player before the Spanish player gets back to his line, the Spanish player must join the Cuban team. If the Cuban player does not catch the Spanish player, the Cuban player returns to his place in line. The game continues with a Cuban player visiting Spain. The game ends when all players are on one side.

MUSIC ACTIVITY

Discuss the islands of the Caribbean with the students. The weather is often sunny and warm. Exotic fruits, trees, and animals live in the Caribbean. Beautiful birds and exotic fish can also be seen. Most people who live in the Caribbean are of European or African descent.

Teach the students the song "Tingalayo," a song from the West Indies. This song can be found in *Wee Sing, Around the World*, on page 15. Steel drums that are made from old oil barrels are instruments you often hear in music from the

336

Caribbean. Play the CD of "Tingalayo" for the students and identify the sound of the steel drums for them when you hear them. Show the students a picture of a steel drum. You can get a picture by searching Yahoo or Google on your computer.

Next, pass out rhythm band instruments. Have the students play to the steady beat of "Tingalayo." If you have more students than instruments, have a group of students play instruments while others sing. Then have the students who sang play instruments, and have the students who played instruments sing.

Conclude the lesson by reviewing what the students learned about the Caribbean islands.

If you are a classroom teacher with limited space, make sure you have plenty of room to play Cuba and Spain. Playing outside if weather permits is ideal. The music lesson may proceed as described.

If you have paraprofessionals or other adults assisting in your classroom, have them monitor a second group of students while you play Cuba and Spain, so that the students may have more opportunities for turns. During the music lesson, have assistants help you distribute and collect instruments.

Lesson 19

Multicultural Days: France (Europe)

National Standards for Physical Education: 5, Exhibits responsible personal and social behavior that respects self and others in physical activity settings.

National Standards for Music Education: 1, Singing, alone and with others, a varied repertoire of music; 2, Performing on instruments, alone and with others, a varied repertoire of music; 9, Understanding music in relation to history and culture.

Equipment: Something for a blindfold for PE, Resonator bells for music.

Lesson Focus:

- Games from the country of France.
- Songs from the country of France.

Related Literature: *Puss in Boots* by Charles Perrault or *Bone Button Borscht* by Aubrey Davis.

READ THE STORY

Read one of the selected stories aloud to the class.

PE ACTIVITY

The activity for today is a game from France. This game is called Swap Chairs by the Numbers. Have all but one of your students sit in a circle. Give all of the students sitting in the circle a number. The student left in the middle of the circle needs to be blindfolded. The blindfolded student calls out two different numbers. The students with the numbers that are called try to exchange places, staying inside the circle. They cannot run. The blindfolded student tries to tag one of the students trying to exchange places before she gets to the other spot. If a student is tagged, she takes the spot in the center and the blindfolded person takes her spot on the circle. Continue until all students get a turn to be blindfolded.

MUSIC ACTIVITY

Ask the students what they know about the country of France. Show them where France is on a map. Tell them that they already know some words that are French (e.g., ballet, croissant, soufflé). Teach the students to sing the traditional song "Frère Jacques." Teach them to sing the song first in French, and then teach them to sing the song in English. Next, pass out resonator bells (boom whackers or xylophones will also work) to play an ostinato while they sing the song. Give each student a note of the I chord or the V chord to play. Chord notes are as follows:

I—F, A, and C
V—C, E, and G

If you have more students than notes available on instruments, have half of the students play while the other half sings the song. Then give the students who were singing a chance to play instruments, and the students who were playing instruments a chance to sing. Make sure that all of your students who play the I chord are together and that all of your students who play the V chord are together. Conduct your students by looking directly at them and holding up their chord number when they are supposed to play. Make sure that they only strike once each time you signal to them to play.

Conclude the lesson by asking the students what they learned about France. The Statue of Liberty was a gift from France to the United States in 1884. France is a country rich in beautiful music, exquisite artwork, and amazing cuisine.

If you are a classroom teacher with limited space, these lessons may proceed as described. If you do not have any classroom instruments, have the children bring xylophones from home. You could also have the students play a high-pitched bell on the I signal and a low-pitched bell on the V signal.

If you have paraprofessionals or other adults assisting in your classroom, have them monitor a second circle of students playing the game Swap Chairs by the Numbers. They can also assist the blindfolded students in knowing where a student they may tag is located. During "Frère Jacques," adults may help distribute and collect instruments. They can also lead a fun song to sing in a round. If you have another adult to help, divide the students in a round. Have the assistant sing part one with a group of students while you sing part two with another group of students.

Lesson 20

Multicultural Days: Iran (Middle East)

⁓⟊⟊⟊⟊⟊⟊⟊⁓

National Standards for Physical Education: 5, Exhibits responsible personal and social behavior that respects self and others in physical activity settings.

National Standards for Music Education: 1, Singing, alone and with others, a varied repertoire of music; 9, Understanding music in relation to history and culture.

Equipment: A large cloth handkerchief with knots tied in it for PE.

Lesson Focus:

• Games and culture from Iran in PE.
• Songs from the Middle East.

Related Literature: *Ali and the Magic Stew* by Shulamith Levey Oppenheim.

READ THE STORY

Read the story aloud to the class.

PE ACTIVITY

This game came from a time in Iranian history when shepherds had to watch sheep and keep them safe from animals that were predators, such as the fox. They also had to watch the sheep to keep them safe from other dangers or thieves. The game is The Fox's Tail. Have your students form a large circle and sit down. The players who are sitting are the shepherds; choose one player to be the fox.

The fox holds onto the handkerchief and runs around the outside of the circle chanting, *the fox goes round and round!* The shepherds respond with the words, *and on his tail there are some knots!* After the chant, the fox tickles a shepherd with the handkerchief. The shepherd who was tickled stands up and chases the fox around the circle. If the fox is tagged before reaching the shepherd's place, then the shepherd becomes the new fox. If the shepherd does not tag the fox, the fox tickles a different shepherd. This game is similar to Duck, Duck, Goose.

MUSIC ACTIVITY

Teach the students some facts about the country of Iran. Iran is one of the oldest countries in the world, and historical archives in Iran date back more than five thousand years. Iran was once a part of the Persian Empire. Iran is known for

340

crude oil (a natural resource) to make gasoline for cars, handmade Persian rugs, and a warm, dry desert climate. Some people use camels as transportation because of a camel's ability to go for long periods of time with no water.

Teach the children the song "Attal Mattal." This song can be found in *Wee Sing, Around the World*, on page 53. After the children know the song, teach them how to play the game that is described with the song. Have the students listen to the recording of the song so they can hear how the Persian language sounds. Show the students the lyrics in Persian by drawing some on a dry-erase board. This shows the students that people around the world write in different ways.

Conclude the lesson by asking the students what they learned about the country and culture of Iran. Tell them that many people in Iran are Muslims, and they celebrate Ramadan. For more information about Ramadan, see Unit 6 Lesson 8.

If you are a classroom teacher with limited space, make sure you have sufficient room to play The Fox's Tail. If you have a rug or padded area, the students can play in a smaller space by crawling instead of running. Make sure the students know how to move safely in the space and they know the boundaries of the game (e.g., they must crawl clockwise around the circle). The music lesson may proceed as described.

If you have paraprofessionals or other adults assisting in your classroom, have them supervise a second group of students so that students get more opportunities to be a fox or a shepherd. During the music lesson have assistants help lead singing.

Lesson 21

Multicultural Days: Brazil (South America)

⊸⊸⫯⫯⫯⊸

National Standards for Physical Education: 5, Exhibits responsible personal and social behavior that respects self and others in physical activity settings.

National Standards for Music Education: 1, Singing, alone and with others, a varied repertoire of music; 9, Understanding music in relation to history and culture.

Equipment: None.

Lesson Focus:

• Games and culture from Brazil.
• Songs from South America.

Related Literature: *The Great Kapok Tree* by Lynne Cherry.

READ THE STORY

Read the story aloud to the class.

PE ACTIVITY

This game from Brazil is Cat and Rat. Choose one student to be the cat and one to be the rat. Have the rest of the students form a circle. The cat stands on the outside of the circle and the rat stands on the inside of the circle.

The cat taps one student from the circle on the shoulder. The circle player says, *What do you want?* The cat replies, *I want to see the rat.* The circle player says, *You cannot see him now.* The cat now says, *When can I see him?* The player replies, *At ten o'clock.* (The player can pick any time he wants.)

The circle now begins to move clockwise in rhythm as they count off the hours by saying, *One o'clock, tick-tock, two o'clock, tick-tock*, and so on until they reach the announced time (in this case ten o'clock). At this point the circle stops moving. The cat steps up again to the player he or she originally tapped.

The circle opens at the original spot and the rat comes out. The cat chases the rat around the circle and tries to catch him. If the rat is caught, choose a new student to be the rat. It would be best to choose a new cat, to keep everyone involved. Begin the game again.

MUSIC ACTIVITY

Show the students where Brazil is located on a map. It is the largest country in South America. The official language of Brazil is Portuguese. Discuss the climate in Brazil. It is usually warm and sunny. Teach the children the song "Ciranda" (circle game). The song and game are located in *Wee Sing, Around the World*, on page 20. The students form a circle. The children sing the song as they skip to the left during verse one. During verse two, the students skip to the right. At the beginning of verse three, the students keep skipping to the right. They call out the name of a child to go to the center of the circle. The students stop skipping and stay in place. The new child recites the poem that accompanies the song "Ciranda." The child joins the circle again, and the game continues.

Conclude the lesson by discussing what the students have learned about Brazil.

If you are a classroom teacher with limited space, make sure you have plenty of room to play Cat and Rat. "Ciranda" can take place in an area that is big enough for circle time.

If you have paraprofessionals or other adults assisting in your classroom, have them supervise a second circle of students playing Cat and Rat so that students can have more turns. During "Ciranda," paraprofessionals can also supervise a second circle of students playing the game.

Lesson 22

Multicultural Days: American Indians

<figure>—◅⫷⫸▻—</figure>

National Standards for Physical Education: 5, Exhibits responsible personal and social behavior that respects self and others in physical activity settings.

National Standards for Music Education: 1, Singing, alone and with others, a varied repertoire of music; 9, Understanding music in relation to history and culture.

Equipment: A fleece ball for each tribe in PE.

Lesson Focus:

- Traditional games of American Indians.
- Traditional music of American Indians.

Related Literature: *Annie and the Old One* by Miska Miles.

READ THE STORY

Read the story aloud to the class.

PE ACTIVITY

This activity is an American Indian ball race. Divide the class into tribes of six players each. Designate areas as paths. Put three members of each tribe on each end of the path. On the *go* signal, one member from each tribe begins pushing the ball (using feet, as in soccer) to the other end where the rest of their tribe is. The next tribe member in line from the other side begins pushing the ball back the other way. This continues until all tribe members have had a turn pushing the ball. The winner is the tribe that finishes first.

Pushing the ball instead of kicking should look like a soccer dribble. In other words, the ball has to stay right by the pusher's foot. Have the students practice what the push looks like before playing the game.

MUSIC ACTIVITY

Discuss American Indian life with the students. There are many tribes of American Indians. They live in many areas of the United States, and they have a long and rich heritage. When colonists first came to what was known as the "New World," the American Indians helped them to learn how to hunt so they could survive. Download pictures of American Indian artifacts and traditional clothing to show the students.

Teach the students the song "Uhe'Basho^N Sho^N" (The Crooked Path). This is a song of the Omaha Indians. It can be found in *Wee Sing, Around the World*, page 12. The Omaha Indians live in Nebraska. Nebraska is in the midwestern

United States. After the children are comfortable singing the song, have them play Follow the Leader while they sing. Omaha Indian children would sing this song as they followed a leader through the forest and over the plains.

Conclude the lesson by asking the students what they know about American Indians.

If you are a classroom teacher with limited space, make sure you have plenty of room to play the ball race and Follow the Leader.

If you have paraprofessionals or other adults assisting in your classroom, have them supervise the ball race. They can also help lead students and sing during Follow the Leader.

Lesson 23

Multicultural Days: Korea

—◦◦◦◦◦—

National Standards for Physical Education: 5, Exhibits responsible personal and social behavior that respects self and others in physical activity settings.

National Standards for Music Education: 1, Singing, alone and with others, a varied repertoire of music; 2, Performing on instruments, alone and with others, a varied repertoire of music; 9, Understanding music in relation to history and culture.

Equipment: Triangles or finger cymbals and a rain stick for music.

Lesson Focus:

• Games and songs from other cultures.

Related Literature: *Yunmi and Halmoni's Trip* by Sook Nyul Choi.

READ THE STORY

Read the story aloud to the class.

PE ACTIVITY

This traditional Korean game is called Sam Pal Sun, which translates to "the line between South Korea and North Korea." It is played by dividing the class into two equal teams. Each team has a safe area. Begin by lining up the teams, facing each other on opposite ends of the playing area. A team's safe area will be on the far side of the direction they are facing. On the *go* signal, the teams begin to move toward each other in an attempt to make it to the opposite end to be safe. If someone from the opposing team tags a student, that student must return to the starting line and begin again. The game is over when one team has all of its members into the safe area.

MUSIC ACTIVITY

Discuss the country of Korea with the students. Korea is located in Northeast Asia. It is located on the Korean peninsula. Korea is divided into two nations: North Korea and South Korea. The south and the west have plains, whereas the east and the north are covered with mountains. When children are born in Korea, they are considered to be a year old that day. People celebrate turning a year older on New Year's Day instead of on their birthday. If a baby were born on December several days before New Year's Day, that child could be considered two years old before he or she were even one week old!

346

Teach the students the song "Arirang." This song can be found in *Wee Sing, Around the World*, on page 56. Play the CD for the students so that they can hear it both in Korean and in English. Show the students some of the lyrics in Korean by drawing them on a dry-erase board.

Next pass out finger cymbals, triangles, and a rain stick for some of the students to play. Have the students playing finger cymbals and triangles play on beat one of every measure. Conduct them so that they know when to play. Have the student who is playing the rain stick play softly throughout the song. If you have more students than instruments, give some students a chance to play the instruments while other students sing.

Conclude the lesson by asking the students what they learned about Korea.

If you are a classroom teacher with limited space, make sure you have plenty of space to play Sam Pal Sun. The music lesson may proceed as described. If you have no classroom instruments, glasses filled with water being struck by a spoon can replace the sound of the triangles and finger cymbals. Rain sticks can be made by taking gift-wrapping tubes, inserting toothpicks through the tube, and filling them with dry beans, rice, or popcorn seeds.

If you have paraprofessionals or other adults assisting in your classroom, have them help distribute and collect instruments and supervise game play.

Lesson 24

Multicultural Days: Germany

National Standards for Physical Education: 5, Exhibits responsible personal and social behavior that respects self and others in physical activity settings.

National Standards for Music Education: 1, Singing, alone and with others, a varied repertoire of music; 9, Understanding music in relation to history and culture.

Equipment: A scarf for music.

Lesson Focus:

- Culture, games, and music of Germany.

Related Literature: *The Fisherman and His Wife* by Rosemary Wells.

READ THE STORY

Read the story aloud to the class.

PE ACTIVITY

This traditional German game is Sardines. Choose a student to be "it." The child who is it hides from the other students. The rest of the class is hiding their eyes and counting to ten. Next, they go looking for the student who is it. When a student finds it, they must hide with him. The game continues until all of the class has found the students who are hiding.

MUSIC ACTIVITY

Teach the students about Germany. Germany is on the continent of Europe. Many great musicians including Beethoven, Schubert, and Schumann were from Germany. The submarine was invented in Germany. Show the students where Germany is located on a map. Download some pictures of Germany for the students to see.

Teach the students the song "Alle Meine Entchen" (All My Little Ducklings). The song can be found in *Wee Sing, Around the World*, on page 38. Play the CD for the students so they can hear the song in German and in English.

When the students are comfortable singing the song, have them make a circle. Choose one child to be a "duckling." Tuck the scarf down the back of the duckling's shirt. The duckling walks around the circle as the students sing the song. When the children sing the phrase *tails are in the air,* the duckling tags a student to chase him or her around the circle and try to grab the tail from the duckling's shirt. If the chaser grabs the scarf, he gets to put the scarf down the back of his shirt and choose a child to chase him while the students sing the song. If the chaser does not get the scarf, he or she return to his or her spot in the circle.

Conclude the lesson by asking the students what they know about Germany.

If you are a classroom teacher with limited space, make sure you have sufficient room to play the circle game that goes with "Alle Meine Entchen" (All My Little Ducklings). You will need to find a space to play Sardines where there are sufficient hiding places.

If you have paraprofessionals or other adults assisting in your classroom, have them supervise a second circle of students playing and singing "Alle Meine Entchen." This way more students will have the opportunity to be a duckling or a chaser. They may also supervise the Sardines game.

Lesson 25

Multicultural Days: England

≈‖♪‖≈

National Standards for Physical Education: 5, Exhibits responsible personal and social behavior that respects self and others in physical activity settings.

National Standards for Music Education: 1, Singing, alone and with others, a varied repertoire of music; 8, Understanding relationships between music, the other arts, and disciplines outside the arts; 9, Understanding music in relation to history and culture.

Equipment: Paper and crayons for music.

Lesson Focus:

• History, games, and songs of England.

Related Literature: *Jack and the Beanstalk* by Ann Keay Beneduce and Gennady Spirin.

READ THE STORY

Read the story aloud to the class.

PE ACTIVITY

This traditional English game is called "Please Mr. Crocodile," and is played on playgrounds all over England. Choose one student to be Mr. Crocodile. The other students stand at the end of the gym. The students chant, *Please Mr. Crocodile, may I cross the water to see my baby daughter who lives in a cup and saucer?* Mr. Crocodile replies with something that involves what the students are wearing, such as, *Only if you are wearing red.* The students wearing what the crocodile called may take one step toward the middle of the gym. The game continues until one student reaches Mr. Crocodile. The student who gets to that spot first becomes the next Mr. Crocodile.

MUSIC ACTIVITY

Teach the students about the country of England. Long ago England was ruled by a king or a queen. This form of government is called a monarchy. Presently the country is ruled using a parliamentary/monarchy form of government. The prime minister and parliament make the laws for England. England still has a royal family because the royal family is a tradition. England still has many old castles and estates where noble families still live. People in England drink lots of tea. Download some pictures of castles and estates found in England to show your students. Show them where England is located on the map.

Teach the students the song "Lavender's Blue." When the students are comfortable singing the song, give each student some crayons and paper. Have the students draw a picture of a large castle where a king or queen and their family might have lived.

Conclude the lesson by asking the students what they learned about England. Let them take their artwork home.

If you are a classroom teacher with limited space, find a larger space to play "Please Mr. Crocodile." The music lesson may proceed as described.

If you have paraprofessionals or other adults assisting in your classroom, have them help lead singing. They can also help distribute paper and crayons and monitor students making pictures. Have them help supervise during the game.

Lesson 26

Multicultural Days: Ireland

National Standards for Physical Education: 5, Exhibits responsible personal and social behavior that respects self and others in physical activity settings.

National Standards for Music Education: 1, Singing, alone and with others, a varied repertoire of musi; 9, Understanding music in relation to history and culture.

Equipment: None.

Lesson Focus:

- History, music, culture, and games of Ireland.

Related Literature: *Brothers* by Yin or *King Puck* by Michael Garland.

READ THE STORY

Read the story aloud to the class.

PE ACTIVITY

Mill and Grab is a traditional Irish game. It is often played on playgrounds because a large number of children can play at one time. The teacher calls a number and the children have to form groups of that number. For instance, if the teacher calls "three," the children form groups of three as quickly as possible. If a student is left out, have him come to you and do a couple of jumping jacks and return to the game. The teacher continues calling different numbers.

MUSIC ACTIVITY

Teach the students about the country of Ireland. Ireland is known as the "Emerald Isle" because of the beautiful green countryside that is covered with rolling hills. Many people came from Ireland to the United States in the mid-1800s. Ireland is famous for handmade lace and crystal. Show the students where Ireland is located on a map. Show the students some pictures of Ireland that you downloaded from the Internet.

Teach the students the song "Wee Falorie Man." This song can be found in *Wee Sing, Around the World*, on page 31. Explain the terms that they may not understand (e.g., *falorie*, *bap*, or *clipe*; these words are also found on page 31). When the students are comfortable singing the song, teach them a jig (dance) to go with the song.

Beat one measure one—right foot heel out, strike floor to the front.

Beat two measure one—right toes cross left foot and strike the floor.

Beat one measure two—right foot heel out strike floor to the front again.

Beat one measure two—both feet back together.

Repeat this pattern with the left foot. You should be able to do the pattern with the right foot and the left foot two times during each verse.

Conclude the lesson by having the students tell you what they learned about Ireland.

If you are a classroom teacher with limited space, make sure each student has a self-space to do the jig while singing "Wee Falorie Man." The Mill and Grab game should be played in the gym or outside.

If you have paraprofessionals or other adults assisting in your classroom, have them help students learn the jig. Some students will learn it quickly, whereas others will need more time. Give the students the experience of enjoying a dance. They can help the children form number groups in the Mill and Grab game.

Lesson 27

Multicultural Days: Japan

National Standards for Physical Education: 5, Exhibits responsible personal and social behavior that respects self and others in physical activity settings.

National Standards for Music Education: 1, Singing, alone and with others, a varied repertoire of music; 9, Understanding music in relation to history and culture.

Equipment: Tiddlywinks or poker chips for PE, Scarves, paper, and crayons for music.

Lesson Focus:

• History, culture, music, and games of Japan.

Related Literature: *Yoshi's Feast* by Kimiko Kajikawa or *Jojofu* by Michael P. Waite.

READ THE STORY

Read one of the selected stories aloud to the class.

PE ACTIVITY

Ohajiki is a traditional Japanese game. Each student will need five tiddlywinks or poker chips. Have the students find a partner. Both players will lay down their chips. Play rock, paper, scissors to see which child goes first. The first person to take a turn gathers all of the chips in one hand and tosses them on the floor from a kneeling position. Next, the first player points to two chips. He or she picks one and using the thumb and index finger, flicks the first chip at the second chip. If he or she hits the second chip, he or she gets to keep it. If the chip is missed, it is the second child's turn. If the chip is hit, the child gets another turn. The winner is the child with the most chips at the end.

MUSIC ACTIVITY

Discuss the country of Japan with the students. Today Japan is a country where many technological advances are being made. Japan has an ancient culture. Sumo wrestling began in Japan. Download pictures of Japan to show the students.

Teach the students the song "Ame Ame" (Rain Song). The song can be found in *Wee Sing, Around the World*, on page 57. Have them listen to the CD so that they can hear the song in English and in Japanese. Show the students some of the Japanese lyrics by writing them on a dry-erase board.

When the students are comfortable singing the song, give each student a colorful scarf. Have the students wave their scarves while they sing "Ame Ame." Next, give each student some paper and crayons. Have the students draw some of the Japanese lyrics on the paper.

Conclude the lesson by asking the students what they know about Japan. Let them take their Japanese lyrics home.

If you are a classroom teacher with limited space, make sure every student has a self-space so that they can move creatively while using their scarves as they sing the song "Ame Ame." The PE plan may proceed as described. If you do not want to use the floor, desks would work fine.

If you have paraprofessionals or other adults assisting in your classroom, have them help distribute scarves, paper, and crayons. They can also assist with singing and drawing lyrics. Have them rotate from game to game in Ohajiki.

Lesson 28

Multicultural Days: Israel

National Standards for Physical Education: 5, Exhibits responsible personal and social behavior that respects self and others in physical activity settings.

National Standards for Music Education: 1, Singing, alone and with others, a varied repertoire of music; 2, Performing on instruments, alone and with others, a varied repertoire of music; 9, Understanding music in relation to history and culture.

Equipment: Scooters, Boom whackers or xylophones for music.

Lesson Focus:

- Culture, music, and games of Israel.

Related Literature: *The Never-Ending Greenness* by Neil Waldman.

READ THE STORY

Read the story aloud to the class.

PE ACTIVITY

A game commonly seen on the playground or PE classes in Israel is relays. The students will do scooter relays today. Put them in small groups of three. Each group will need a scooter. Line up the groups on the end line of the gym. Some of the scooter activities you can do are: sitting on their bottom, putting their knees on the scooter, and lying on their belly. After each student has a turn, he returns to the end of the line.

MUSIC ACTIVITY

Israel has an ancient heritage. Israel is located in the Middle East. Israel is the birthplace of Christianity, Judaism, and Islam, three of the world's major religions. Show the students where Israel is located on a map. Download pictures of Israel to show the students.

Teach the students the song "Zum Gali Gali." It is located in *Wee Sing, Around the World*, on page 52. Have the students listen to the CD so that they can hear it in Hebrew and in English. Show the students what the lyrics look like in Hebrew by writing some of them on a dry-erase board.

When the students are comfortable singing the song, pass out a boom whacker or xylophone to each student and instruct them to play a note in the E minor chord (i.e., E, G, or B). Have each student play only one note. Have all of the students strike their notes together on beat one of each measure. Have them only strike once. Conduct them so that they know when to play. If you have more students than instruments, have some students play while others sing. Then have the singers play the instruments and the students who played previously sing.

Conclude the lesson by asking the students what they learned about Israel.

If you are a classroom teacher with limited space, the music lesson may proceed as described. If you do not have boom whackers or xylophones, have students bring toy xylophones from home or use homemade percussion instruments from previous lessons. Have the students strike the instruments on beat one of every measure. The PE activity must be done in a large space with a smooth surface.

If you have paraprofessionals or other adults assisting in your classroom, have them help sing the "chant" part of the song with a group of students while you sing the verses of the song with another group of students. Have assistants also distribute and collect instruments. They can help supervise during the scooter relays.

Lesson 29

Multicultural Days: Greece

National Standards for Physical Education: 5, Exhibits responsible personal and social behavior that respects self and others in physical activity settings.

National Standards for Music Education: 1, Singing, alone and with others, a varied repertoire of music; 9, Understanding music in relation to history and culture.

Equipment: One carpet sample for every three students, A small ring for music.

Lesson Focus:

• History, songs, and games from Greece.

Related Literature: *I Have an Olive Tree* by Eve Bunting.

READ THE STORY

Read the story aloud to the class.

PE ACTIVITY

This traditional Greek game can be played in any large space; it is called Sharks. Place the carpet samples on the floor in a scattered formation. Choose one student to be the shark. There can never be more than three people on a carpet at a time. If four students are on a carpet, it sinks and they are out. Children move from carpet to carpet trying not to get tagged by the shark. If the shark tags a student, he is out. To keep children actively involved, only have them stay out for fifteen seconds and then have them rejoin the game. Change sharks often.

MUSIC ACTIVITY

Discuss the country of Greece with the students. Greek history, art, science, literature, and other facets of Greek culture have been influential in many other cultures and societies. Ancient Greek ruins date back more than 1400 years. The Olympic Games and the marathon race originated in Greece. Download pictures of Greek ruins to show the students.

Teach the students the song "Pou'n-do to Dachtilidi" (Where Is the Ring?). The song can be found in *Wee Sing, Around the World*, on page 42. Have the students listen to the CD so that they can hear the song in both Greek and in English.

When the students are comfortable singing the song, have them play the game described on page 42. The children form a circle. They sit pretzel-style with their hands open and their palms facing up but cupped so that it would be hard to see if there is something in their hands. A leader is chosen. As the students sing the song, the leader goes around the circle and pretends to place a ring in the students' hands. The leader places the ring in only one student's hand. When the song is over, the leader chooses another student to guess who has the ring. If the student guesses who has the ring, she becomes the new leader. If she does not correctly guess who has the ring, the same student remains the leader. If you want to make sure that all students get a turn, use more than one ring and have more than one leader. You may also have the student who was chosen to guess who had the ring be the next leader even if her guess was incorrect.

Conclude the lesson by discussing what the students learned about Greece.

If you are a classroom teacher with limited space, this lesson may proceed as described. The PE activity needs to be played in a large, open space.

If you have paraprofessionals or other adults assisting in your classroom, have them supervise a second group of students playing so that students have more opportunities for turns. They can supervise the Sharks game.

Lesson 30

Multicultural Days: Italy

National Standards for Physical Education: 5, Exhibits responsible personal and social behavior that respects self and others in physical activity settings.

National Standards for Music Education: 1, Singing, alone and with others, a varied repertoire of music; 9, Understanding music in relation to history and culture.

Equipment: None.

Lesson Focus:

• Culture, games, and music of Italy.

Related Literature: *The Orphan Singer* by Emily Arnold McCully.

READ THE STORY

Read the story aloud to the class.

PE ACTIVITY

Strega Comanda Color is the name of this traditional Italian game. In English, it would be called "Witch Says Colors." Select a student to be the "witch." The witch stands in the middle of the gym and calls out a color. The rest of the students leave the starting line and try to find something to touch that is the color the witch called. If they are tagged before they touch something, they must join the witch. Have the students come back to the starting line, and the witch calls a new color. Change the witch often.

MUSIC ACTIVITY

Italy has made many significant contributions to government, art, culture, and music of Western society. Opera originated in Italy. Many famous musicians, including Bellini and Verdi, are from Italy. All over the world people enjoy Italian foods, such as spaghetti, pizza, ravioli, and tiramisu. Roman architecture influenced many structures all over the world. Download some pictures of ancient structures from Italy to show your students.

Teach the students the song "Mio Galleto" (My Rooster). This song can be found in *Wee Sing, Around the World*, on page 39. Have the students listen to the song recorded on the CD so that they can hear it in Italian and in English.

When the students are comfortable singing the song, have them form a circle. Choose a student to be the "rooster." As the students sing the song, the rooster walks around the outside of the circle. At the end of the song, the rooster tags another student to chase him around the circle to find him. If the rooster is caught, he must sit down and the child who was chasing the rooster is the new rooster. If the rooster is not caught, he or she remains the rooster. To ensure that more students have a turn, consider having the chaser be the new rooster even if he does not catch the old rooster.

Conclude the lesson by asking the students what they know about Italy.

If you are a classroom teacher with limited space, make sure you have enough space for a circle with students running around it. Emphasize safety when the students are running around the circle. Run in the same direction. Do not leave the perimeter of the circle. Hands and feet should remain in the center of the circle. The Witch Calls Color should be played in a large, open area.

If you have paraprofessionals or other adults assisting in your classroom, have them supervise a second circle of students playing and singing "Mio Galleto." This way more students have an opportunity to be it. They can also supervise during the PE activity.

Lesson 31

Summer Olympics

National Standards for Physical Education: 1, Demonstrates competency in motor skills and movement patterns needed to perform a variety of physical activities.

National Standards for Music Education: 1, Singing, alone and with others, a varied repertoire of music; 2, Performing on instruments, alone and with others, a varied repertoire of music; 6, Listening to, analyzing, and describing music; 9, Understanding music in relation to history and culture.

Equipment: Scooters, music, and balls for PE, A recording of the "Olympic Theme" (download from iTunes) and xylophones for music.

Lesson Focus:

- Sports of the Summer Games in PE.
- Singing and playing instruments in music.

Related Literature: *Make the Team, Baby Duck!* by Amy Hest.

READ THE STORY

Read the story aloud to the class.

PE ACTIVITY

Have an "Opening Ceremony" to begin your Olympic celebration. Have the students form a line in pairs. Give every two students a flag from a different country to carry in the parade. Use the "Olympic Theme" and have students march around the gym to the steady beat.

Play "The Swimming Song" by The Learning Station (*Tony Chestnut* CD, #9). Have the students perform the movements that are on the song. Play the song several times and let the students enjoy the swimming movements.

MUSIC ACTIVITY

Discuss the Olympics with the students. Ask them about their favorite events. Play the "Olympic Theme" (also known as "Summon the Heroes" by John Williams) for the students. Have them notice the dynamic changes and tempo changes. Teach the children to sing the main theme on the syllable *la*. Have them move their hands high when the pitch is high and low when the pitch is low. Play the song several times until the students are comfortable singing the main theme. Play "The Star-Spangled Banner" for the students so they recognize it when they hear it being played.

Conclude the lessons by asking the students what they learned about the Olympics.

If you are a classroom teacher with limited space, make sure you have sufficient space for the Olympic activities. If you do not have xylophones, have the students bring their toy xylophones from home. If this is not possible, have students move to the "Olympic Theme" using scarves or streamers.

If you have paraprofessionals or other adults assisting in your classroom, have them help distribute and collect equipment and instruments. They can help supervise activities. Students who need help finding the correct notes to play on the xylophones can also use some paraprofessional help.

Olympic Theme (Summon the Heroes)

John Williams; simplified by C. Wilson

Lesson 32

Summer Olympics

National Standards for Physical Education: 1, Demonstrates competency in motor skills and movement patterns needed to perform a variety of physical activities.

National Standards for Music Education: 1, Singing, alone and with others, a varied repertoire of music; 2, Performing on instruments, alone and with others, a varied repertoire of music; 9, Understanding music in relation to history and culture.

Equipment: Scooters, music, and balls for PE, A recording of the "Olympic Theme" (download from iTunes) and xylophones for music.

Lesson Focus:

• Sports of the Summer Games in PE.
• Singing and playing instruments in music.

Related Literature: *Paperboy* by Mary Kay Kroeger.

READ THE STORY

Read the story aloud to the class.

PE ACTIVITY

Download "Eye of the Tiger" from iTunes. Discuss boxing with the students. There are rules for boxing. Boxers may not strike below the belt or grab onto their opponent and hold onto him. Boxers must be free to move around the ring. The ultimate goal is to knock out the opponent. If there is no knockout, judges decide who wins the boxing match by scoring boxing technique and numbers of hits to the opponent. Have the students shadowbox to the song "Eye of the Tiger." Training for boxing is rigorous. In between bouts of shadowboxing, have the students jog through the gym.

MUSIC ACTIVITY

Review the "Olympic Theme" (also known as "Summon the Heroes" by John Williams) with the students. Have them sing the main theme on the syllable *la*. Have them march in place to the music of the slow section. Have them jog in place to the fast section. Discuss how the main theme is heard at the beginning and the end of the piece, and how the section in the middle is faster. Play "The Star-Spangled Banner" for the students to hear again.

Conclude the lessons by asking the students what they learned about the Olympics.

If you are a classroom teacher with limited space, make sure you have sufficient space for the Olympic activities. If you do not have xylophones, have the students bring their toy xylophones from home. If this is not possible, have students move to the "Olympic Theme" using scarves or streamers.

If you have paraprofessionals or other adults assisting in your classroom, have them help distribute and collect equipment and instruments. They can help supervise activities. Students who need help finding the correct notes to play on the xylophones can also use some paraprofessional help.

Lesson 33

Summer Olympics

National Standards for Physical Education: 1, Demonstrates competency in motor skills and movement patterns needed to perform a variety of physical activities.

National Standards for Music Education: 1, Singing, alone and with others, a varied repertoire of music; 2, Performing on instruments, alone and with others, a varied repertoire of music; 6, Listening to, analyzing, and describing music; 9, Understanding music in relation to history and culture.

Equipment: Scooters, music, and balls for PE, A recording of the "Olympic Theme" (download from iTunes) and xylophones for music.

Lesson Focus:

- Sports of the Summer Games in PE.
- Singing and playing instruments in music.

Related Literature: *One-Dog Canoe* by Mary Casanova.

READ THE STORY

Read the story aloud to the class.

PE ACTIVITY

Discuss canoeing with the students. Canoe races are an exiting event during the Olympics. One- and two-person canoe races are events.

Place cones around the perimeter of the gym to make a "race track" for the "canoes." Have students get on scooters and race around the cones to simulate the canoe race. Make sure they sit on their bottom at all times while on the scooters. Race several times.

MUSIC ACTIVITY

Review all previous Olympic lessons with the students. Make sure each student has a xylophone to play, or have a group of students play the xylophones while others sing with you. Sing the simplified version of the "Olympic Theme" for the students using note names. Have them slowly play the theme while you slowly sing the note names. Give each student a chance to play.

Conclude the lessons by asking the students what they learned about the Olympics.

If you are a classroom teacher with limited space, make sure you have sufficient space for the Olympic activities. If you do not have xylophones, have the students bring their toy xylophones from home. If this is not possible, have students move to the "Olympic Theme" using scarves or streamers.

If you have paraprofessionals or other adults assisting in your classroom, have them help distribute and collect equipment and instruments. They can help supervise activities. Students need help finding the correct notes to play on the xylophones can also use some paraprofessional help.

Lesson 34

Summer Olympics

National Standards for Physical Education: 1, Demonstrates competency in motor skills and movement patterns needed to perform a variety of physical activities.

National Standards for Music Education: 1, Singing, alone and with others, a varied repertoire of music; 2, Performing on instruments, alone and with others, a varied repertoire of music; 6, Listening to, analyzing, and describing music; 9, Understanding music in relation to history and culture.

Equipment: Scooters, music, and balls for PE, A recording of the "Olympic Theme" (download from iTunes) and xylophones for music.

Lesson Focus:

- Sports of the Summer Games in PE.
- Singing and playing instruments in music.

Related Literature: *A Pony for Keeps* by Elizabeth Henning Sutton.

READ THE STORY

Read the story aloud to the class.

PE ACTIVITY

Discuss equestrian sports with the students. Equestrian sports are scored not only by how fast a handler can get her horse to race, but also by the beauty of the routine when the handler and the horse are performing.

Play the song "Gallop" for the students. This song is by The Learning Station on the *Physical Ed* CD, #15. The students gallop through general space. Play the song several times to let the students enjoy galloping like a horse.

MUSIC ACTIVITY

Once again, have the students play the xylophones to the "Olympic Theme" as in Unit 6 Lesson 33. Discuss the country where the Olympics are being hosted. If it is one of the countries listed in this book, have the students sing the song that is from that country.

Conclude the lessons by asking the students what they learned about the Olympics.

If you are a classroom teacher with limited space, make sure you have sufficient space for the Olympic activities. If you do not have xylophones, have the students bring their toy xylophones from home. If this is not possible, have students move to the "Olympic Theme" using scarves or streamers.

If you have paraprofessionals or other adults assisting in your classroom, have them help distribute and collect equipment and instruments. They can help supervise activities. Students who need help finding the correct notes to play on the xylophones can also use some paraprofessional help.

Lesson 35

Summer Olympics

National Standards for Physical Education: 1, Demonstrates competency in motor skills and movement patterns needed to perform a variety of physical activities.

National Standards for Music Education: 1, Singing, alone and with others, a varied repertoire of music; 2, Performing on instruments, alone and with others, a varied repertoire of music; 6, Listening to, analyzing, and describing music; 9, Understanding music in relation to history and culture.

Equipment: Scooters, music, and balls for PE, A recording of the "Olympic Theme" (download from iTunes) and xylophones for music.

Lesson Focus:

• Sports of the Summer Games in PE.
• Singing and playing instruments in music.

Related Literature: *Froggy Plays Soccer* by Jonathan London.

READ THE STORY

Read the story aloud to the class.

PE ACTIVITY

Discuss soccer with the students. Turn on some music for the students. Have the students dribble the soccer ball with their feet as the music plays. When the music stops, have the students freeze. Turn on the music and have them continue dribbling. Keep having the students play, using the music as a cue to freeze and to go.

MUSIC ACTIVITY

Have the students review all Olympic musical activities. Play the "Olympic Theme" on the xylophones. Have them sing the "Olympic Theme" on the syllable *la*. Review "The Star-Spangled Banner." Once again, discuss the country that is hosting the Olympics. Download information about the musical traditions of that country to share with your students.

Conclude the lessons by asking the students what they learned about the Olympics.

If you are a classroom teacher with limited space, make sure you have sufficient space for the Olympic activities. If you do not have xylophones, have the students bring their toy xylophones from home. If this is not possible, have students move to the "Olympic Theme" using scarves or streamers.

If you have paraprofessionals or other adults assisting in your classroom, have them help distribute and collect equipment and instruments. They can help supervise activities. Students who need help finding the correct notes to play on the xylophones can also use some paraprofessional help.

Lesson 36

Winter Olympics

National Standards for Physical Education: 1, Demonstrates competency in motor skills and movement patterns needed to perform a variety of physical activities.

National Standards for Music Education: 2, Improvising melodies, variations, and accompaniments; 6, Listening to, analyzing, and describing music.

Equipment: Paper flags from other countries, a box, mats, scooters, cones, paper plates, hockey sticks, small soft balls, and relay batons for PE, A recording of the "Olympic Theme" and xylophones for music.

Lesson Focus:

- Sports of the Winter Games in PE.
- Olympic theme song in music.

Related Literature: *Celebrate the Fire Within* by Kathy Larsen.

READ THE STORY

Read the story aloud to the class.

PE ACTIVITY

Have an "Opening Ceremony" to begin your Olympic celebration. Have the students form a line in pairs. Give every two students a flag from a different country to carry in the parade. Use the "Olympic Theme" and have them march around the gym to the steady beat. Next, have the students divide into relay teams. Have them relay a baton like the Olympic torch. Give all of the students a chance to run with the "torch."

MUSIC ACTIVITY

Discuss the Olympics with the students. Ask them about their favorite events. Play the "Olympic Theme" (also known as "Summon the Heroes" by John Williams) for the students. Have them notice the dynamic changes and tempo changes. Teach the children to sing the main theme on the syllable *la*. Have them move their hands high when the pitch is high and low when the pitch is low. Play the song several times until the students are comfortable singing the main theme. Play "The Star-Spangled Banner" for the students so they recognize it when they hear it being played.

Conclude the lessons by asking the students what they learned about the Olympics.

If you are a classroom teacher with limited space, make sure you have sufficient space for the Olympic activities. If you do not have xylophones, have the students bring their toy xylophones from home. If this is not possible, have students move to the "Olympic Theme" using scarves or streamers.

If you have paraprofessionals or other adults assisting in your classroom, have them help distribute and collect equipment and instruments. They can help supervise activities. Students who need help finding the correct notes to play on the xylophones can also use some paraprofessional help.

Olympic Theme (Summon the Heroes)

John Williams; simplified by C. Wilson

Lesson 37

Winter Olympics

⟞⟋⟍⟞

National Standards for Physical Education: 1, Demonstrates competency in motor skills and movement patterns needed to perform a variety of physical activities.

National Standards for Music Education: 2, Performing on instruments, alone and with others, a varied repertoire of music; 6, Listening to, analyzing, and describing music.

Equipment: Paper flags from other countries, a box, mats, scooters, cones, paper plates, hockey sticks, small soft balls, and relay batons for PE, A recording of the "Olympic Theme" and xylophones for music.

Lesson Focus:

• Sports of the Winter Games in PE.
• Olympic theme song in music.

Related Literature: *Tacky and the Winter Games* by Helen Lester.

READ THE STORY

Read the story aloud to the class.

PE ACTIVITY

Today the students will enjoy the ski jump. Have the students get on top of a sturdy box one at a time and jump into the air, landing on a mat. They can try to make fun shapes while they are in the air. Download pictures of ski jumpers in the air to show to your students.

MUSIC ACTIVITY

Review the "Olympic Theme" (also known as "Summon the Heroes" by John Williams) with the students. Have them sing the main theme on the syllable *la*. Have them march in place to the music of the slow section. Have them jog in place to the fast section. Discuss how the main theme is heard at the beginning and the end of the piece, and how the section in the middle is faster. Play "The Star-Spangled Banner" for the students to hear again.

Conclude the lessons by asking the students what they learned about the Olympics.

If you are a classroom teacher with limited space, make sure you have sufficient space for the Olympic activities. If you do not have xylophones, have the students bring their toy xylophones from home. If this is not possible, have students move to the "Olympic Theme" using scarves or streamers.

If you have paraprofessionals or other adults assisting in your classroom, have them help distribute and collect equipment and instruments. They can help supervise activities. Students who need help finding the correct notes to play on the xylophones can also use some paraprofessional help.

Lesson 38

Winter Olympics

National Standards for Physical Education: 1, Demonstrates competency in motor skills and movement patterns needed to perform a variety of physical activities.

National Standards for Music Education: 2, Performing on instruments, alone and with others, a varied repertoire of music; 6, Listening to, analyzing, and describing music.

Equipment: Paper flags from other countries, a box, mats, scooters, cones, paper plates, hockey sticks, small soft balls, and relay batons for PE, A recording of the "Olympic Theme" and xylophones for music.

Lesson Focus:

- Sports of the Winter Games in PE.
- Olympic theme song in music.

Related Literature: *Old Turtle's Winter Games* by Leonard Kessler.

READ THE STORY

Read the story aloud to the class.

PE ACTIVITY

Discuss the luge with the students. Show them pictures of teams racing on the luge. Give each student a scooter to ride to simulate the luge race. Use cones or dome markers to set up a course for the students to follow riding their scooters. Have the students' race around the gym on the scooters. Make sure students remain on their bottoms when they are riding on the scooters.

MUSIC ACTIVITY

Review all previous Olympic lessons with the students. Make sure each student has a xylophone to play, or have a group of students play the xylophones while others sing with you. Sing the simplified version of the "Olympic Theme" for the students using note names. Have them slowly play the theme while you slowly sing the note names. Give each student a chance to play.

Conclude the lessons by asking the students what they learned about the Olympics.

If you are a classroom teacher with limited space, make sure you have sufficient space for the Olympic activities. If you do not have xylophones, have the students bring their toy xylophones from home. If this is not possible, have students move to the "Olympic Theme" using scarves or streamers.

If you have paraprofessionals or other adults assisting in your classroom, have them help distribute and collect equipment and instruments. They can help supervise activities. Students who need help finding the correct notes to play on the xylophones can also use some paraprofessional help.

Lesson 39

Winter Olympics

National Standards for Physical Education: 1, Demonstrates competency in motor skills and movement patterns needed to perform a variety of physical activities.

National Standards for Music Education: 2, Performing on instruments, alone and with others, a varied repertoire of music; 6, Listening to, analyzing, and describing music.

Equipment: Paper flags from other countries, a box, mats, scooters, cones, paper plates, hockey sticks, small soft balls, and relay batons for PE, A recording of the "Olympic Theme" and xylophones for music.

Lesson Focus:

- Sports of the Winter Games in PE.
- Olympic theme song in music.

Related Literature: *A Is for Axel* by Kurt Browning.

READ THE STORY

Read the story aloud to the class.

PE ACTIVITY

This next activity simulates ice skating and it is a lot of fun. Give each student two paper plates. Put on some fun music and have the students put the plates under their feet. They will slide on the plates or skates dancing to the music, just as a figure skater would do.

MUSIC ACTIVITY

Once again, have the students play the xylophones to the "Olympic Theme" as in Unit 6 Lesson 38. Discuss the country where the Olympics are being hosted. If it is one of the countries listed in this book, have the students sing the song that is from that country.

Conclude the lessons by asking the students what they learned about the Olympics.

If you are a classroom teacher with limited space, make sure you have sufficient space for the Olympic activities. If you do not have xylophones, have the students bring their toy xylophones from home. If this is not possible, have students move to the "Olympic Theme" using scarves or streamers.

If you have paraprofessionals or other adults assisting in your classroom, have them help distribute and collect equipment and instruments. They can help supervise activities. Students who need help finding the correct notes to play on the xylophones can also use some paraprofessional help.

Lesson 40

Winter Olympics

National Standards for Physical Education: 1, Demonstrates competency in motor skills and movement patterns needed to perform a variety of physical activities.

National Standards for Music Education: 2, Performing on instruments, alone and with others, a varied repertoire of music; 6, Listening to, analyzing, and describing music.

Equipment: Paper flags from other countries, a box, mats, scooters, cones, paper plates, hockey sticks, small soft balls, and relay batons for PE, A recording of the "Olympic Theme" and xylophones for music.

Lesson Focus:

- Sports of the Winter Games in PE.
- Olympic theme song in music.

Related Literature: *Z Is for Zamboni* by Matt Napier.

READ THE STORY

Read the story aloud to the class.

PE ACTIVITY

The last activity of the Winter Games is hockey. Give each student a hockey stick and a small soft ball. Show the students how to dribble the hockey ball using small taps and keeping the ball close to their stick. Remind them to never raise the stick higher than their knees.

MUSIC ACTIVITY

Have the students review all Olympic musical activities. Play the "Olympic Theme" on the xylophones. Have them sing the "Olympic Theme" on the syllable *la*. Review "The Star-Spangled Banner." Once again, discuss the country that is hosting the Olympics. Download information about the musical traditions of that country to share with your students.

Conclude the lessons by asking the students what they learned about the Olympics.

If you are a classroom teacher with limited space, make sure you have sufficient space for the Olympic activities. If you do not have xylophones, have the students bring their toy xylophones from home. If this is not possible, have students move to the "Olympic Theme" using scarves or streamers.

If you have paraprofessionals or other adults assisting in your classroom, have them help distribute and collect equipment and instruments. They can help supervise activities. Students who need help finding the correct notes to play on the xylophones can also use some paraprofessional help.

Lesson 41

Anniversary or Opening of a School

National Standards for Physical Education: 1, Demonstrates competency in motor skills and movement patterns needed to perform a variety of physical activities.

National Standards for Music Education: 1, Singing, alone and with others, a varied repertoire of music.

Equipment: A recording of "Pomp and Circumstance" by Edward Elgar (download from iTunes), paper, and crayons or markers for PE, Scarves for music.

Lesson Focus:

• Celebrating the birthday of a special place.

Related Literature: *A One-Room School* by Bobbie Kalman.

READ THE STORY

Read the story aloud to the class.

PE ACTIVITY

Have the students think of things about their school they are thankful for. Have them color a picture of an item they are thankful for. Have them form a line with their pictures. Play the "Pomp and Circumstance" music as the students march in a parade-style procession with their pictures. Play "Pomp and Circumstance" again. Have the students march in general space around the gym while the music is playing. When you stop the music, have each student go to the nearest person and tell him about his picture. The students can explain what is in their pictures that they are thankful for.

MUSIC ACTIVITY

Discuss the importance of the celebration with the students. Teach the students the song "We Are the Light of the World." Teach the refrain first. Once the students are comfortable singing the refrain, have them all wave colorful scarves as they sing.

Conclude the lesson by asking the students what other things they will be doing that are a special way of celebrating their school.

If you are a classroom teacher with limited space, these lessons may proceed as described.

If you have paraprofessionals or other adults assisting in your classroom, have them help students think of ideas for pictures. They can also help lead the parade, help with singing, and distributing and collecting scarves.

We Are the Light of the World

C. Wilson

38. hope for all__ the good that there can be. Our lives will grow and__ change,__ And

42. we will go our sep-ar - ate ways. We will al - ways re mem ber__ the friends that we made here, And the

1st time D.S. al Coda

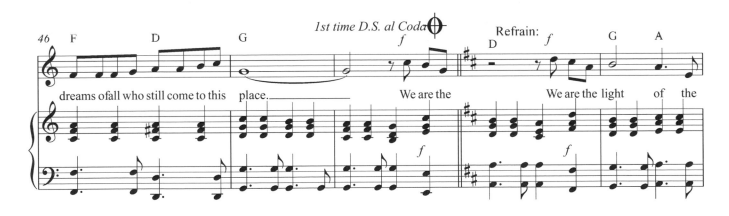

46. dreams of all who still come to this place._____ We are the *Refrain:* We are the light of the

51. world, The fut-ure is in our hands. We are the salt of the Earth, We are the

seed on fer-tile ground Some-day we'll rise up and shine, Rise up and shine for all to

see.

Lesson 42

Last Day of School

National Standards for Physical Education: 5, Exhibits responsible personal and social behavior that respects self and others in physical activity settings.
National Standards for Music Education: 1, Singing, alone and with others, a varied repertoire of music.
Equipment: Buckets of water and plastic cups for PE.
Lesson Focus:

• Steady movement and concentration in PE.
• Singing and remembering the school year for music.

Related Literature: *The Last Day of School* by Louise Borden and Adam Gustavson.

READ THE STORY

Read the story aloud to the class.

PE ACTIVITY

These water relays are such fun to do on the last day of school if the weather is nice outside.

Fill up buckets with water and place them outside. Give each student a plastic cup filled to the top with water. Place students in teams of four each.

Have the students do relays such as skipping or jogging, but do not allow them to put their water cups down. Add some fun exercises such as jumping jacks or walk around the play area, trying not to spill the water.

At the end of the class period, have each team dump their remaining water in an empty bucket. Measure how much water each team was able to keep in their cups. The team that had the most water left would win the game.

If possible, give the students a special treat after this event. A popsicle or a sports drink makes a good treat to end this special day.

MUSIC ACTIVITY

Talk to the children about the school year that is ending. Have them recall all of the things they learned in music. Have a sing-along and review some of their favorite songs from the year. Ask them about orchestral music and stories they heard. Ask them about instrument families, quarter notes, eighth notes, and quarter rests. Ask them to tell you about the instruments they learned how to play. Teach the students the song "Time to Say Goodbye."

Conclude the lesson by telling the students to have a wonderful summer and that you will look forward to seeing them next year. Remind them to sing a lot during the summer. Maybe they will come back to school with a new song to sing for you.

If you are a classroom teacher with limited space, make sure you have a space outside for the water relays. The music lesson may proceed as described.

If you have paraprofessionals or other adults assisting in your classroom, have them help you give each student a cup filled with water. The extra supervision and assistance will be invaluable. During the music lesson, they can help remember songs and lead singing.

Physical Education Resources

BOOKS

Graham, George, Shirley Ann Holt/Hale, Melissa Parker. (2007). *Children Moving: A Reflective Approach to Teaching Physical Education*, 7th ed. New York: McGraw-Hill.

Mehrhof, Joella H, Kathy Ermler. (2001). *Physical Essentials: Kindergarten–5th Grade Physical Education Curriculum*. Emporia, KS: Mirror Publishing.

MUSIC CDS

Jim Gill
  Make it Noisy in Boise, Idaho (1996)
  The Sneezing Song and Other Contagious Tunes (1994)
  Do Re Mi on his Toe Leg Knee (1999)
The Learning Station from Monopoli Productions (2000–2006)
  Physical Ed
  Tony Chestnut
  Rock and Roll Songs That Teach
Dr. Jean, also known as Jean Feldman (1997–2006)
  Kiss Your Brain
  Dr. Jean and Friends
Hap Palmer from Educational Activities (1987)
  Sally the Swinging Snake
Sesame Street (1997)
  Hot! Hot! Hot! Dance Songs
Tom Chapin (1994)
  Zig Zag

Literature, PE Equipment, and Music Resource List

The equipment and resources are listed in unit and lesson order.

UNIT 1: MY BODY AND MELODIC VOICE

Lesson 1

Book: *The Hare and the Tortoise* by Carol Jones
PE: The Learning Station, *Physical Ed*, song #14 "The Run Walk Song"
Music: *Peer Gynt Suite* by Edvard Grieg from *Music Smart* by Gwen Hotchkiss (New York: Parker Publishing Company, 1990)

Lesson 2

Book: *Peter's Chair* by Ezra Jack Keats or *My Secret Place* by Eric Magnus
PE: Jim Gill, *The Sneezing Song and Other Contagious Tunes*, song #8 "The Silly Dance Contest"
Music: Orff instruments, resonator bells, or boom whackers
"La Boomba" by Theresa Jennings, arr. Paul Jennings from *Music K–8*, Vol. 14, #3 (January/February 2004)

Lesson 3

Book: *Beach Ball Left, Right* by Bruce McMillan
PE: Sesame Street, *Hot! Hot! Hot! Dance Songs*, song #8 "A New Way to Walk"
Music: Drum and rhythm sticks
"Spicy Hot" by Theresa Jennings, from *Music K–8*, Vol. 13, #4 (March/ April 2003)

Lesson 4

Book: *Cross-Country Cat* by Mary Calhoun
PE: Paper plates (thin ones) and pictures of skaters and skiers from magazines
Music: "Forte Piano" by Theresa Jennings, from *Music K–8*, Vol. 13, #1 (September/October 2002)

Lesson 5

Book: *Even More Parts* by Tedd Arnold
PE: The Learning Station, *Tony Chestnut and Fun Time Action Songs*, song #1 "Tony Chestnut" and Jim Gill, *Do Re Mi*, song #5 *Toe Leg Knee*
Music: Orff instruments and www.classicsforkids.com

Lesson 6

Book: *I Can Move* by Mandy Suhr
PE: Jim Gill, *The Sneezing Song and Other Contagious Tunes,* song #12 "Spaghetti Legs"
Music: Orff instruments

Lesson 7

Book: *Red Riding Hood* by James Marshall
PE: Tom Chapin, *Zig Zag,* song #6 "Zig Zag"
Music: Scarves, *Singin', Sweatin', and Story Time* CD

Lesson 8

Book: *Elephants Aloft* by Kathi Appelt
PE: None
Music: *Singin', Sweatin', and Story Time* CD

Lesson 9

Book: *Brown Rabbit's Shape Book* by Alan Baker
PE: Hap Palmer, *Sally the Swinging Snake*, song #3 "Everything has a Shape"
Music: Pencils and paper
"Hot Cross Buns," traditional, arr. by Wayne Roe, from *The Music Connection*, Grade 1, (Glenville, IL: Silver Burdett Ginn Inc., 2000)

Lesson 10

Book: *Applebaums Have a Robot!* by Jane Thayer or *Hello, Robots* by Bob Staake
PE: If extending the lesson, Styrofoam plates
Music: Orff instruments, boom whackers, or drinking glass xylophones

Lesson 11

Book: *Thundercake* by Patricia Polacco
PE: Pictures of sumo wrestlers and copies of the cake recipe *(optional)*
Music: Review songs from previous lessons

Lesson 12

Book: *Stand Tall, Molly Lou Melon* by Patty Lovell, *Enemy Pie* by Derek Munson, or *Harry and the Terrible Whatzit* by Dick Gackenbach
PE: The Learning Station, *Tony Chestnut*, song #6 *Mr. Mirror*
Music: "Down by the Station," traditional, from *Wee Sing, Sing-Alongs* by Pamela Conn Beall and Susan Hagen Nipp (New York: Price Stern Sloan, 1990), 39

Lesson 13

Book: *Gingerbread Man* retold by Jim Aylesworth or *Ready, Set, Skip!* by Jane O'Connor
PE: The Learning Station, *Physical Ed,* song #14 "The Run Walk Song"
Music: Scarves
"My Bonnie Lies Over the Ocean," traditional Scottish folk song from *Get America Singing Again*, Vol. 1, arranged by Hal Leonard

Lesson 14

Book: *Wiggle Waggle* by Jonathan London

PE: Choose an animal song from what you have *(optional)*; most artists who cater to young children will have an animal song on their CD

Music: "Old MacDonald," traditional, from *Music and You*, Grade 1 (New York: Macmillan Publishing Company, 1991) or *Wee Sing, The Best of* by Pamela Conn Beall and Susan Hagen Nipp (New York: Price Stern Sloan, 2007)

UNIT 2: HAPPY, HEALTHY, MUSICAL ME

Lesson 1

Book: *Wiggle* by Doreen Cronin or *The Heart* by Anne Fitzpatrick

PE: Hap Palmer, *Sally the Swinging Snake*, song #3 "Wiggy Wiggy Wiggles"

Music: Rhythm band instruments, *Singin', Sweatin', and Story Time* CD

"Head and Shoulders" from *Wee Sing, The Best of* by Pamela Conn Beall and Susan Hagen Nipp (New York: Price Stern Sloan, 2007)

Lesson 2

Book: *The Skeleton Inside You* by Philip Balestrino

PE: Copies of the skeleton printout *(optional)* and *Bones* by Jim Valley from Rainbow Planet

Music: "Dry Bones" African American spiritual from *Music and You*, Grade 6 (New York: Macmillan Publishing Company, 1991)

Lesson 3

Book: *No One Like You* by Jillian Harker

PE: None

Music: Rhythm band instruments, *Singin', Sweatin', and Story Time* CD

"Kids Are Different" by Catherine Wilson (2004)

Lesson 4

Book: *Just Big Enough* by Mercer Mayer or *Bend and Stretch* by Pamela Hill Nettleton

PE: The Learning Station, *Tony Chestnut*, song #12 "Pump Pump Shuffle"

Music: Orff instruments or boom whackers or resonator bells

"My Muscles" by Catherine Wilson (2004)

Lesson 5

Book: *You Dirty Dog* by Stephen Caitlin

PE: A soft object for tagging

Music: Orff instruments

"Don't Put Your Fingers in Your Mouth" by Catherine Wilson (2004)

Lesson 6

Book: *Dinosaurs Get Well Soon* by Jane Yolen and Mark Teague

PE: A soft ball for tagging, Jim Gill, *The Sneezing Song and Other Contagious Tunes*, song #1 "Sneezing Song," and #4 "I Took a Bath in a Washing Machine"

Music: Lummi sticks

"Wash Your Hands" by Catherine Wilson (2004)

Lesson 7

Book: *Jane vs. the Tooth Fairy* by Betsy Jay
PE: Signs for each of the teeth; enough sets so that all children have one
Music: "The Tooth Hop" by Catherine Wilson (2004)
"I Lost My Tooth Today," words composed by Catherine Wilson

Lesson 8

Book: *Tooth Fairy's First Night* by Anne Bowen
PE: A short nerf noodle and beanbags
Music: "Ouch, I Have a Sore Tooth" by Catherine Wilson (2004)
"I Lost My Tooth Today," words composed by Catherine Wilson

Lesson 9

Book: *This Is the Way We Go to School* by Edith Baer
PE: www.walktoschool.com
Music: Rhythm chart with quarter notes, eighth notes, and quarter rests

Lesson 10

Book: *Moses Goes to a Concert* by Isaac Millman
PE: Small bags with objects for the children to feel and describe
Music: Rhythm cards with quarter notes and eighth notes, rhythm sticks, and hand drums
"Five Senses Jive" created by Catherine Wilson and Rebecca Hamik

Lesson 11

Book: *What Your Nose Knows!* by Jane Belk Moncure
PE: None
Music: "Looby Loo," traditional, from *Wee Sing, The Best of* by Pamela Conn Beall and Susan Hagen Nipp (New York: Price Stern Sloan, 2007)

Lesson 12

Book: *Mickey McGuffin's Ear* by John Hall
PE: Jim Gill, *Make it Noisy in Boise*, song #12 "Sound Effects Song"
Music: Musical instruments
Peter and the Wolf by Sergei Prokofiev from *Music Smart* by Gwen Hotchkiss (New York: Parker Publishing Company, 1990)

Lesson 13

Book: *A Tasting Party* by Jane Belk Moncure
PE: A variety of food for tasting
Music: Orff instruments or pitched instruments
"Hot Cross Buns" traditional folk song (Unit 1 Lesson 9)

Lesson 14

Book: *Spectacles* by Ellen Raskin
PE: One white paper plate per student, crayons, and items to decorate with such as ribbon

Music: "Beauty and the Beast" by Maurice Ravel from *Music and You*, Grade 2 (New York: Macmillan Publishing Company, 1991)

Lesson 15

Book: *The Berenstain Bears Visit the Dentist* by Stan and Jan Berenstain or *Tabitha's Terrifically Tough Tooth* by Charlotte Middleton
PE: A short nerf noodle and beanbags
Music: "The Tooth Hop," "Ouch, I Have a Sore Tooth," and "I Lost My Tooth Today" by Catherine Wilson (2004)

Lesson 16

Book: *Eating the Alphabet* by Lois Ehlert
PE: Food ads from your local newspaper
Music: Pitched instruments
"Twinkle, Twinkle, Little Star" from *Wee Sing, Nursery Rhymes and Lullabies* by Pamela Conn Beall and Susan Hagen Nipp (New York: Price Stern Sloan, 2002)

Lesson 17

Book: *Bread, Bread, Bread* by Ann Morris
PE: A soft ball for tagging
Music: A hand drum or rhythm sticks
"The Bread Jam" by Catherine Wilson and Rebecca Hamik (2004)

Lesson 18

Book: *The Seven Silly Eaters* by Mary Ann Hoberman
PE: Food cards or food ads from your local newspaper
Music: Instrument cards
Peter and the Wolf by Sergei Prokofiev from *Music Smart* by Gwen Hotchkiss (New York: Parker Publishing Company, 1990)

Lesson 19

Book: *Potluck* by Anne Shelby
PE: Signs with the words *healthy* and *not healthy*
Music: Instruments and other objects that make sounds
"The Little Train of the Caipira" from *Brachianas Brasilieras No. 2* by Heitor Villa-Lobos from *Music and You*, Grade 2 (New York, Macmillan Publishing Company, 1990) and download from iTunes, "The Train" by Quad City DJ

Lesson 20

Book: *Cloudy With a Chance of Meatballs* by Judi Barrett
PE and Music: This is a review day; choose equipment accordingly.

UNIT 3: POSITIVE PERSONALITY

Lesson 1

Book: *The Pig Who Went Home on Sunday* by Donald Davis
PE: The Learning Station, *Tony Chestnut* song #7 "I Like Friends"

Music: *Singin', Sweatin', and Story Time*
"If You Look Inside" by Catherine Wilson (2004)

Lesson 2

Book: *I Like Myself!* by Karen Beaumont
PE: None
Music: "Mind Your Manners" by Theresa Jennings from *Music K–8,* Vol. 13, #5 (May/June 2003)

Lesson 3

Book: *The Ant Bully* by John Nickle
PE: Beanbags
Music: "I'll Be There" by Theresa Jennings from *Music K–8*, Vol. 13, # 3 (January/February 2003)

Lesson 4

Book: *All the Colors of the Earth* by Sheila Hamanaka or *Too Many Pears!* by Jackie French
PE: Assorted equipment to play catch with
Music: Unpitched percussion instruments

Lesson 5

Book: *The Ugly Vegetables* by Grace Lin
PE: Signs that have the words *Do* and *Do not*
Music: Handheld percussion instruments
"Upstanding Citizen" by Theresa and Paul Jennings from *Music K–8,* Vol. 15, #4 (March/April 2005)

Lesson 6

Book: *Fat Cat* by Margaret MacDonald
PE: None
Music: "Three Little Monkeys," traditional, from *Wee Sing, Songs and Finger Plays* by Pamela Conn Beall and Susan
    Hagen Nipp (New York: Price Stern Sloan, 2006)

Lesson 7

Book: *It's Up to You Griffin* by Susan T. Pickford or *Stink Soup* by Jill Esbaum
PE: Plenty of pieces of equipment that the children can sort
Music: Rhythm band instruments
"Clean Up!" by Catherine Wilson (2004)

Lesson 8

Book: *Pedrito's Day* by Luis Garay or "*It's Not My Job!*" by Ted Lish
PE: Fleece balls
Music: Rhythm band instruments
"Clean Up!" by Catherine Wilson and "I'm Gonna Clean My Bedroom" by Catherine Wilson (2004)

Lesson 9

Book: *Ruby and the Muddy Dog* by Helen Stephens
PE: Something soft for tagging

Music: "The Mulberry Bush," traditional, from *Wee Sing, Songs and Finger Plays* by Pamela Conn Beall and Susan Hagen Nipp (New York: Price Stern Sloan, 2006)

Lesson 10

Book: *The Firekeeper's Son* by Linda Sue Park
PE: Magazines for the children to cut pictures from, glue sticks, and poster paper
Music: "The Mulberry Bush," traditional, from *Wee Sing, Songs and Finger Plays* by Pamela Conn Beall and Susan Hagen Nipp (New York: Price Stern Sloan, 2006)

Lesson 11

Book: *Eagle Boy* by Richard Lee Vaughan
PE: One plastic garbage or grocery bag per student
Music: "Big Beautiful Planet" by Raffi from *The Music Connection* (Glenview, IL: Silver Burdett Ginn, 2000)

Lesson 12

Book: *Uncle Willie and the Soup Kitchen* by DyAnne DiSalvo-Ryan
PE: Letter to parents asking them to send a food item with the student to give to the food pantry and boxes to carry the items.
Music: "It Starts with Me" by Catherine Wilson (2004)

Lesson 13

Book: *Duck for President* by Doreen Cronin
PE: Ballots for the children to vote and pencils
Music: "You're a Grand Old Flag," "The Star-Spangled Banner," and "My Country, 'Tis of Thee," also known as "America," words by Samuel Francis Smith, 1832, from *Wee Sing, America* by Pamela Conn Beall and Susan Hagen Nipp (New York: Price Stern Sloan, 1987)

Lesson 14

Book: *My Teacher for President* by Kay Winters
PE: A picture of the flag and red and blue crayons
Music: Percussion instruments for music
"You're a Grand Old Flag" by George M. Cohan from *Wee Sing, America* by Pamela Conn Beall and Susan Hagen Nipp (New York: Price Stern Sloan, 1987)

Lesson 15

Book: *We the Kids* by David Catrow
PE: None
Music: Resonator bells
"I Love the Mountains," traditional, from *Wee Sing, Sing-Alongs* by Pamela Conn Beall and Susan Hagen Nipp (New York: Price Stern Sloan, 1990)

Lesson 16

Book: *The Farmer* by Mark Ludy
PE: None
Music: "Old Brass Wagon," traditional, from *Wee Sing, Sing and Play* by Pamela Conn Beall and Susan Hagen Nipp (New York: Price Stern Sloan, 2006)

Lesson 17

Book: *Tops & Bottoms* by Janet Stevens
PE: Two small pieces of equipment per group (e.g., a tennis ball and a die)
Music: Rhythm band instruments
"Old Brass Wagon," traditional, from *Wee Sing, Sing and Play* by Pamela Conn Beall and Susan Hagen Nipp (New York: Price Stern Sloan, 2006)

Lesson 18

Book: *The Old Woman Who Lived in a Vinegar Bottle* by Margaret Read MacDonald
PE: Small pieces of equipment (e.g., dice, balls, beanbags, and so on)
Music: A small rock
"Obwisana," traditional song from Ghana, from *Music and You*, Grade 2 (New York: Macmillan Publishing Company, 1991)

Lesson 19

Book: *The King of the Birds* by Helen Ward
PE: Several kinds of balls
Music: "Roll That Red Ball," traditional, from *Wee Sing, Sing and Play* by Pamela Conn Beall and Susan Hagen Nipp (New York: Price Stern Sloan, 2006)

Lesson 20

Book: *The True Story of the 3 Little Pigs!* by Jon Scieszka
PE: Soft objects for tagging
Music: "We Are Playing in the Forest," traditional, from *Music and You,* Grade 2 (New York: Macmillan Publishing Company, 1991)

Lesson 21

Book: *What's So Terrible about Swallowing an Apple Seed?* by Harriet Lerner and Susan Goldhor
PE: None
Music: Lummi sticks

Lesson 22

Book: *Believing Sophie* by Hazel Hutchins
PE: None
Music: "You Could Be My Friend" by Mike Wilson from *Music K–8,* Vol. 16, #3 (January/February 2006), and "I'll Be There" by Teresa Jennings from *Music K–8* (January/February 2003)

Lesson 23

Book: *King Bob's New Clothes* by Dom DeLuise
PE: None
Music: Orff instruments, boom whackers, resonator bells, or other pitched instruments and rhythm band percussion instruments

Lesson 24

Book: *My Big Lie* by Bill Cosby or *Edwurd Fudwupper Fibbed Big* by Berkeley Breathed
PE: Scarves or crepe paper streamers
Music: "Follow the Rainbow" by Theresa Jennings from *Music K–8*, Vol. 15, #4 (March/April 2005)

Lesson 25

Book: *A Day's Work* by Eve Bunting or *A Big Fat Enormous Lie* by Marjorie Weinman Sharmat
PE: Something soft to tag with
Music: "Hush Little Baby" and "Sleep Baby Sleep" from *Wee Sing, Nursery Rhymes and Lullabies*, by Pamela Conn Beall and Susan Hagen Nipp (New York: Price Stern Sloan, 2002)

Lesson 26

Book: *Alexander and the Wind-Up Mouse* by Leo Lionni
PE: None
Music: "Skip to My Lou," traditional, from *Wee Sing, Sing and Play* by Pamela Conn Beall and Susan Hagen Nipp (New York: Price Stern Sloan, 2006)

Lesson 27

Book: *Tico and the Golden Wings* by Leo Lionni
PE: Construction paper, scissors, and crayons
Music: Camera or recording device
"If You're Happy," traditional, from *Wee Sing, The Best of* by Pamela Conn Beall and Susan Hagen Nipp (New York: Price Stern Sloan, 2007)

Lesson 28

Book: *Rosie and Michael* by Judith Viorst
PE: None
Music: "What Are You Wearing?" traditional, from Hap Palmer, *Basic Skills through Music Vol. 1* (1986)

Lesson 29

Book: *The Wednesday Surprise* by Eve Bunting
PE: Poly spots or dome markers
Music: Rhythm band instruments
"Skidamarink," traditional, from *Wee Sing, The Best of* by Pamela Conn Beall and Susan Hagen Nipp (New York: Price Stern Sloan, 2007)

Lesson 30

Book: *The Flower Man* by Mark Ludy or *Daisy Comes Home* by Jan Brett
PE: Something soft for tagging
Music: "One Elephant Went Out to Play," traditional, from *Wee Sing, Songs and Finger Plays* by Pamela Conn Beall and Susan Hagen Nipp (New York: Price Stern Sloan, 2006)

UNIT 4: SKILLS AND THRILLS

Lesson 1

Book: *One, Two, Three, Jump!* by Penelope Lively
PE: None
Music: Orff instruments or resonator bells
"Hey Diddle Diddle" by J. W. Elliot from *Wee Sing, Nursery Rhymes and Lullabies* by Pamela Conn Beall and Susan Hagen Nipp (New York: Price Stern Sloan, 2002)

Lesson 2

Book: *Jumpers* by Jillian Powell or *Bounce* by Doreen Cronin
PE: Poly spots
Music: "Pop Goes the Weasel," traditional, from *Wee Sing, The Best of* by Pamela Conn Beall and Susan Hagen Nipp (New York: Price Stern Sloan, 2007)

Lesson 3

Book: *Dancing in the Wings* by Debbie Allen
PE: Yardstick, balloon, and colored tape
Music: Xylophones
"One, Two, Buckle My Shoe," traditional, from *Wee Sing, Songs and Finger Plays* by Pamela Conn Beall and Susan Hagen Nipp (New York: Price Stern Sloan, 2006)

Lesson 4

Book: *Madeline and the Gypsies* by Ludwig Bemelmans
PE: None
Music: "All the Pretty Little Horses," traditional, from *Wee Sing, Nursery Rhymes and Lullabies* by Pamela Conn Beall and Susan Hagen Nipp (New York: Price Stern Sloan, 2002)

Lesson 5

Book: *Clifford at the Circus* by Norman Bridwell
PE: None
Music: "Fiddle-Dee-Dee" by W. Crane (1879) from *Wee Sing, Nursery Rhymes and Lullabies* by Pamela Conn Beall and Susan Hagen Nipp (New York: Price Stern Sloan, 2002)

Lesson 6

Book: *Silly Sally* by Audrey Wood
PE: Tumbling mats
Music: Number songs
"The Ants Go Marching," traditional, from *Wee Sing, Silly Songs* by Pamela Conn Beall and Susan Hagen Nipp (New York: Price Stern Sloan, 2005)

Lesson 7

Book: *The Catspring Somersault Flying One-Handed Flip-Flop* by Suann Kiser
PE: Tumbling mats
Music: "London Bridge," traditional, from *Wee Sing, Sing and Play* by Pamela Conn Beall and Susan Hagen Nipp (New York: Price Stern Sloan, 2006)

Lesson 8

Book: *Hey Batta Batta Swing!* by Sally Cook and James Charlton
PE: Colorful scarves
Music: "Peas Porridge Hot," traditional, from *Wee Sing, The Best of* by Pamela Conn Beall and Susan Hagen Nipp (New York: Price Stern Sloan, 2007)

Lesson 9

Book: *Stop That Ball!* by Mike McClintock, *Balls!* by Michael J. Rosen, or *Out of the Ballpark* by Alex Rodriguez
PE: Beanbags

Music: Playground ball
"One, Two, Three O'Leary," traditional, from *Wee Sing, Sing and Play* by Pamela Conn Beall and Susan Hagen Nipp (New York: Price Stern Sloan, 2006)

Lesson 10

Book: *Mouse Practice* by Emily Arnold McCully
PE: Plastic grocery bags
Music: Poster board with a staff drawn on it and beanbag animals

Lesson 11

Book: *H is for Home Run* by Brad Herzog
PE: Clothespins
Music: Copies of large staff on paper and a marker for each student

Lesson 12

Book: *J is for Jump Shot* by Michael Ulmer
PE: Beanbags
Music: Large sheets of paper, washable markers, and xylophones

Lesson 13

Book: *By My Brother's Side* by Tiki Barber and Ronde Barber
PE: Clothespins
Music: "Row, Row, Row Your Boat," traditional, from *Wee Sing, Sing-Alongs* by Pamela Conn Beall and Susan Hagen Nipp (New York: Price Stern Sloan, 1990)

Lesson 14

Book: *T is for Touchdown* by Brad Herzog
PE: Shuttlecocks
Music: Paper, crayons, and a paper clip for each student and a pretend goalpost

Lesson 15

Book: *Miss Nelson Has a Field Day* by Harry Allard
PE: Beanbags
Music: "The Green Grass Grows All Around," traditional, from The Countdown Kids, *100 Silly Songs* (Madacy Kids, 2004)

Lesson 16

Book: *K is for Kicking* by Brad Herzog
PE: Balls for kicking
Music: Orff instruments or resonator bells
"The Green Grass Grows All Around," traditional, from The Countdown Kids, *100 Silly Songs* (Madacy Kids, 2004)

Lesson 17

Book: *Winners Never Quit!* by Mia Hamm
PE: Balls to kick
Music: "Today Is Monday," traditional, from *Wee Sing, Sing-Alongs* by Pamela Conn Beall and Susan Hagen Nipp (New York: Price Stern Sloan, 1990)

Lesson 18

Book: *Froggy Plays Soccer* by Jonathan London
PE: Balls for kicking
Music: "Oh Shenandoah," traditional, from *Wee Sing, Sing-Alongs* by Pamela Conn Beall and Susan Hagen Nipp (New York: Price Stern Sloan, 1990)

Lesson 19

Book: *The Dog That Stole Football Plays* by Matt Christopher
PE: Balls for kicking
Music: Review previous songs

Lesson 20

Book: *Salt in His Shoes* by Delores Jordan
PE: Basketballs
Music: Resonator bells or Orff instruments
"Michael Row the Boat Ashore," traditional, from *Wee Sing, Sing-Alongs* by Pamela Conn Beall and Susan Hagen Nipp (New York: Price Stern Sloan, 1990)

Lesson 21

Book: *Gus and Grandpa at Basketball* by Claudia Mills
PE: Basketballs
Music: Resonator bells, two triangles, and two drums
"Down in the Valley," traditional, from *Wee Sing, Sing-Alongs* by Pamela Conn Beall and Susan Hagen Nipp (New York: Price Stern Sloan, 1990)

Lesson 22

Book: *The Princesses Have a Ball* by Teresa Bateman
PE: Basketballs
Music: "Sarasponda," traditional, from *Wee Sing, Sing-Alongs* by Pamela Conn Beall and Susan Hagen Nipp (New York: Price Stern Sloan, 1990)

Lesson 23

Book: *Play Ball, Joey Kangaroo!* by Donna Lugg Pape or *Play Ball* by Margaret Hillet
PE: Balloons
Music: Lummi sticks
Review songs

Lesson 24

Book: *Clifford The Big Red Dog: The Missing Beach Ball* by Sonali Fry
PE: Balloons
Music: A penny and a pin that you might wear
Who Has the Penny/Who Has the Pin," traditional game, from *Music and You*, Grade 2 (New York: Macmillan Publishing Company, 1991)

Lesson 25

Book: *Volleyball for Fun!* by Darcy Lockman
PE: Balls that bounce

Music: "I've Been Working On the Railroad," traditional, from *Wee Sing, Sing-Alongs* by Pamela Conn Beall and Susan Hagen Nipp (New York: Price Stern Sloan, 1990)

Lesson 26

Book: *Bump! Set! Spike!* by Nick Fauchald
PE: Balls that bounce
Music: Bass xylophone, alto xylophone, alto glockenspiel, and finger cymbals
"Sweetly Sings the Donkey," traditional, from *Wee Sing, Sing-Alongs* by Pamela Conn Beall and Susan Hagen Nipp (New York: Price Stern Sloan, 1990)

Lesson 27

Book: *The ABC's of Tennis* by Cheryl Lagunilla
PE: Short-handled paddles and balloons
Music: Bass xylophone, alto xylophone, alto glockenspiel, and finger cymbals
Review songs

Lesson 28

Book: *Girl Wonder* by Deborah Hopkinson or *Batter Up* by Neil Johnson
PE: Batting tees, soft bats, and balls
Music: Lummi sticks
"A Ram Sam Sam," traditional, from *Wee Sing, Sing-Alongs* by Pamela Conn Beall and Susan Hagen Nipp (New York: Price Stern Sloan, 1990)

Lesson 29

Book: *P is for Putting* by Brad Herzog
PE: Croquet mallets or plastic golf clubs
Music: Rhythm band instruments
"*Viva La Compagnie*," traditional, from *Wee Sing, Sing Alongs* by Pamela Conn Beall and Susan Hagen Nipp (New York: Price Stern Sloan, 1990)

Lesson 30

Book: *Hat Tricks Count* by Matt Napier
PE: Hockey sticks and balls
Music: Paper, crayons, and three voice-flexing cards that have been made ahead

Lesson 31

Book: *I Want to Play Tennis* by Ann S. Bartek
PE: Rackets and balloons
Music: Resonator bells and mallets
"Hey, Ho! Nobody Home," traditional, from *Wee Sing, Sing-Alongs* by Pamela Conn Beall and Susan Hagen Nipp (New York: Price Stern Sloan, 1990)

Lesson 32

Book: *M is for Melody* by Kathy-jo Wargin
PE: Objects to catch
Music: *Carnival of the Animals* by Camille Saint-Saëns from *Music Smart* by Gwen Hotchkiss (New York: Parker Publishing Company, 1990)

Lesson 33

Book: *Berlioz the Bear* by Jan Brett
PE: Soccer balls
Music: Review songs

Lesson 34

Book: *Zin! Zin! Zin! a Violin* by Lloyd Moss
PE: Basketballs
Music: Review songs

Lesson 35

Book: *Our Marching Band* by Lloyd Moss or *Music Is* by Lloyd Moss
PE: CDs review previous movement songs
Music: "Music Alone Shall Live," traditional, from *Wee Sing, Sing-Alongs* by Pamela Conn Beall and Susan Hagen Nipp (New York: Price Stern Sloan, 1990)

Lesson 36

Book: *The Remarkable Farkle McBride* by John Lithgow
PE: One hula hoop per student
Music: Review songs

Lesson 37

Book: *I Know a Shy Fellow Who Swallowed a Cello* by Barbara S. Garriel
PE: Poly spots and balls
Music: Pictures of orchestral instruments
Peter and the Wolf, from *Music Smart* by Gwen Hotchkiss (New York: Parker Publishing Company, 1990)

Lesson 38

Book: *Mozart Finds a Melody* by Stephen Costanza
PE: Poly spots
Music: Xylophones and *Moving with Mozart* CD for music
"Twinkle, Twinkle, Little Star," traditional, (Taylor) from *Wee Sing, Nursery Rhymes and Lullabies* by Pamela Conn Beall and Susan Hagen Nipp (New York: Price Stern Sloan, 2002)

Lesson 39

Book: *What Charlie Heard* by Mordicai Gerstein
PE: Balls that bounce
Music: A recording of "Putnam's Camp, Redding Connecticut" by Charles Ives

Lesson 40

Book: *The Farewell Symphony* by Anna Harwell Celenza
PE: Paper and crayons
Music: Paper and crayons

Lesson 41

Book: *The Farewell Symphony* by Anna Harwell Celenza
PE: Paper and crayons
Music: Paper and crayons

Lesson 42

Book: *Bach's Goldberg Variations* by Anna Harwell Celenza
PE: Paper and crayons
Music: Scarves

Lesson 43

Book: *Bach's Goldberg Variations* by Anna Harwell Celenza
PE: Paper and crayons
Music: Scarves

Lesson 44

Book: *The Beethoven's Heroic Symphony* by Anna Harwell Celenza
PE: Lummi sticks
Music: Lummi sticks and scarves

Lesson 45

Book: *The Beethoven's Heroic Symphony* by Anna Harwell Celenza
PE: Lummi sticks
Music: Lummi sticks and scarves

Lesson 46

Book: *Bats Around the Clock* by Kathi Appelt
PE: CDs with favorite dance tunes
Music: CDs of favorite dance songs

Lesson 47

Book: *Pigs Rock* by Melanie Jones and Bob Staake
PE: CDs with favorite dance tunes
Music: CDs of favorite dance songs

Lesson 48

Book: *The Three Little Pigs* by James Marshall
PE: Construction paper, small white paper bags, crayons, cue cards with words from the story, and pieces from the book to make the puppets
Music: "A Three Piggy Opera in One Act"

Lesson 49

Book: *Bantam of the Opera* by Mary Jane Auch
PE: Construction paper, small white paper bags, crayons, cue cards with words from the story, and pieces from the book to make the puppets
Music: "A Three Piggy Opera in One Act"

Lesson 50

Book: *Opera Cat* by Tess Weaver
PE: Construction paper, small white paper bags, crayons, cue cards with words from the story, and pieces from the book to make the puppets
Music: "A Three Piggy Opera in One Act"

Lesson 51

Book: *The Dog Who Sang at the Opera* by Marshall Izen and Jim West
PE: Construction paper, small white paper bags, crayons, cue cards with words from the story, and pieces from the book to make the puppets
Music: "A Three Piggy Opera in One Act"

Lesson 52

Book: *Lookin' for Bird in the Big City* by Robert Burleigh
PE: Recordings of jazz music
Music: A recording of "Sir Duke" by Stevie Wonder

Lesson 53

Book: *Charlie Parker Played Be Bop* by Chris Raschka
PE: Small balls
Music: Jazz recordings, paper, and crayons

Lesson 54

Book: *Rent Party Jazz* by William Miller
PE: Poly spots with letters, poker chips, and index cards with jazz-related words
Music: A recording of "What a Wonderful World" sung by Louis Armstrong

Lesson 55

Book: *The Old Banjo* by Dennis Haseley
PE: Dance music for the polka or simple square dances
Music: The words to "The Farmer in the Dell"

Lesson 56

Book: *The Little Red Hen* by Jerry Pinkney
PE: Music to review the student's favorite dances
Music: "The Farmer in the Dell," traditional, from *Wee Sing, Sing and Play* by Pamela Conn Beall and Susan Hagen Nipp (New York: Price Stern Sloan, 2006)

Lesson 57

Book: *The Little Red Hen* by Barrry Downard
PE: Review music from previous lessons
Music: Review music from previous lessons

Lesson 58

Book: *Barnyard Boogie* by Jim and Janet Post or *Today Is Monday* by Eric Carle
PE: None
Music: Review music from previous lessons

Lesson 59

Book: *Goldilocks* by James Marshall
PE: Fun country music
Music: Square dance music

Lesson 60

Book: *Hansel and Gretel* by James Marshall
PE: Scarves and the Jim Gill CD, *Make it Noisy in Boise*, song # 7, "5 Strings on my Banjo"
Music: "Three Blind Mice," traditional, from *Wee Sing, Sing-Alongs* by Pamela Conn Beall and Susan Hagen Nipp (New York: Price Stern Sloan, 1990)

UNIT 5: GAMES, SONGS, AND SEASONS OF OTHER LANDS

Lesson 1

Book: *Turtle Spring* by Deborah Turney Zagwyn or *Pumpkin Fiesta* by Caryn Yacowitz
PE: None
Music: "Mi Chacra," Argentinean folk song from *Music and You*, Grade 1 (New York: Macmillan Publishing Company 1991)

Lesson 2

Book: *Erandi's Braids* by Antonio Hernández Madrigal
PE: Strips of crepe paper
Music: "El Coqui," folk song from Puerto Rico from *The Music Connection*, Grade 1 (Glenview, IL: Silver Burdett Ginn, 2000)

Lesson 3

Book: *Under the Lemon Moon* by Edith Hope Fine
PE: Plastic lids and poly spots
Music: Rhythm band instruments
"La Raspa" (Mexican Dance) from *Diez Ditos* (*Ten Little Fingers and Other Play Rhymes and Action Songs from Latin America*) by Jose Luis Orozco

Lesson 4

Book: *Mice and Beans* by Pam Muñoz Ryan
PE: Review from previous lessons
Music: Review songs from previous lessons

Lesson 5

Book: *Summer* by Barrons Publishing
PE: None
Music: A medium-sized rock or small stuffed animal
"Obwisana," traditional, from Ghana from *Music and You*, Grade 2 (New York: Macmillan Publishing Company, 1991)

Lesson 6

Book: *Pinduli* by Janell Cannon
PE: None
Music: Hand drums and maracas

Lesson 7

Book: *Water Hole Waiting* by Jane and Christopher Kurtz
PE: Batting tee, beanbags, and fleece balls
Music: Rhythm band instruments and scarves

Lesson 8

Book: *Mufaro's Beautiful Daughters* by John Steptoe
PE: Cups or cans and small balls
Music: "Che Che Koolay," traditional song from Ghana from *Music and You*, Grade 2 (New York: Macmillan Publishing Company, 1991)

Lesson 9

Book: *Do Cows Turn Colors in the Fall?* by Viki Woodworth
PE: Hula hoops and cones
Music: "Kookaburra," traditional song from Australia from *Wee Sing, Sing-Alongs* by Pamela Conn Beall and Susan Hagen Nipp (New York: Price Stern Sloan, 1990)

Lesson 10

Book: *The Old Woman Who Loved to Read* by John Winch
PE: Something soft to tag with
Music: Xylophones

Lesson 11

Book: *The Pumpkin Runner* by Marsha Diane Arnold
PE: Beanbags
Music: "Waltzing Matilda," the official National Anthem of Australia, arranged for accordion/guitar by Pietrs Deire, Jr., music by Marie Cowan, and words by AB Patterson. Can be found on www.sheetmusicplus.com

Lesson 12

Book: *Wombat Stew* by Marsha K. Vaughn and Pamela Lofts
PE: Something soft to tag with
Music: Review songs from previous lesson

Lesson 13

Book: *Winter* by Barrons Publishing
PE: Poker chips or coins
Music: *Nutcracker Suite* by Pyotr Ilyich Tchaikovsky from *Music Smart* by Gwen Hotchkiss (New York: Parker Publishing Company, 1990)

Lesson 14

Book: *A Symphony of Whales* by Steve Schuch
PE: A large animal and a small ball
Music: Scarves and songs from previous lesson, paper, and crayons

Lesson 15

Book: *Latkes Latkes Good to Eat* by Naomi Howland
PE: A scarf
Music: "Russian Slumber Song," traditional, from *The Music Connection*, Grade 1 (Glenview, IL: Silver Burdett Ginn, 2000)

Lesson 16

Book: *The Elf's Hat* by Brigitte Weninger
PE: Hula hoops
Music: Bass xylophones, alto xylophones, alto glockenspiels, and finger cymbals

UNIT 6: HOLIDAYS AND SPECIAL TIMES

Lesson 1

Book: *I Am Too Absolutely Small for School* by Lauren Child
PE: None
Music: "The More We Get Together," traditional, from *Wee Sing, Sing-Alongs* by Pamela Conn Beall and Susan Hagen Nipp (New York: Price Stern Sloan, 1990)

Lesson 2

Book: *Hoodwinked* by Arthur Howard
PE: Halloween paper plates and beanbags
Music: Rhythm band instruments

Lesson 3

Book: *By the Dawn's Early Light* by Steven Kroll
PE: Something soft to tag with
Music: "The Star Spangled Banner" (and other patriotic songs) from *Wee Sing, America* by Pamela Conn Beall and Susan Hagen Nipp (New York: Price Stern Sloan, 1987)

Lesson 4

Book: *'Twas the Night Before Thanksgiving* by Dav Pilkey
PE: Construction paper turkey feathers

Music: "Jingle Bells" and "Over the River," traditional, from *Music and You*, Grade 2 (New York: Macmillan Publishing Company, 1990)

Lesson 5

Book: *Papa's Latkes* by Michelle Edwards
PE: Enough empty two-liter pop bottles for every six students and ten pennies each
Music: Sleigh bells
"Hanukah is Here" by Theresa Jennings, *Music K–8*, November/December 2002
"My Dreydl," traditional, from *Music and You*, Grade 1 (New York: Macmillan Publishing Company, 1990)

Lesson 6

Book: *The Christmas Hat* by A. J. Wood
PE: Fleece balls
Music: Xylophones, hand drum, and finger cymbals
"We Wish You a Merry Christmas" and " Christmas is Coming," traditional, from *Wee Sing for Christmas* by Pamela Conn Beall and Susan Hagen Nipp (New York: Price Stern Sloan, 2005)

Lesson 7

Book: *Seven Candles for Kwanzaa* by Andrea Davis Pinkney
PE: Seven large cones with different color construction paper and beanbags
Music: "O Kwanzaa" by Theresa Jennings from *Music K–8*, Vol. 13, #2, November/December 2002

Lesson 8

Book: *Celebrating Ramadan* by Diane Hoyt-Goldsmith
PE: Milk cartons and poker chips
Music: "Sleep," music on http://www.mamalisa.com

Lesson 9

Book: *What Is Martin Luther King, Jr. Day?* by David Adler or *Let Them Play Ball* by Margot Theis Raven
PE: Lummi sticks
Music: "Martin Luther King" by Theresa Fulbright from *Music and You*, Grade 2 (New York: Macmillan Publishing Company, 1990)

Lesson 10

Book: *Go to Sleep, Groundhog!* by Judy Cox
PE: Hula hoops and something soft to tag with
Music: Resonator bells and finger cymbals
"Time to Wake Up!" by B.S. from *Music and You*, Grade 2 (New York: Macmillan Publishing Company, 1990)

Lesson 11

Book: *Heart to Heart* by George Shannon
PE: Dome markers or poly spots
Music: "Skidamarink," traditional, from *Wee Sing, The Best Of* by Pamela Conn Beall and Susan Hagen Nipp (New York: Price Stern Sloan, 2007)

Lesson 12

Book: *The Leprechaun's Gold* Pamela Duncan Edwards
PE: Scarves
Music: "Mrs. Murphy's Chowder" from *Music and You*, Grade 5 (New York: Macmillan Publishing Company, 1990)

Lesson 13

Book: *Earth Day* by Mir Tamim Ansary or *Earth Day—Hooray!* by Stuart J. Murphy
PE: None
Music: Resonator bells
"I Love the Mountains," traditional, from *Wee Sing, Sing-Alongs* by Pamela Conn Beall and Susan Hagen Nipp (New York: Price Stern Sloan, 1990)
"Big Beautiful Planet" by Raffi from *The Music Connection* (Glenview, IL: Silver Burdett Ginn, 2000)

Lesson 14

Book: *Rechenka's Egg* by Patricia Polacco
PE: Plastic eggs with exercises written on slips of paper inside
Music: Resonator bells
"Little Peter Rabbit," traditional, from *Singin' Sweatin', and Story Time* CD

Lesson 15

Book: *Miss Flora McFlimsey's May Day* by Mariana
PE: Maypole and artificial flowers
Music: "Las Mananitas," traditional, from Mexico; see the book *Diez Ditos* from Unit 5.
"Little Green Frog," available at www.songsforteaching.com

Lesson 16

Book: *Mars Needs Moms* by Berkeley Breathed or *I Like Noisy, Mom Likes Quiet* by Eileen Spinelli
PE: None
Music: Scarves and songs from previous lessons

Lesson 17

Book: *The Seven Chinese Brothers* by Margaret Mahy or *Grandfather Tang's Story* by Ann Tompert
PE: None
Music: Paper, crayons, or markers
"Fong Swei," from *Wee Sing, Around the World* by Pamela Conn Beall and Susan Hagen Nipp (New York: Price Stern Sloan, 2006), 55

Lesson 18

Book: *Isla* by Arthur Dorros or *Sugar Cane* by Patricia Storace
PE: None
Music: Rhythm band instruments
"Tingalayo" from *Wee Sing, Around the World* by Pamela Conn Beall and Susan Hagen Nipp (New York: Price Stern Sloan, 2006), 15

Lesson 19

Book: *Puss in Boots* by Charles Perrault or *Bone Button Borscht* by Aubrey Davis
PE: Something for blindfolds
Music: Resonator bells
"Frère Jacques," from *Wee Sing, Around the World* by Pamela Conn Beall and Susan Hagen Nipp (New York: Price Stern Sloan, 2006), 20

Lesson 20

Book: *Ali and the Magic Stew* by Shulamith Levey Oppenheim or *The Golden Sandal* by Rebecca Hickox
PE: A large handkerchief with knots tied in it
Music: "Attal Mattal," from *Wee Sing, Around the World* by Pamela Conn Beall and Susan Hagen Nipp (New York: Price Stern Sloan, 2006), 53

Lesson 21

Book: *The Great Kapok Tree* by Lynne Cherry or *The Dancing Turtle* by Pleasant DeSpain
PE: None
Music: "Ciranda," from *Wee Sing, Around the World* by Pamela Conn Beall and Susan Hagen Nipp (New York: Price Stern Sloan, 2006)

Lesson 22

Book: *Annie and the Old One* by Miska Miles
PE: Fleece balls
Music: Rhythm band instruments
"Uhe'Basho Sho," from *Wee Sing, Around the World* by Pamela Conn Beall and Susan Hagen Nipp (New York: Price Stern Sloan, 2006), 12

Lesson 23

Book: *Yunmi and Halmoni's Trip* by Sook Nyul Choi
PE: None
Music: Triangles, finger cymbals, and a rain stick
"Arirang," from *Wee Sing, Around the World* by Pamela Conn Beall and Susan Hagen Nipp (New York: Price Stern Sloan, 2006), 56

Lesson 24

Book: *The Fisherman and His Wife* by Rosemary Wells
PE: None
Music: A scarf
"Alle Meine Entchen," from *Wee Sing, Around the World* by Pamela Conn Beall and Susan Hagen Nipp (New York: Price Stern Sloan, 2006), 38

Lesson 25

Book: *Jack and the Beanstalk* by Ann Keay Beneduce and Gennady Spirin
PE: None
Music: Paper and crayons
"Lavender's Blue" from *Wee Sing, Around the World* by Pamela Conn Beall and Susan Hagen Nipp (New York: Price Stern Sloan, 2006), 33

Lesson 26

Book: *Brothers* by Yin or *King Puck* by Michael Garland
PE: None
Music: "Wee Falorie Man," from *Wee Sing, Around the World* by Pamela Conn Beall and Susan Hagen Nipp (New York: Price Stern Sloan, 2006), 31

Lesson 27

Book: *Yoshi's Feast* by Kimiko Kajikawa or *Jojofu* by Michael P. Waite
PE: Tiddlywinks or poker chips
Music: Scarves, paper, and crayons
"Ame Ame," from *Wee Sing, Around the World* by Pamela Conn Beall and Susan Hagen Nipp (New York: Price Stern Sloan, 2006), 57

Lesson 28

Book: *The Never-Ending Greenness* by Neil Waldman
PE: Scooters
Music: Boom whackers or xylophones
"Zum Gali Gali," from *Wee Sing, Around the World* by Pamela Conn Beall and Susan Hagen Nipp (New York: Price Stern Sloan, 2006), 52

Lesson 29

Book: *I Have an Olive Tree* by Eve Bunting
PE: Carpet samples
Music: A small ring
"Pou' n-do to Dachtilidi," from *Wee Sing, Around the World* by Pamela Conn Beall and Susan Hagen Nipp (New York: Price Stern Sloan, 2006), 42

Lesson 30

Book: *The Orphan Singer* by Emily Arnold McCully
PE: None
Music: "Mio Galleto," from *Wee Sing, Around the World* by Pamela Conn Beall and Susan Hagen Nipp (New York: Price Stern Sloan, 2006), 39

Lesson 31

Book: *Make the Team, Baby Duck!* by Amy Hest
PE: Scooters, music, and balls
Music: Xylophones
"Olympic Theme," available at iTunes

Lesson 32

Book: *Paperboy* by Mary Kay Kroeger
PE: Scooters, music, and balls
Music: Xylophones
"Olympic Theme," available at iTunes

Lesson 33

Book: *One-Dog Canoe* by Mary Casanova
PE: Scooters, music, and balls
Music: Xylophones
"Olympic Theme," available at iTunes

Lesson 34

Book: *A Pony for Keeps* by Elizabeth Henning Sutton
PE: Scooters, music, and balls
Music: Xylophones
"Olympic Theme," available at iTunes

Lesson 35

Book: *Froggy Plays Soccer* by Jonathan London
PE: Scooters, music, and balls
Music: Xylophones
"Olympic Theme," available at iTunes

Lesson 36

Book: *Celebrate The Fire Within* by Kathy Larsen
PE: Paper flags from other countries, a box, mats, scooters, cones, paper plates, hockey sticks, small soft balls, and relay
  batons
Music: "Olympic Theme," available at iTunes, and "The Star-Spangled Banner"

Lesson 37

Book: *Tacky and the Winter Games* by Helen Lester
PE: Paper flags from other countries, a box, mats, scooters, cones, paper plates, hockey sticks, small soft balls, and relay
  batons
Music: "Olympic Theme," available at iTunes, and "The Star-Spangled Banner"

Lesson 38

Book: *Old Turtle's Winter Games* by Leonard Kessler
PE: Paper flags from other countries, a box, mats, scooters, cones, paper plates, hockey sticks, small soft balls, and relay
  batons
Music: "Olympic Theme," available at iTunes, and "The Star-Spangled Banner"

Lesson 39

Book: *A Is for Axel* by Kurt Browning
PE: Paper flags from other countries, a box, mats, scooters, cones, paper plates, hockey sticks, small soft balls, and relay
  batons
Music: "Olympic Theme," available at iTunes, and "The Star-Spangled Banner"

Lesson 40

Book: *Z Is for Zamboni* by Matt Napier
PE: Paper flags from other countries, a box, mats, scooters, cones, paper plates, hockey sticks, small soft balls, and relay
  batons
Music: "Olympic Theme," available at iTunes, and "The Star-Spangled Banner"

Lesson 41

Book: *A One-Room School* by Bobbie Kalman
PE: A recording of "Pomp and Circumstance," available at iTunes, and paper, markers, and crayons
Music: Scarves
"We Are the Light of the World" by Catherine Wilson, 2006

Lesson 42

Book: *The Last Day of School* by Louise Borden and Adam Gustavson
PE: Buckets of water and plastic cups
Music: "Time to Say Goodbye" by Theresa Jennings from *Music K–8*